Teaching First-Year College Students

BETTE LASERE ERICKSON

CALVIN B. PETERS

DIANE WELTNER STROMMER

Teaching First-Year College Students

Revised and
Expanded Edition of
Teaching College Freshmen

JOSSEY-BASS
A Wiley Imprint
www.josseybass.com

Published by Jossey-Bass
A Wiley Imprint
989 Market Street, San Francisco, CA 94103-1741   www.josseybass.com

Jossey-Bass books and products are available through most bookstores. To contact Jossey-Bass directly call our Customer Care Department within the U.S. at 800-956-7739, outside the U.S. at 317-572-3986, or fax 317-572-4002.

Jossey-Bass also publishes its books in a variety of electronic formats. Some content that appears in print may not be available in electronic books.

Library of Congress Cataloging-in-Publication Data

Erickson, Bette LaSere, 1945-
    Teaching first-year college students / Bette LaSere Erickson, Calvin B. Peters,
Diane Weltner Strommer.— Rev. and expanded ed.
        p. cm.
    Rev. ed. of: Teaching College Freshmen. 1991.
    Includes bibliographical references and index.
    ISBN-13: 978-0-7879-6439-9 (cloth)
    ISBN-10: 0-7879-6439-5 (cloth)
    1. College teaching—United States. 2. College freshmen—United States.
I. Peters, Calvin B. II. Strommer, Diane Weltner, 1935- III. Erickson, Bette LaSere,
1945- Teaching College Freshmen. IV. Title.
    LB2331.E76 2006
    378.1'2—dc22
                                                                    2006005273

Printed in the United States of America
FIRST EDITION
PB Printing   10 9 8 7 6 5 4 3 2 1

The Jossey-Bass
Higher and Adult Education Series

CONTENTS

PREFACE

In the years since the first edition of this book appeared, millions of first-year students have entered our nation's colleges and universities. By most estimates, only about half have completed their studies and emerged four, five, or six years later as freshly minted graduates. Some, of course, were not prepared for the challenges of college and academic life; others found the financial burden too much to bear, and still others tired of the classroom and abandoned academic routine to take their chances in life beyond the campus. But many more, perhaps most, were first-year students brimming with potential who encountered an institution out of step with their needs, a campus climate that was unwelcoming and unsupportive, and faculty who were all too often aloof, distant, and seemingly disinterested in students' struggles to fit in socially and succeed academically.

We in higher education have known for some time that the lives of students who enter colleges or universities are profoundly affected by their experiences in their first semesters, if not their first weeks on campus. If they feel welcomed, challenged, and supported, first-year students flourish. They persist in their studies, grow as human beings, and eventually become the sort of informed and inquiring citizens so essential for our times. If they feel abandoned and adrift, at once ignored and overwhelmed, they do what we all would do in similar circumstances: flee to places that are more comforting and more affirming.

The attrition of so many new college students exacts a high price—in dollars, in missed opportunity, and in human lives. Of course, the movement to direct the academy's attention to the experiences of first-year students recognized this fact more than two decades ago, and a number of committed faculty members and administrators on campuses across the country invested considerable energy attending to the needs of first-year students. They have much to show for those efforts. There are two national centers devoted to first-year student experience, and nearly every institution in the United States now conducts some form of focused seminar for its incoming students.

The heart of a student's first-year college experience remains in those interactions that occur in classrooms, laboratories, recital halls, and studios: teaching and learning. It is, after all, what drew them to college in the first place, and their relationships with faculty members, as instructors and as mentors, are the foundation for successful college careers. If more first-year students are going to persist and succeed in college—and the need is urgent that they do—then the instruction they receive demands our renewed attention. That is the focus of this book.

Audience

Teaching First-Year College Students was written primarily for those college and university faculty who teach first-year students. Although we draw on the research and theory of learning, our emphasis throughout is on practical application of these insights in the classroom. In nearly every chapter there are concrete suggestions about approaches and practices that we believe will improve the quality of instruction in first-year courses.

New faculty, who are often assigned to teach first-year courses, will find discussion ranging from the initial steps of course design through the conduct of class sessions and creation of assignments, to assessment of student performance and assigning of grades. Although our focus is on the first-year student and the first-year course, we believe faculty new to the professoriate will find our treatment of teaching and learning a useful general introduction to a crucial aspect of faculty careers.

For more experienced faculty, our discussion of the characteristics of first-year students and the practices that meet their needs will be a helpful review. Some may be returning to entry-level courses after teaching upper-division or graduate students, only to find that those techniques that worked so well with seniors or juniors are much less effective with first-year students. Others, for whom first-year instruction has been a way of life, may need a fresh start, a new approach, a different sort of assignment to reinvigorate courses that have grown a bit stale. *Teaching First-Year College Students* offers an extensive menu of theoretically informed practices that should allow both these groups of veteran faculty to bring renewed enthusiasm and intellectual excitement to their first-year courses.

Although our primary audience is our colleagues who teach first-year students, our treatment of the academic experience in the first semesters of students' college careers is also appropriate for administrators and others whose portfolios includes ensuring the quality of undergraduate programs and supporting campus efforts to improve instruction. Deans, department chairs, and faculty development professionals play important roles in developing the educational policies that steer institutional resources. We hope this book reminds them that teaching first-year students places special demands on faculty—for engagement, creativity, and time devoted to student learning.

Themes

Our discussion of teaching and learning in the first year of college is knitted together by three themes. First, we argue that those of us who teach first-year students need to meet them where they are, with *reasonable rigor and appropriate support*. This may seem to be a gloss on the obvious, but what it demands is not easily accomplished. Designing and conducting courses for first-year students that ask neither too much nor too little is a craft that requires considerable informed reflection and a deft touch. Likewise, supporting first-year students in their endeavors requires more than encouragement and empathy. Finding the right tasks, prompting the right practice, giving the right feedback to meet the diverse needs of first-year students is a challenge of the first order.

Second, we argue that first-year instruction demands *variety*—in approaches, examples, presentation style, assignments, evaluation, and nearly everything we do as instructors. First-year students bring to our campuses a range of learning styles, educational experiences, and cultural practices. Instruction that asks all of them to attend to the same things in the same way inevitably marginalizes some, obscuring their talents and potentials. Our emphasis on variety is not a call to spice up dull courses. Rather, it grows out of our deep appreciation for the insights produced by the research on learning styles, and our awareness that first-year students approach and accomplish learning in divergent ways.

Third, we argue that instruction in our first-year courses is effective only to the extent that it succeeds in *engaging* our students. There is, of course, no shortage of advice along these lines, and we are happy to join the chorus. But engaging first-year students is both more difficult and more important than the usual recommendations for active learning might suggest. Many first-year students enter our courses underpracticed in doing much more than committing things to memory. When we seek to engage them in activities and assignments that require deeper learning, they (and often we) founder. Yet it is in our first-year courses that students lay the foundation for future courses, not only in terms of content but also with regard to their academic skills and intellectual development. Unless we engage first-year students in those practices that sustain deep learning, we shortchange both them and our institutions.

Overview of the Contents

The three parts of the book reflect one way of thinking about the academic experience of first-year students. Part One presents a variety of information that allows us to see first-year students for who they are and to begin understanding what reasonable rigor and appropriate support mean in concrete terms. Chapter One draws a broad-brush portrait of first-year students. Our approach here is forward-looking in that we focus on what incoming students expect to encounter in college and how accurate those expectations are. We also spend some time discussing those aspects of academic life that first-year students find especially disconcerting. Chapters Two and Three include reviews of the literature on intellectual development in college students and the extensive research on learning styles. These reviews are practical in their intent and implications. How first-year students learn and what they think constitutes learning are the bases for our suggestions on how we can engage them by using a variety of instructional practices.

Part Two comprises a comprehensive catalogue of considerations and practices for faculty who teach first-year students. Chapter Four opens with an examination of appropriate goals for first-year courses and develops some working definitions of the sort of learning we often stress in them. It also notes how first-year students are likely to respond to the challenges they confront in our courses, with some initial suggestions about teaching methods and evaluation procedures. Chapter Five focuses on translating our goals into the syllabus that outlines for students what they can expect and what we expect of them. We also devote attention to how we conduct our first class sessions—the real introduction of first-year students to the core of college life. We turn to presenting and explaining information in Chapter Six. Lecturing remains a staple of collegiate instruction, and we offer a number of suggestions on how to engage students actively even when we feel we need to "cover the material."

The next four chapters in Part Two take a direct approach to the issue of engaging students. Chapter Seven includes an extensive list of activities that instructors can use during class to encourage involvement and deep learning. The activities we discuss can be used singly or in combination to appeal to a variety of student interests and needs. Chapter Eight shifts our attention to engaging students out of class, focusing on strategies to help them do (and learn from doing) their reading. We continue our discussion in Chapter Nine, offering a number of assignments, some individual, some cooperative, to structure the studying of first-year students productively. Chapter Ten includes our treatment of some ways to redesign entire courses to enhance student engagement. Here we offer suggestions about how problem-based learning, learning communities, and service learning can help us meet the needs of first-year students.

Part Two concludes with our examination of the procedures we employ to assess student learning and our discussion of grading in first-year courses. Chapter Eleven reviews a variety of evaluation techniques and offers a number of examples of good evaluation procedures. We discuss construction of examinations, focusing on developing items that measure more than memory. In addition, we present several examples of techniques to score essay exams and papers efficiently and reliably. Translating all that evaluation into grades is the topic of Chapter Twelve. We offer suggestions on which, and how much, various assignments should count, a review of procedures to sustain a climate of academic integrity in our courses, and brief consideration of grade inflation.

Part Three calls out three aspects of higher education that merit special consideration because they present particular opportunities and challenges in first-year instruction. Two of them, the issues of diversity and difference and the role of advising, have consequences well beyond the first-year, but they deserve our focused attention here because of the powerful effects they have on entering students. The remaining issue, large-class instruction, also warrants some extended discussion because large-enrollment courses are heavily populated by first-year students and present unique problems for the challenging, supportive, and engaging instruction we advocate.

We look at the issues of inclusion in first-year courses and classrooms in Chapter Thirteen. Although we refer to the importance of diversity in approaches and materials throughout our discussion, we think that some direct attention to the roles of race, gender, sexual orientation, religion, and more in teaching first-year students is appropriate. We again revisit some of the advice of earlier chapters and offer some suggestions for dealing with those difficult dialogues that can emerge in our classrooms. Chapter Fourteen tackles the problem of the large course. We offer a number of ways to overcome the alienation and disaffiliation that often infect large-enrollment courses, and we also revisit some of the advice of earlier chapters with an eye toward encouraging engagement when there are hundreds of students and only one of us.

Chapter Fifteen focuses on the interaction of faculty with first-year students as advisors and in first-year seminars. The encounters students have with faculty both in and out of the classroom are crucial to their success. We share some ideas about how to make advising sessions more productive for our students and more enjoyable for us. The final chapter offers our commentary on how institutions can enhance the academic experience of first-year students and how colleges and universities can build and sustain support for those who teach them.

A Last Word

Naturally, we hope that faculty will read all of *Teaching First-Year College Students,* but we recognize that with busy lives and numerous demands on their time the cover-to-cover approach may not always be feasible. The book can be sampled profitably; the practices discussed in Part Two are grounded in the discussion of Part One, but most of them can be adopted (and adapted) on a more ad hoc basis. We know that good teaching takes considerable time and attention. But we also know that trying out new assignments, including new examples, and employing new evaluation techniques is risky business. So whether you read from beginning to end or dip in here and there, we suggest you find one or two ideas of interest, try them out, and once you're comfortable with them come back later for more.

There is much more to be said about both first-year students and how we teach them than we have had room to include. Our portrait of first-year students could be expanded to include more discussion of those who are nontraditional, and our examples of assignments, exam questions, and course designs could have covered more disciplines, more types of courses, and more kinds of campuses. Nevertheless, we believe that the outlines of who first-year students are and what they require from us to succeed are here. There may be factors that sometimes and in some places make some needs more acute than others, but the basic challenge remains: to meet our first-year students with reasonable rigor and appropriate support. If we do that, their lives—and ours—will be richer.

ACKNOWLEDGMENTS

Projects such as this are never accomplished by only those whose names appear on the cover. There are always scores of people behind the scenes who provide ideas, advice, feedback, support, and more. Our work on *Teaching First-Year College Students* has benefited from the participation of many of our friends.

Ed Neal, of the University of North Carolina, Chapel Hill, made major contributions as we tried to envision a revised version of *Teaching College Freshmen*. Ed's wise counsel was instrumental in helping us see the project as a coherent whole. We hope he will be happy with the completed product.

Two anonymous reviewers of the first draft of this manuscript helped us clarify our thinking and pointed out several oversights and omissions. Mary Ellen Weimer, who also reviewed the draft manuscript, sharpened our focus in various places and reminded us of several valuable resources we had inadvertently overlooked. The book is better because of these reviews.

We are also grateful to David Brightman, our editor at Jossey-Bass. He saw the project through several dramatic changes and numerous postponements. His faith in us and in *Teaching First-Year College Students* has established a new benchmark for patience and support.

Our colleagues at the University of Rhode Island, some of whom are mentioned in the text, have for thirty years supported us with their creativity, wisdom, and wit, and with their unselfish willingness to share their ideas, their classroom successes, and their (rare) failures. Without them, we could not have undertaken this project, much less completed it.

Finally, we are deeply grateful to the literally thousands of first-year students we have encountered over the years. Some of them graciously shared their voices as part of the manuscript. All of them shared a bit of their lives with us. They have challenged us to be creative, thoughtful, caring, and young at heart. We hope those who follow in their footsteps will benefit from the work our first-year students have inspired.

B.L.E.
C.B.P.
D.W.S.

ABOUT THE AUTHORS

Teaching First-Year College Students is an extensive revision of the 1991 book *Teaching College Freshmen*. Although nearly all the text and most examples and illustrations in this book are new, it rests on the foundation laid in the earlier edition. For her contributions to that edition, we respectfully acknowledge Diane Weltner Strommer.

B.L.E.
C.B.P.

BETTE LaSERE ERICKSON is the director of the Instructional Development Program at the University of Rhode Island. She received her B.A. in English (1967) from Saint Olaf College and earned her Ed.D. (1975) from the University of Massachusetts, Amherst. Erickson is an authority on faculty development and course design and has published articles on faculty development programs and teaching techniques. She has also conducted numerous workshops and seminars at colleges and universities throughout the country. She is a founding member of the Professional and Organizational Development Network (POD) and has also served as its executive director.

CALVIN B. PETERS is professor of sociology at the University of Rhode Island. He is a graduate of Westmont College (B.A. 1971) and the University of Kentucky (M.A. 1973; Ph.D. 1977). His scholarly expertise is in cultural sociology and the sociology of knowledge. In addition to his sociological books and articles, Peters has published papers and presented workshops and seminars on teaching and instructional design. For the last thirty years, he has been heavily involved in instructing and advising first-year students, regularly teaching introductory sociology to enrollments of more than five hundred.

DIANE WELTNER STROMMER earned an A.B. in English from the University of North Carolina, Chapel Hill, and an M.A. (1965) and Ph.D. (1969) from the Ohio State University. She retired as dean emerita of University College and Special Academic Programs at the University of Rhode Island in 2001. Since 1998, Strommer has worked abroad, serving as the founding dean at Zayed University in Dubai and Abu Dhabi, United Arab Emirates; as an administrator at the American University in Bulgaria, Blagoevgrad, Bulgaria; and as the accreditation advisor for the Glion Institute for Higher Education and Les Roches Schools of Hotel Management in Switzerland.

PART ONE

Understanding First-Year Students

The challenges of our time make college education indispensable to a fulfilling life and responsible citizenship. Persistence in college and eventual degree completion depend heavily on the instruction students encounter during their first semesters on campus. Effective instruction in turn depends on understanding who first-year students are: their expectations, their attitudes, their intellectual development, their views of learning.

Chapter One gives an overview of entering college students. We discuss their expectations for college and the difficulties of adjusting to a higher education environment that is very different from secondary school. We outline some of the particular challenges faculty confront when they look out over a classroom full of first-year students and also sketch out some of the factors that make this generation of college entrants somewhat different from their predecessors. Chapter Two focuses on the intellectual development of first-year students and why they present special challenges (and opportunities) to those who teach them. Although the chapter is designed to lay a foundation for the instructional practices that are discussed in Part Two, it does contain some general suggestions for constructing first-year curricula in ways that encourage and support student learning. Chapter Three contains a selected review of the literature on learning styles and offers broad advice on how faculty can accommodate the variety of approaches to and understanding of learning that first-year students bring to their classrooms.

CHAPTER 1

First-Year Students in Perspective

On a warm September morning, Professor O'Keefe's computer chimes as an e-mail message arrives. O'Keefe's first class of the day concluded just over an hour ago, and he is reflecting on what went well and what he needs to do in preparation for the next session. The e-mail chimes again, and O'Keefe begins scrolling through the unread and newly arrived messages. After deleting a couple that apparently slipped past the university's spam filter, he stops at a message tagged with a university address and a subject heading that reads "Wow What an Intense Read!"

Intrigued, O'Keefe double-clicks to open the message. A bemused smile spreads across his face as the text of the message fills his screen:

> Wow what an intense read, Taylor is. What does that guy do for fun geez. I have become fond of the dictionary through this book. Yet I still have a few questions: 2nd paragraph on page 17 huh wha? Also bottom of page 19 to pg 20 paragraph. Woah, that's a little to deep for me. Could you shed some light on these paragraphs please? and the key phrases "Soft relativism and Soft despotism." i have been outlining and noting each paragraph so i think i am on track, i will be attending thursday nite services.
> Over and Out for now.
> Even though it's a class of 500 you really do well, I like it even though i'm from a small town. (my entire high school could fit in your class) WOW.
> Margaret (I always sit in front)

Although "Professor O'Keefe" is our creation, the message embedded in the vignette is verbatim, a text drafted and sent by a first-year student during the first two weeks of classes. The message is charming in its enthusiasm, typical in its inattention to the strictures of standard English, amusing in its word choice ("thursday nite services" refers to a scheduled help session), and challenging in its implicit acknowledgment of the difficulty of college-level work and the subsequent requests for assistance.

The message is emblematic of the first-year students who populate American college and university campuses each fall. The claim may be surprising. We have all heard descriptions (and perhaps even made them ourselves) of first-year students that are a less-than-flattering assessment of their intellectual skills, their motivation, and their general ability to negotiate the complexities of an academic landscape. For all its informality, Margaret's e-mail belies a grumbling account of the first-year student. If motivation can be judged by enthusiasm, it is certainly present, and if getting acquainted with the dictionary reflects willingness to engage in intellectual labor, there is evidence of that as well. Indeed, the entire message, with its questions and its promise to attend the "services," shows at least the beginning of a sense of what is necessary to succeed in an academic community.

Why They Come

There is plenty of evidence to support the idea that these qualities can be extrapolated across the more than one million full-time, first-year students enrolling in institutions across the country. The American Freshman Project, a long-term study of first-year students, has consistently reported that an overwhelming majority of incoming students decide to go to college for what most of us would regard as good reasons: to learn more about things that interest them (77 percent), to get training for a specific career (75 percent), to gain a general education and appreciation of ideas (65 percent), or to prepare for graduate or professional school (57 percent; Sax and others, 2004). Similarly, at least by their own estimation, first-year students possess the requisite character and ability to succeed. A significant majority of them (60 percent or more in each case) rate themselves to be above average in their drive to succeed, academic ability, persistence, and intellectual self-confidence (Sax and others, 2004). Although they don't necessarily confirm these self-assessments, recent standardized testing results are at least consistent with them. Math and verbal SAT averages have inched upward over the last decade, with the math average currently at its highest point since 1967 (all scores recentered). These changes are not dramatic, but they do (within the limits of standardized testing) fly in the face of the grousing that students are now less prepared for college than they once were.

If incoming students enroll in colleges or universities to get a general education and prepare for graduate school, their reflections of first-year experience suggest that in general they haven't been disappointed. The National Survey of Student Engagement (NSSE) indicates that more than 80 percent of first-year students report a "substantial" gain in their ability to think critically and analytically and in acquiring a broad general education. Additionally, more than half of them said they had made similar gains in acquiring job- or work-related skills (NSSE, 2004).

Yet something seems not quite right about this. The confident, well-prepared, intellectually curious students who are interested in general education seem much less common in the first-year classroom than in tables of survey data and the publicity of admissions and advancement offices. For every Margaret, there seem to be others (and many of them) who are less engaged, less enthusiastic, and less willing to ask questions, seek help, or even attend the "services" we schedule for them. For all the confidence first-year students express in their abilities, the faculty teaching them are more likely to hear the worry and self-doubt expressed by another student: "No matter how much I study, I still feel like I'm not prepared. . . . Some people are good with writing and know a lot of big words, but I don't." Somehow, the promise implicit in Margaret's e-mail fades in light of the less buoyant reality we confront reading our first set of essays, recording midterm grades, and meeting with students who "just don't understand anything."

In a sense, both impressions of first-year students are right. They *are* enthusiastic, intellectually curious, and reasonably well prepared for academic life. Yet at the same time they *are* easily discouraged, unnerved, and overwhelmed. George D. Kuh puts the matter this way: "For many new students . . . the initial weeks of the first academic term are like being in a foreign land. With only intermittent feedback and classes meeting but two or three times a week, students who think they are doing well are sometimes surprised to discover after their first midterm exam reports that their academic performance is subpar. After six or eight weeks, some have dug a hole so deep that getting back to ground level seems almost impossible" (2005, p. 86). Kuh (2005) goes on to argue that the strangeness of college and university life to the uninitiated causes first-year students to underestimate the challenges they will confront, both in and out of the classroom, and to overestimate their capacity to bring plans and practices in line with the new environment they confront.

There is nothing novel in the observation that the move from high school to college is a difficult one. Students have been told this repeatedly by teachers, counselors, parents, and even those of us at universities in various Welcome Day and orientation presentations.

In spite of the prosaic nature of the observation, it is worth our while to spend some time reflecting on just why the transition is so difficult, and on how the challenges inherent in the "foreign land" of the college campus affect the teaching and learning of first-year students.

A Backward Glance

Why do students who have succeeded in high school and who seem well prepared for college life struggle and sometimes fail when they arrive on campus? Perhaps the most common explanation casts the American high school as the culprit. Students are not challenged. They do not write. They do not read. They take their senior year off. All of these observations (and more) have been used, alone or in combination, to account for why the student who never got lower than a B and who did well on the SAT is not succeeding in philosophy or physics or psychology. Although the criticism of the American high school (or more properly, the institution of the American high school) on which these explanations turn cannot be easily dismissed, we think the finger-pointing many of us in higher education engage in is both counterproductive and just this side of smug.

The high school in the United States faces an array of challenges that make those confronted by higher education (particularly at four-year institutions) seem significantly less daunting. Moreover, new national standards that require all students to be prepared for post-secondary education without remediation (Reich, 2003) have dramatically raised the stakes, adding political pressure to the already complex educational tasks assigned to American secondary schools. Some may see the movement to impose new standards and new means of assessment—exit exams, portfolios, certificates of mastery, senior projects, and the like—on high schools and their graduates as proof that the difficulties first-year students encounter stem primarily from lack of preparation.

The American Diploma Project (2004), for example, argues bluntly that "the preparation students receive in high school is the greatest predictor of bachelor's degree attainment" (p. 2). The merit of the argument cannot be dismissed out of hand: better-prepared students do succeed more often. But at the same time, we need to remind ourselves that one of the strongest arguments that successful students are better prepared is that they do succeed. If preparation predicts student success, student success acts as the sign and seal of preparation.

All of this tends to deflect attention from what happens in the classrooms and laboratories at colleges and universities. If students succeed, they were, against the odds, well prepared. If they fail, well, perhaps when the high schools get straightened out that will not happen so often. Such a passive stance is neither accurate—what happens in college instruction *does* matter—nor viable in the long run. After all, the same forces that have begun to demand more accountability and more assessment from secondary schools are also arrayed around the wall of academe. In the words of the American Diploma Project (2004), the states backed by the clout of the federal Higher Education Act should "hold postsecondary institutions accountable for the academic success of the students they admit——including learning, persistence and degree completion——rather than allowing them to continue to place ill-prepared students in remedial, non-credit-bearing courses and then replace dropouts with new students the following year" (p. 7).

Our point here is not that the preparation of students is of no concern to faculty teaching first-year students. Nor is it that American high schools are functioning adequately or that they are beyond our capacity to improve or even transform. Rather, what we think makes most sense is for those who teach first-year students to try to devise some means to meet them where they are, academically, intellectually, and emotionally, without abandoning reasonable rigor and appropriately high standards. This is a difficult task. To accomplish it, we first need to acknowledge more clearly than most of us have just how "foreign" the land we inhabit is. If we can get a sense of how alien things must seem to first-year students, we can perhaps begin to see their preparation (or lack of it) in a different and perhaps more illuminating light.

Touching Down

A number of us who have been in college since we first enrolled (and that counts many faculty, both full- and part-time, as well as many administrators) can no longer recall when the land we currently inhabit seemed strange. But if we listen to the voices of students as they reflect on their first few weeks on campus, our initial feelings when we first encountered academe may begin to come back to us:

> I'm worried that my classes may be too difficult and if I have a problem it might not be too easy to get in touch with the teachers. I am worried that teachers may have too many students to keep in contact with them all. I hope all our coursework will be explained effectively in class. (Stephanie)

> In college, the course load is much greater and I get much more work. It is also easier to put things off in college. In high school, every class was five days a week so I had to do the homework for that class every day. But here there is a day between classes, so it's hard not to put homework off until the night before it is due. I am worried that I may get overwhelmed with the work and not be able to handle it all at once. (Christine)

> In chemistry, there's only three exams and they're spaced very far apart. That's a lot of information you have to know and I don't even know how to begin studying. Also, anatomy. There's so much to memorize and I'm worried my study habits aren't up to par. (Christina)

> I don't know how I am going to do on tests, papers, and assignments. The workload is not out of control, but most of it is reading and I hate to read. I guess I better get used to it. I still haven't had any tests in any of my classes so I have no idea what to expect or what to study. (Louis)

The conduct and pace of a typical college course is something with which we are intimately familiar, and so it is difficult for us to recall any longer how stark the contrast is between the routinized curriculum of the secondary school and the more idiosyncratic character of the college classroom. But students notice it right away. Their courses are larger and seem less personal; the structure is looser and the support less evident; expectations seem less clear and evaluation is less frequent. Given the abruptness of these changes—it is important to remember that there is no real *transition* from high school to college, only a stopping and a starting—it is not surprising that many first-year students' initial concerns revolve around the course load and the work it entails.

To some extent, of course, incoming students have been primed to shudder at the amount of work they are assigned. As we mentioned earlier, they have been barraged with the advice that college is different from high school, and most of those observations center around the amount and difficulty of course work. The Faculty Survey of Student Engagement (NSSE, 2004) quantifies that point, reporting that on average full-time faculty expect students to study six hours per week per course (the figure is slightly lower for part-time faculty). For a student enrolled in four or five courses, those faculty expectations come close to transforming studying into a full-time job.

As those expectations are communicated to students, in orientation or during the first few days of class, it is little wonder that college begins to seem like a place different from any they have ever experienced. Their last year in high school was indeed spent in another land. More than 80 percent of incoming college students report studying ten hours or fewer per week during that final high school year, and a mere 3 percent report studying more than twenty hours per week, a figure that would bring them in line with faculty expectations (Sax and others, 2004). The dramatic difference between students' past practice and their future as they hear it portrayed would be enough to overwhelm most anyone's sense of efficacy:

> "I feel like I am totally overwhelmed already with all my schoolwork. It is only three weeks into the semester and I feel I am behind in every class. I just hope that I learn to manage my time better and get ahead

of the game very quickly. I am just really worried I won't do well. (Michaela)

The issue of time management looms large in any number of first-year student comments, but the simple quantity of work expected is not the only thing that eats away at their confidence:

> I have never studied any subjects as challenging as these. My courses are very in-depth and require a lot of careful reading and understanding of hard topics. Many times it is hard to grasp exactly the concepts without the help of the teacher. (Matthew)

The "hard topics" of college course work are often linked to assignments that require students to move beyond memorization or simple comprehension of a text to application of ideas to solve new problems or extension of ideas to new, yet to be discussed, areas. More than eight in ten faculty report that their course work emphasizes applying concepts to practical problems (NSSE, 2004)—something many, if not most, incoming students have little experience in doing, let alone studying for.

A good deal of the anxiety first-year students experience crystallizes around this issue. They enter college believing that they will need to do more work to succeed, and they indicate they are willing to do it. For example, nearly 50 percent say they anticipate studying sixteen or more hours per week during their first year in college (Kuh, 2005). Although this does not fully meet faculty expectations, it does indicate a significant change in attitude and willingness to try to engage the alien nature of academe on its own terms. Yet when confronted with a complex text and a series of questions that ask them to extend, extrapolate from, and respond to an author's argument, their good intentions run headlong into a paucity of experience in doing what is expected:

> When I went to college, everyone told me, "You'll do fine." However, my classes are so different at college. There are no cut-and-dried problems in most of my courses, and no neatly written notes on the board. I hope it will get easier as I go on. (Christopher)

These intellectual challenges are exacerbated by students' perception of the effect of class size on their ability to seek and receive help from their instructors. For all the criticisms of American high schools as large, cold, impersonal places, many students entering college recall their relationships with high school teachers as both personal and helpful. More than 40 percent report talking with teachers outside of class between one and five hours a week, and a quarter of them indicated they spent time in a teacher's home (Sax and others, 2004). The strange world of college seems to put such relationships and the assistance and support they offer beyond their reach:

> One thing that has me worried is class size. I am used to a class size that does not exceed twenty-five, and here I do not have a class smaller than fifty. Up till this year all students have been exposed to a teacher one on one for their entire academic careers. I have always had great relationships with my teachers, and now I don't feel that sense of comfort that I have been used to for the last twelve years. I understand that every professor has office hours, but my worry is more in the sense that they won't even know my name when I get there. (Marissa)

The manner in which many college courses are conducted offers little solace to first-year students eager to do well but anxious because of the newness and the difficulty of the challenges they confront. Lecturing remains the predominant method of instruction in college classrooms, particularly those with sizable enrollments, and the rate at which material is presented can quickly outpace the note-taking skills developed in a smaller, more leisurely setting. The accumulation of lecture after lecture in course after course often leaves students at a loss to understand how class time contributes anything to their learning except more notes to master before the next exam:

> In my chemistry class I just write the notes and do not understand anything. My professor does not help much. (Jerelyn)

In large measure then, first-year students experience their initial weeks in the classroom separated from the support structures that sustained them throughout high school. Reading assignments asking only that chapter two in the text be read for Monday or merely announcing pages 23–157 will be covered on the exam have replaced the frequent homework that, annoying as it sometimes seemed, at least gave clear direction. Classes no longer meet daily but are a scattered patchwork, gathering sometimes two or three times a week, with nothing in particular to do between one session and the next. Instructors seem distant and a bit forbidding as they fill notebook pages with the four causes of this, the three parts of that, and the formula for calculating something or other.

It is little wonder that many first-year students share a similar lament:

> Some of my teachers expect you to teach yourself. (Kiera)

The Bargain

The encounter between first-year students and college we have so far sketched is a familiar one. Adjusting to the rigors of academic life, learning how to budget time, "pulling all-nighters" to ensure success on those first exams, all the while battling the rigid requirements of a demanding professor, are among the recurring themes in the standard narrative of how success in college is attained. Many of us have probably told some version of that story in recounting our own college years. Obviously, there is some truth to the tale. Students *do* find themselves struggling with their course work, and many *do* learn how to manage the heavy load, while gaining knowledge, skills, and self-satisfaction along the way. Of course, the tale also has a less happy variant in which students cannot adjust and must face the consequences of that failing. We know that story too.

If those two accounts of first-year academic life exhausted the range of student experiences, it would be a fairly straightforward task to think about teaching first-year students. Institutions and their faculties could devote themselves to easing the abrupt change from high school to college, working to hone study skills, investing resources to reduce the alienation of large classes, and nurturing sound curricular design and effective instructional practice. Many institutions are, in fact, doing precisely these things with an eye toward enhancing student success and, not incidentally, reaping the rewards of the higher retention sure to follow. Those efforts are all to the good.

Another account of first-year students' experiences emerges from the data on faculty and student expectations, and the tale told is troubling. As we have seen, when faculty members describe their courses and the demands they impose on students, they indicate that students are going to have to spend a significant amount of time preparing to engage in extending and applying ideas to analyze practical problems. Moreover, only a third of the faculty say their courses emphasize memorization (NSSE, 2004). None of this is surprising; expectations of this sort make college what it is—college.

At the same time, we have also seen that first-year students anticipate spending less time (decidedly so) working on course material outside of class than the faculty who teach them expect, and as it turns out, even those expectations are a bit optimistic. The College Student Experiences Questionnaire, administered at the end of the first college year, shows fully 40 percent of first-year students actually spent ten or fewer hours per week preparing for class, with nearly two-thirds reporting spending fifteen or fewer hours (Kuh, 2005). That is less than half the amount of time the faculty who teach them say they expect. Additionally, students also report that a substantial majority of their coursework (about 70 percent) stresses memorization, a figure significantly larger than the one in the faculty account (NSSE, 2004).

In the traditional narrative of the first year of college, this gap between faculty expectations and student expectations and behavior is filled with anxiety. It is why students feel overwhelmed, why they struggle, and why the transition to college is so demanding. In the usual account, studying replaces student anxiety, skill development replaces their struggle, and adapting to the intellectual life and rhythms of the academy replaces the rough transition. At least this is how we account for those who succeed.

Yet what students report is not fully consistent with the story we are so used to telling. They study more, but not nearly so much as we want. They may develop some new analytic skills, but most of their time is spent doing what they already know how to do—committing things to memory. They may adapt to the life of the university, but it is also more likely than we may suspect that we, the university and its faculty, adapt to them. There is some evidence that this is so. Eighty percent of first-year students report receiving grades of mostly B or higher (NSSE, 2004).

Our point here is not to launch an attack on methods of evaluation or join the national sputtering about grade inflation. Rather, we want to encourage some reflection on just how our stated expectations for first-year students fit with the actual practice of our instruction. We say students need to invest six hours per week per course, yet they succeed by doing significantly less. We say students need to develop higher-order intellectual skills, yet they say we mostly ask them to memorize. We say we want students to develop the skills that will sustain lifelong learning, but many of our courses seem to demand only that they do more, and more frequently, of the things we already know they can do.

We are suggesting that in the reality of the classroom encounter between our expectations and first-year student abilities, a bargain is often struck that allows both sides to remain in the comfort of familiar territory. For our part as faculty, we relax the demands that students immerse themselves in reading by highlighting the major ideas of the text in our classroom discussion. We ease the difficulty of applying ideas to practical problems by illustrating how it is done and then asking only that students recapitulate our demonstration. For their part, students soon learn how and how much of the reading is really necessary and that learning to apply ideas really means learning to memorize those applications we have performed. Once the bargain is struck, often in the wake of the first assignment, paper, or exam, we can settle into our familiar rhythm of teaching without having to worry too much about their reading skills and work habits. Students can return to the old practices that have served them well without having to worry too much about how it will all turn out.

This bargain is understandable in many ways. Teaching first-year students is a challenging task that all too often goes under-rewarded. Courses are frequently large, and students often enroll merely to complete a general education requirement rather than out of interest or intellectual curiosity. In such circumstances, the enthusiasm that characterizes students on the verge of their college careers can easily wane, leaving only the hard work of learning new skills and new material at a startlingly fast rate. Not infrequently, student resistance and resignation emerge—many of the comments we hear about faculty "not helping much" or "just not caring" are probably indicators—and when that happens, courses teeter precariously on the edge of disaster.

We rescue our courses, our students, and ourselves by changing the rules of the game in subtle rather than overt ways. Part of the bargain is never having to announce you will ask them only to memorize what you say in class. But somehow the message is communicated. Courses morph into something less than they were intended to be, and students begin to realize that in spite of all the talk college is not so different after all.

It is difficult to tell how widespread and how frequent such bargaining is. We suspect, however, that it is neither isolated nor uncommon. Students learn what college is like and how to manage its demands in the first semester or quarter on campus. They discover what they need to do to succeed in their courses, and they settle into the pattern of studying that has worked for them. The pattern does not change much over their academic career. Full-time first-year students report studying an average of thirteen hours per week; full-time seniors looking toward graduation say they study fourteen hours per week (NSSE, 2004). It is difficult to account for the discrepancy between what students—successful students at both the beginning and the end of their college experience—say they do and what we faculty say they need to do to succeed without concluding there is some significant bargaining going on in many first-year classrooms.

Again, we are not pointing an accusing finger at those faculty who teach first-year students, or at the students themselves. As we have said, the bargain is an understandable response to what seem to be intractable problems inherent in first-year courses. Nevertheless, once the bargain is struck the opportunity to bridge the gap between first-year students and their instructors' expectations with creative instruction, sufficient practice, and appropriate support is squandered. Instead, we adapt our courses to what we think students are able and willing to do (the willing part is a major aspect here), thus setting the tone not only for their first semesters but very probably for their last semesters as well.

There is no little irony in the bargain. As Karen Shilling and Karl Shilling (2005) point out, students' hopes for college are quite similar to what we in higher education expect them to accomplish. When we bargain that point of connection away, we shortchange ourselves; but more important, we deprive our students of what they genuinely seek—an authentic college classroom.

Who They Are

Going to college does not merely continue a student's classroom instruction in another venue. It is an important rite of passage that announces, at least for many, the initial move from adolescence to adulthood, and from an ethos of dependence to one of independence. The newfound freedom from the regimented confines of high school curricula is often joined to a world where parental supervision is significantly reduced, if not absent entirely. The passage is, of course, most clearly delineated for those students who enroll in college full-time immediately after completing their secondary education, but the decision to attend college is a culturally important marker for all first-time students.

In spite of some evidence to the contrary, a substantial majority of first-time college students continue to fit within the broad outlines of a "traditional" educational career. They applied to colleges and universities during their final year of high school and chose to attend immediately following graduation. They attend college full-time, rely on parents or other family members for at least some financial support, and work or plan on working part-time at the most. The American Freshman Project estimated that 1.2 million full-time students would begin their careers at four-year colleges in the autumn of 2004. Nearly all had completed high school earlier that year and were nineteen years of age or younger. Eighty percent expected some financial assistance from their families, and although nearly half expect to "get a job to help pay for college," fewer than 7 percent anticipate working full-time (Sax and others, 2004).

Of course, not all first-year students attend a four-year college; nor do all follow the traditional educational trajectory. Community college populations are often different, especially in the proportion of first-year students who attend part-time or who work full-time. The National Center for Education Statistics (Choy, 2002) reports that undergraduate students are increasingly likely to attend part-time, work full-time, and delay entry into higher education, factors that are most common at two-year institutions. Over time, these developments have expanded the number of "nontraditional" students on college campuses, something our now-dated image of "Joe College" often obscures (Ishler, 2005).

Among first-year students, the balance of the "traditional" and "nontraditional" varies by institution, largely reflecting varied missions and applicant populations. But those features that most commonly make first-year students "nontraditional" may not transform the nature of the challenges they confront as profoundly as we might think. On the contrary, perhaps the characteristics of nontraditional students are best understood as factors that intensify the initial difficulty of confronting a college environment. Full-time work makes the already knotty issue of time management more pressing, if not intractable. Delaying enrollment exacerbates anxiety about (now rusty) academic skills. Part-time enrollment limits the opportunity to connect with fellow students as well as instructors, making overcoming the "foreignness of the land" a more daunting task. Those challenges are real, but they are substantially the same as the issues that originally persuaded us that first-year students had distinctive needs that deserved particular attention.

If we move beyond the discussion of employment patterns, the increase in delayed enrollment, and the like, we find there are other characteristics of the contemporary cohort of first-year students that are worthy of note. Perhaps the most dramatic has to do with gender. Over the last thirty-five years, women have gone from a minority of entering students (45 percent in 1966) to a distinct majority (55 percent in 2001; Astin, Oseguera, Sax, and Korn, 2002). Additionally, women entering college for the first time express a marked increase in intention to pursue a postgraduate degree, with more than three-quarters indicating it was one of their academic goals. This is also a sea change; women are now more interested in pursuing a graduate degree than are men, a dramatic reversal from the situation a generation ago (Astin, Oseguera, Sax, and Korn, 2002).

Changes in the racial composition of first-time college students are marked. In 1971, 90 percent of first-time, full-time college students were white. By 2003, white students composed only three-quarters of the incoming class. This change has been accompanied by an increase in the number of African American, Latino/Latina, and Asian American students. The proportion of Native American students has remained relatively constant over the same time (Astin, Oseguera, Sax, and Korn, 2002).

The most dramatic growth has been in the proportion of Asian American students. Thirty years ago, Asian Americans constituted a mere 1 percent of first-time college students. Now, nearly 8 percent of incoming students are Asian American, a representation more than double that in the population as a whole. Latino students have also made substantial gains. In the last ten years alone, Latinos have grown from about 4 percent of first-time students to nearly 7 percent. African American enrollment has also trended upward, but at a slower and less consistent rate. A generation ago, just under 8 percent of first-time college students were African American; now the figure is slightly under 10 percent. Although that represents an increase since the 1970s, in the last decade the proportion of entering college students who are African American has actually declined from a peak of about 12 percent in the early 1990s (all figures from Astin, Oseguera, Sax, and Korn, 2002).

Beyond its race and gender composition, today's cohort of first-year students differs from those of the past in other ways that might be noticed by faculty. Protestants are no longer in the majority, and first-year students expressing no religious preference have risen to about one in six, nearly double the level of twenty years ago (Astin, Oseguera, Sax, and Korn, 2002). The presence of gay, lesbian, bisexual, and transsexual (GLBT) students on our campuses is no longer a secret, though their proportion in an incoming class is difficult to determine. Estimates put the figure at 7 percent, but some observers argue that prejudice and harassment—some of it violent—prevent some students from disclosing, making most estimates too low (Ishler, 2005). The presence of GLBT organizations on most campuses (and the presence of queer studies on some) serves to make the needs and concerns of GLBT students an increasingly visible part of the culture of the academy.

These changes are, of course, long overdue, and although the cohort of first-year college students doesn't yet "look like America" it has begun to move in that direction. This diversity brings to the college campus and classroom at least some of the same political and cultural struggles that regularly roil our life in the public square. We think this is a positive development. At the same time, however, the dynamics of classroom instruction and student-faculty interaction are affected in ways we have been slow to anticipate. Our patterns of instruction, our heuristic examples, and even our humor often continue to reflect our experience with a student population that was more white and male than is now the case, and the potential for misunderstanding and alienation is frequently overlooked. We devote considerable attention to these issues throughout the coming chapters, but for now this is worth noting because our students are more varied than they were in the past. Meeting students where they are with reasonable rigor and appropriate challenges requires faculty who are more attuned to the communities students represent and more appreciative of the opportunities for educational enrichment inherent in today's classrooms.

Getting Overwhelmed

Much more could be said about first-year college students. Their attitudes, hopes, and political and social views are the stuff for rich and varied reflection. In the midst of percentages and trends it is, however, easy to lose track of the fundamental fact that the young women and men who come to college campuses come primarily as *students.* The centrality of this status may well be affected by a variety of other factors, but in the end those who enroll in college for the first time will measure their success in the academic environment by how they perform as students.

That simple fact sets up a high-stakes game. As we have noted, the college campus is a strange land brimming with new experiences, new opportunities, and new challenges. Sorting out how to have it all—an unfettered social life and academic success as a student—is no small task. Not surprisingly, the act of balancing new friends, new surroundings, and new classes creates considerable strain on first-year students. Their worries run a wide gamut, from weight gain to homesickness, from alcohol consumption to diversity, from not finding friends to failing academically. Listen to a sampling of voices:

> I have to say that the first day I got here I wanted to leave. I felt so uncomfortable and as if I had just been dropped off to fight a battle I would inevitably lose. I spent most of my day on the phone and was worried I would never have a close group of friends like I did in high school. (Deven)

> Although it may sound somewhat selfish or self-centered, I am worried about gaining the "freshman fifteen." I have been trying to eat healthy here, but it can get difficult. I don't want college to be the cause of me gaining weight. (Monica)

> Back in high school, I could slack off and still get B's. Here at college I know I can't do this. I am worried that the first day I oversleep and miss class, that will lead to another, and another. I am trying hard not to mess up, but if I do, I will have to work harder to not let it become a pattern. (Alex)

> I drink but I don't smoke. But I don't drink every day of the week either. People have a lot of different styles and it takes some getting used to. (Brittany)

> I am very happy with the diversity here, but it also frightens me. I am not used to others celebrating holidays in different ways and that some do not believe in God. I have never been in a situation where I have met people who are Jewish, Muslim, atheist, born-again, and many more. I came from a tiny private school and it is overwhelming. (Kylie)

Kylie's sense of being overwhelmed is probably more widely shared than she imagines. More than a quarter of all first-year students, and fully one-third of first-year women, report they "felt overwhelmed by all they had to do" during their last year in high school (Sax and others, 2004). Given the strange land they find when the arrive at college for the first time in late summer and the anxiety that their impending encounters with faculty and classrooms produces, the feeling of being engulfed in too much, too fast is probably a common response.

The initial anxiety of first-year students is often exacerbated by two forces that tend to pull students in opposing directions. On the one hand, most of them desperately want to fit into their new environment and what, for all practical purposes, is their new life. On the other hand, many of them are desperately homesick, longing for known routine, old friends, and familiar faces. As we might guess, managing the challenges of the college classroom while worrying about making new friends one moment and missing younger siblings left at home the next can be more than a little stressful.

In their early days on campus, first-year students are often more concerned about fitting in socially than they are about meeting the academic and intellectual demands of their courses (Terenzini and others, 1996). The urgency of "finding a place" can, of course, make first-year students long for home even more earnestly. High school friends seem dearer, and the high school that students could not wait to get out of is remembered as a warm and caring place compared to the anonymity of the college campus. As one student put it:

> Unlike high school, no one is here to tell you everything you need to do. It's a big difference knowing you need to do everything yourself. No one is here to do anything for you. (Julie)

This somewhat forlorn comment returns us to the encounter between first-year students and their faculty. We do not often see ourselves as "telling them everything they need to do," although that is perhaps more of our role than we like to imagine. Patrick Terenzini (Terenzini and others, 1996) suggests that we seek ways to "humanize" our relationships with students to assure them that we value them both as members of our academic community and as persons. Making an effort to learn and use the names of first-year students in our courses or treating our students as if they were our own daughters and sons (two of Terenzini's suggestions) will not cure their homesickness or reduce their sense of alienation, but it at least reminds us that there is more going on in their lives than reading chapter one in the text or writing that short essay due next Thursday.

In the end, however, our relationship with first-year students is primarily academic. To fulfill the obligations inherent in that relationship, we are called to challenge them, support them, assess them—in a word, teach them. We have outlined who our first-year students are (and who they are not) because we believe seeing them clearly makes it more likely that we can meet them where they are. We do so not to join them in a bargain that leaves them and us unchanged, but rather to begin the process of developing those intellectual, social, and citizenly skills that our nation's needs (and the world's) demand they possess.

Reprise

With a shake of his head, Professor O'Keefe leans back in his chair, preparing to return to that bit of reading he promised himself he would get done before the week's end. But Margaret's message reclaims his attention; she had him at "wow." He decides that, given her enthusiasm, he probably should respond promptly. He clicks the Reply button and begins to type:

Hi Margaret: Thanks for the note. I'm glad you. . . .

When O'Keefe begins his response to Margaret, there is a gap separating him from her and her classmates that is wider than even what the whimsical text of her message might indicate. In addition to their experiences in high school and their expectations of and anxiety about college, the Margarets in our classes bring with them a variety of ways of learning as well as a variety of definitions of just what learning is. How first-year students learn and how they think about their learning have profound effects for faculty who teach them. Understanding the intellectual development of college students and the classroom consequences of a variety of learning styles is crucial if we are to provide appropriate challenges and support to first-year students. We turn our attention to those tasks now.

For Further Exploration

- The American Freshman Project. Higher Education Research Institute. University of California, Los Angeles.

  The yearly publications of the American Freshman Project offer invaluable insight into the demographics, attitudes, values, expectations, and experiences of incoming first-year students. The project also publishes longitudinal data covering the last four decades.

- The National Survey of Student Engagement. Center for Postsecondary Research, Indiana University.

  This national survey complements the American Freshman Project. The National Survey of Student Engagement data tabulate students' self-reports about their academic practices during their first year and last year of college. The data are especially useful in understanding what students expect of, and what they actually do in, college.

- Nathan, R. *My Freshman Year: What a Professor Learned by Becoming a Student.* Ithaca, N.Y.: Cornell University Press, 2005.

  Rebekah Nathan (the pseudonym of Northern Arizona University anthropologist Cathy Small) "returned to college" and produced an ethnography of her experience as a "first-year" student. Her account of student life in and out of the classroom is worth a look.

CHAPTER 2

Intellectual Development in College

Students differ. We all know that at some level. Still, many of us teach our courses as our favorite teachers taught them. We assume that most able and talented students will respond as we did; we forget that *our* favorite professors were not necessarily our classmates' favorites. When we confront student differences in concrete terms—in comments in a course evaluation, for example—we are often surprised. These comments written anonymously by first-year students enrolled in the same course reveal how dramatic the differences can be:

> I find the course very interesting. [The instructor] insists on group discussions, which I find to be an outstanding method of learning. He also provides demonstrations in many of his lectures, which makes the concepts we are studying easier to visualize. I've learned a lot and I can honestly say it's the best course I've ever had.

> I felt that I didn't learn half as much as I should have. Going to class was a waste of time. . . . For the first time in my life I became *very* apathetic toward a course in school.

> The group discussions are a very good idea. They gave me a chance to work out problems with people who are on my level. This is more effective than watching someone do it on the blackboard.

> Too much group work wasted class time. More of the problems should have been explained by the instructor.

How do we make sense of such conflicting views? How do we respond to student evaluations and recommendations when a practice that one student considers "outstanding" another sees as "a waste of time"? Research on student development sheds light on both questions. In this chapter, we summarize the findings from this research that are most pertinent to first-year students. The chapters on teaching in Part Two draw on the developmental and stylistic differences among first-year students, and many of our suggestions reflect a concern for responding to students' needs in ways that are inclusive rather than exclusive, supportive instead of frustrating.

Among the many changes students undergo during the college years, one of the most significant is in their perception of learning. William Perry ([1968] 1999), among the first to study the intellectual development of college students, found that students' assumptions and expectations about teaching and learning change while they are in college and that the changes follow a predictable pattern. Our discussion of student development first traces the developmental path as outlined by Perry, then briefly summarizes more recent research, and finally offers some general suggestions on how we might use these findings.

Perry's Research on Student Development

Perry distinguished nine "positions" in the developmental sequence, which are usually categorized in four groups: dualism, multiplicity, relativism, and commitment in relativism.

Dualism

Students in the positions of dualism view knowledge as truth—as factual information, correct theories, right answers. They view the professor as an authority who knows these truths and believe that teaching constitutes explaining them to students. Learning means taking notes on what the authority says, committing them to memory, and feeding them back as answers on exams.

Students in these positions expect to receive important information and right answers, and they become anxious or impatient if they sense they are missing either. A first-year chemistry student, for example, criticized the instructor for "leaving things out when he covers a chapter. . . . I think the instructor should go over topics a little more carefully . . . writing concepts and theories on the blackboard so we can copy down the concepts. There are not enough notes." A first-year student in English suggested: "I think more time should be spent on each story so that I can get a clearer picture about what is the most important aspect in the story." Students in positions of dualism and received knowledge are uncomfortable if we skip a section of the text, which is, of course, another authoritative source. They can handle abstraction and discussion, but in the end they want "a clear picture," the "most important aspect," and "enough notes."

Class activities or assignments that ask students to learn from their peers are a second source of frustration for students in a position of dualism. The instructor knows the right answers; students do not. Therefore little, if anything, can be learned from other students. Class discussion is "a waste of time," and classes would be better spent listening to the instructor explain things. Asking students to critique one another's papers sometimes provokes a similar response. One student complained: "I think [the instructor] should grade our assignments. I don't think students know what he wants; at least I didn't."

Assignments that ask students to think independently, state their own opinions, or draw their own conclusions are a third source of bewilderment and criticism from dualists. Because students assume that right answers exist and that authorities know them, they wonder why their professors do not reveal the answers. They may even conclude it is because the professors are not doing their job very well. A student in a philosophy course commented that the course was disorganized and confusing "because you're answering questions with questions and you never get a complete picture." In an English course, a student expressed a widely shared feeling: "I'm not really sure how my essay answers can be improved to give her what she wants."

Although students in early developmental positions talk about learning to think in their courses, their comments reveal that they view thinking quite differently than we do. To them, our challenge to think appears to be an academic game in which we "answer questions with questions" or ask them to guess "the meaning of a poem." Whatever thinking is, it is not learning, and they tolerate the diversion only so long. A first-year student in chemistry most clearly expressed this sentiment: "The teacher is good in his field. He encourages us to think. But he doesn't define things. Thinking is fine, but learning is what I'm here for."

Because dualists depend on an authority as a source of knowledge, few things are more unsettling to them than uncertainty or disagreement among authorities. One first-year student, commenting on a team-taught course, described the mixed feelings that disagreement among professors often elicits:

> I'd never seen two professors disagree with each other. Both of these guys seemed really smart, but they disagreed all the time. I mean, I don't think they were playing devil's advocate. They *really* disagreed. It was interesting to see how they looked at things. But at times that really drove you crazy! You couldn't figure out what you were supposed to assume. . . . Lots of times I never did figure out who was right. And they wouldn't tell you. They left you hanging. That bothered me.

Disagreement between professors can drive you crazy, but this student remained sane by assuming one of the professors was right. Being left hanging did not disturb the student's faith in right answers

Such faith in authority and right answers gradually erodes, however. Many introductory courses emphasize multiple perspectives and diverse interpretations. Again and again, professors ask first-year students what they think and praise them for offering original answers. Students discover more disagreement in texts and among professors. Eventually, they conclude that in some areas, at least, no one knows the answers.

Multiplicity

Once students realize that in some areas or on some issues no one yet has a definitive answer, they revise their assumptions about teaching and learning. Knowledge no longer consists of right and wrong answers; it becomes a matter of opinion. Therefore faculty are not authorities who know the answers; they are people with opinions or theories. When it comes to opinion, everyone, including the student, has a right to have one.

Initially these new assumptions prompt students to claim equal status with faculty. One opinion is as good as another, so teachers "have no right to call [the student] wrong" (Perry, [1968] 1999, p. 107). Convinced that all positions are equally valid, students in early multiplicity see little need to justify or support their conclusions. Because they do not yet appreciate the difference between a gut reaction and an informed opinion, they wonder how and why we criticize their work. In fact, many students conclude that it is merely because we disagree with their positions.

A first-year student in an English course wrote: "The professor . . . has to be more open to other views of stories besides her own. Not everyone gets exactly the same thing out of every story. The other person's view is not wrong." Another criticized an art history professor for similar reasons: "Art is interpreted in different ways, and there should be no wrong answer. There is no way anyone should get below a B on any of the essays." Although students tend to hold onto dualistic views about the sciences longer, eventually they question authority even in this area. A student wrote: "Lab is about experiments. It shouldn't be graded like a test with right and wrong answers. Everyone sees something different in an experiment. Science is not exact and shouldn't be graded as right and wrong."

Joanne Kurfiss (1988, p. 54) remains especially insightful in summarizing such views: "Students at this level recognize complexity but have not yet learned how to navigate its waters. They perceive no basis other than intuition, feeling, or 'common sense' on which to judge the merits of . . . opinions." Meanwhile, as faculty continue to insist on *informed* opinions, *reasoned* judgments, *evidence* and *documentation*, students begin to temper their claims.

Students in late multiplicity still see knowledge as opinion or theory, but they realize they must support an opinion or offer evidence for a theory—at least in an academic setting. They see too that faculty know the rules for finding support or evidence and now assume that teaching means helping students learn those rules. Grading continues to be a major worry and topic for criticism, but the focus shifts. Students criticize their professors not for being opinionated but for failing to make evaluation criteria clear. As one student put it: "The essays are graded hard and the grading is not really explained thoroughly enough. I don't really know what to write and not to write, how to support my interpretation."

As students in multiplicity gain skill in supporting their opinions, the transition to relativism occurs. In the process, students learn to consider counterarguments and alternative conclusions. They begin to weigh evidence and distinguish strong support from weak. They recognize that what they initially viewed as "academic" rules for argumentation, analysis, or problem solving lead in fact to more informed and more persuasive conclusions. Developing these skills brings new insight about what it means to know and to learn.

Perry's work and subsequent research suggest that most first-year students hold views similar to those described in dualism and multiplicity (Baxter Magolda, 2002; Clinchy, 2002; King and Kitchener, 1994; Kurfiss, 1988; Perry, [1968] 1999). Indeed, most of these researchers find that only a minority of college undergraduates at any level express views characteristic of later developmental positions—a finding that perhaps should concern us. Nevertheless, to provide a complete picture, we include a brief discussion of the subsequent positions.

Relativism

Students in the positions of relativism recognize that knowledge is contextual. What one "knows" about something or concludes in a situation is colored by one's perspective, assumptions, and methods of inquiry, which make most questions and problems more complex. Recognizing the need to consider many factors, look at them from differing perspectives, use systematic methods of analysis, and supply evidence, these students view faculty as resources who can help them learn disciplinary methods of analysis. Learning becomes the use of those methods to understand complexity.

Students in positions of relativism often find that the more they analyze complexity the less able they are to make a decision or draw a conclusion because doing so seems to neglect some important factor or insight. They prefer exposing the complexity. An assignment that asks them to take a position or commit to some action is especially challenging. Of course, professors regularly ask students to take a position or recommend action, and students do so, secure in knowing that they can change their minds and that their decisions have no dire consequences. The academic environment thus allows them to test choices and commitments tentatively until they find those they can hold more permanently.

Commitment in Relativism

To recognize that choice and commitment must eventually be made casts learning in a somewhat different light. Students seek to understand complexity and diverse perspectives not only as an academic pursuit but as a way to create personal worldviews from which they will make choices and commitments. The progression through positions in this stage finds students making an initial commitment in an area (perhaps selecting a career), then exploring stylistic dimensions of that commitment (how one goes about that career), and finally developing a sense of oneself in that context.

Several researchers have challenged Perry's model for its ambiguity about what happens in these later positions. Perry acknowledged that development at this stage was more stylistic than structural and not characterized by any major changes in form. Instead, he wrote, "Positions 7, 8, and 9 express degrees of ripening in an art" and described them as "degrees of seasoning which we felt to be broadly distinguishable in our students' reports" ([1968] 1999, p. 170). Research conducted after Perry's work sheds additional light on what happens as people mature and come to grips with uncertainty and the contextual nature of knowing. Faculty who also teach upper-division and graduate courses may wish to consult references listed at the end of this chapter. The issues and challenges for students in these later positions are, however, well beyond the developmental positions of most first-year students.

Research over the last two decades has both clarified and extended our understanding of the developmental path first outlined by Perry. Before suggesting how research on intellectual development might guide faculty in planning their courses, we offer a brief synopsis of these findings.

Belenky, Clinchy, Goldberger, and Tarule: Women's Ways of Knowing

Concerned that Perry's description of development was based on research with male subjects, Mary Field Belenky, Blythe McVicker Clinchy, Nancy Rule Goldberger, and Jill Mattuck Tarule studied women. Their research, reported in *Women's Ways of Knowing* (1986), found women's views of knowledge were similar in broad outline to those of Perry's men, but they often differed in emphasis and in voice, prompting these scholars to relabel the major stages of development. Our summary notes similarities and highlights some of the differences between Perry's findings and those reported in *Women's Ways of Knowing* (*WWK*).

Received Knowledge

Like Perry's men in positions of dualism, *WWK*'s women in early positions viewed knowledge as factual and faculty as authorities who know the facts. In contrast to the male subjects in Perry's studies who seemed to view themselves as "authorities-in-the-making" and often professed their knowledge almost as if to show it off or prove themselves, the women subjects interviewed by *WWK* authors did not seem to identify with authorities and were far less assertive in proclaiming what they knew. *WWK* women subjects "received" knowledge, but they were quiet about it. Although this may strike some as appropriate humility on the part of novice learners, *WWK* authors expressed concern that women's passivity deprived them not only of deserved recognition but also of constructive feedback that might contribute to their learning.

Subjective Knowledge

Recognition that truth is not yet known, at least in some areas, was expressed by both women and men in research reported by Perry and *WWK* authors, but differences again surfaced in the *WWK* research. Perry's men responded to uncertainty with vigor, proclaiming their right to their own opinions; *WWK* women seemed more tentative, saying "it's just my opinion." Perry's men learned to justify their opinions with reason and evidence; they welcomed debate to sharpen their views. In contrast, women tended to rely more on personal experience as a source of knowing (hence the label "subjective" knowing) and expressed concern that differences in opinion might sever their connection with others.

Procedural Knowledge

Both men and women at later stages of development talked about the uncertainty and complexity of knowledge and the need for systematic procedures for sorting things out. In their interviews with women, however, *WWK* authors heard two procedural approaches described. Most women talked about traditionally academic procedures for knowing—looking at things objectively, distancing oneself to avoid bias, relying on reason and argument—procedures they labeled "separate knowing." Some women also talked about an alternative way of knowing, using procedures that involved "imagining oneself into" (p. 121) a situation and placing greater value on insight gained through their own and others' personal experiences. *WWK* called this "connected knowing." For these women, empathy and personal experience represented not only alternative procedures for understanding but also the primary procedures for learning important things. Although they speculated that preferences for separate and connected knowing might be gender-related, *WWK* researchers stressed that many women in their study would be described as separate knowers and that there likely were men who would be described as connected knowers.

Constructed Knowledge

WWK women came to recognize that all knowledge is constructed, that one's frame of reference makes a difference in the construction, and that frames of reference can be changed. They talked about the need to reevaluate knowledge regularly as new information emerges or as context changes. They also saw the need to make commitments—to work, to relationships, to communities. In these ways, they resembled Perry's men. Some women, however, faced an additional task of integrating their contrasting procedures for knowing. As they prepared to complete their studies, women spoke, often passionately, of the struggle to integrate "feeling and care into their work" (*WWK*, p. 152).

The distinction between separate and connected knowing is one of the most important contributions of *WWK* researchers. Identification of these contrasting ways of knowing helps us understand the struggle of some students in some later developmental positions. The distinction also begs us to pay closer attention to themes heard in interviews with students in earlier stages of development: the reluctance of some to speak out and show what they know, their tendency to feel uncomfortable with argumentation lest it sever their connection with others, their preference for collaboration and consensus over debate, and their inclination to value things learned from experience.

In their effort to master separate-knowing procedures, *WWK* women talked about neglecting or giving up part of themselves; some said they left the discipline and its professions for those reasons. Concerned about this loss of women, several of the scientific and professional disciplines have, over the last decade, looked to this and other feminist research for guidance in retaining women students. Much of the attrition of women from scientific, technical, and professional disciplines has its origin in their experiences in first-year classrooms.

Being attuned to the dimensions of separate and connected knowing is especially crucial for those of us who teach first-year students.

Baxter Magolda: Gender-Related Patterns

Curious about the role gender might play in epistemological assumptions, Marcia Baxter Magolda conducted a five-year longitudinal study including men and women as subjects. Her findings, reported in *Knowing and Reasoning in College* (1992), identify four developmental categories: absolute knowing, transitional knowing, independent knowing, and contextual knowing. These categories generally parallel those described by Perry and by Belenky and colleagues, but Baxter Magolda found other patterns of reasoning within each of the first three categories. One trajectory, the mastering-impersonal-individual patterns, describes students who participate initially in order to show what they know and later on to test themselves. These students value involvement with peers as a way to sharpen their thinking, and they tend to rely on challenge, debate, and argumentation. In contrast, the receiving-interpersonal-interindividual trajectory of reasoning patterns is characteristic of students who are more likely to listen quietly to authority in early stages and then rely more and more on peer interactions as a way to gain understanding. These students tend to value sharing and discussion rather than debate.

Description of the two trajectories is reminiscent of Belenky and her colleagues' description of separate and connected knowing, which *WWK* authors recognized at later stages of development. Baxter Magolda's account of patterns helps us "hear" these contrasting approaches even earlier. Baxter Magolda found that use of the various patterns was gender-related; women used some patterns more often than men did, and vice versa. Men and women, however, used both contrasting patterns at each stage of development, and their preference for one more than the other did not necessarily follow a simple trajectory.

King and Kitchener: The Reflective Judgment Model

Influenced by Perry's research on development, and interested especially in how critical thinking develops, Patricia M. King and Karen Strohm Kitchener (1994; 2002) examine how people reason about "ill-structured problems"—those that are ambiguous and often controversial in definition and solution. The problems used in their interviews, for example, asked subjects to state and justify their opinions about conflicting views on how the pyramids were built, on whether news stories can be objective, on creation stories, and on the safety of chemical additives in foods (King and Kitchener, 1994). Drawn from interviews of more than seventeen hundred participants, *Developing Reflective Judgment* (King and Kitchener, 1994) articulated a seven-stage model with three levels that we briefly summarize here.

Prereflective Level

At this level (stages one to three), students assume that knowledge is certain and is gained from authority or firsthand observation. At stage three comes recognition that answers to some questions or in some areas are not *yet* known. This temporary uncertainty permits personal opinion, but only until true answers still assumed to exist are discovered.

Quasi-Reflective Level

Students at stages four and five come to see that knowledge is uncertain in more (and eventually all) areas because what is known is always shaped by the perspective and perception of the knower. Students see the need to support interpretation and belief with reason and evidence, but they do not see qualitative differences in justification. Responses at stage four are much like Perry's multiplists; everyone has a right to an opinion. At stage five, like Perry's relativists students focus on rules of inquiry and interpretation within a context or discipline, but they do not yet compare and contrast or synthesize evidence across contexts.

Reflective Thinking Level

At this level (stages six and seven), students recognize that legitimate and important controversy requires thinking across contexts and that any solution must be constructed rather than found. Stage five skills in trying multiple perspectives help, but more is required (for example, abstracting common elements across domains, integrating tools of inquiry, synthesizing) if a solution is to be reached. Solutions are evaluated on the basis of what is most plausible given current evidence and may be reconsidered as new evidence becomes available.

King and Kitchener are widely credited for fleshing out the upper stages of Perry's scheme, and faculty who teach upper-division or graduate courses may find it useful to examine further the reflective judgment model. A contribution more pertinent for our attention to first-year students is the focus on reasoning about complex problems. Although most of us believe this is the most important goal for higher education, many of our colleagues feel that first-year courses are too early to begin working on this goal. Our view is that it is not too early to address this issue. Instructional approaches that incorporate this type of complex, real-life problem—approaches such as problem-based learning, service learning, field experiences—tend to engage students more deeply and more actively in their studies. We advocate such approaches in later chapters, especially in Chapter Ten; but we recognize the risk in using them with first-year students and our discussion there is guided by King and Kitchener's research.

Implications of Research on Development for Instruction

In their review of Perry's research and the investigation into intellectual development that it spawned, Barbara K. Hofer and Paul R. Pintrich (1997, p. 121) concluded: "In spite of the various approaches, methodologies, samples, and designs, there is agreement across studies as to the general trend of development. Within these models it appears that the view of knowledge is transformed from one in which knowledge is right or wrong to a position of relativism and then to a position in which individuals are active constructors of meaning, able to make judgments and commitments in a relativistic context."

This general pattern of intellectual development has clear implications for nearly all of our instructional decisions. Although later chapters discuss many of those decisions at length, there are some general issues that we want to highlight now.

First, we need to pay more attention to the challenges we pose in a first-year course. Too often, we require memorization and little more. This practice undermines student motivation, fails to develop thinking skills, and reinforces beliefs that knowledge is factual, known to authorities, and acquired through memorization. In Chapter Four we outline a broader range of goals for first-year courses, including thinking about ill-structured problems. To be sure, many first-year students find these challenges daunting and we must extend appropriate support, but if we omit the challenge, we place unnecessary constraints on student development.

Second, first-year students especially need faculty support. We do not dwell here on what happens when students feel bewildered or confused by assignments and class activities, frustrated by grading practices they do not understand, or abandoned because they believe faculty are too busy to see them. The consequences are, however, worth mentioning. In a nutshell, they stop coming to class, ignore assignments, and do everything they can to avoid the course. They may look elsewhere—to other courses or other disciplines—for a more supportive environment. If they do not find it, they may leave the university altogether.

We need to remember too that course content and assignments often elicit powerful emotional reactions. As King and Kitchener point out, when we ask students how we could know what really happened at My Lai, the stakes are high for students whose parents or grandparents fought in Vietnam or who were caught up in that war. Discussion of evolution, ecology, comparative religion, alternative lifestyles and family structures, poverty and wealth, race and ethnicity, and virtually every issue we examine have the potential to challenge family relationships, religious beliefs, and deeply held traditions. Structure, repeated explanation about why we ask students to do what we ask them, feedback that is encouraging and not solely critical, and reassurance that we care and will keep students company are among the supports suggested in later chapters.

Third, as Perry (1989, p. 1) noted, the developmental scheme is useful to us "less as a way of classifying students than as a way of hearing 'where students are speaking from' so that communication can be more fruitful." Although some suggest it, we do not advocate trying to assess the developmental position of the individual student. Formal assessment is too costly and time-consuming to be practical, and informal assessment is too unreliable. We think it is enough to know that even though students on our campus represent a range of developmental positions, it is likely that most first-year students are in earlier positions and find many of our practices puzzling and troubling. We can anticipate, for example, that many first-year students will criticize peer learning activities and recommend that professors who use them lecture more and "give more notes." Listening with an ear to hear "where students are speaking from," we might also note a desire for right answers, dependence on authority, and anxiety about not getting either. Fruitful responses, we believe, include looking for ways to reduce students' anxieties but probably not following their advice to lecture more and give more notes.

Finally, we suggest proactively using the developmental progression as a template for reviewing course plans, anticipating possible reaction from students in various developmental positions, and strengthening support structures. As we prepare courses, for example, we might ask ourselves these questions:

- How might students in each developmental position or level interpret and react to the range of course goals?

- How might students in differing developmental positions interpret each assignment and class activity planned?

- What aspects of assignments and activities will students at each developmental position likely find challenging or unsettling?
- What can I do to encourage and support students as they work through these tasks?

If we take care to consider students' intellectual development, our courses will likely pose challenges that are appropriate for them. Our task, however, is still far from complete. As we noted earlier, students have their own ideas about what it means to learn; they also learn in their own ways. Creating courses that accommodate diverse learning styles is something to which we need to attend as well. Chapter Three addresses that challenge.

For Further Exploration

- Hofer, B. K., and Pintrich, P. R. (eds.). *Personal Epistemology: The Psychology of Beliefs About Knowledge and Knowing.* Hillsdale, N.J.: Erlbaum, 2002.

  This volume includes chapters by several major researchers updating their studies of student development. The contributors delineate multiple perspectives useful to faculty in a variety of disciplines.

CHAPTER 3

Learning Styles

Some time ago, we attended a conference where Peter Briggs-Myers introduced a discussion of learning styles by inviting members of his audience to try a simple experiment: to write our names first with one hand and then with the other. In doing so, we learned two lessons. First, we all could write with both hands. Second, writing with the hand we do not normally use felt awkward, required concentration, and took longer.

The analogy between right- or left-handedness and learning styles may be overly simple, but it highlights some important considerations. The term *learning style* loosely refers to a preference for certain kinds of learning activities over others. We examine some dimensions of those preferences here, but we stress at the outset that we are discussing *how* people learn, not *whether they can* learn. Just as we can write our name with either hand, students with different learning styles are capable of learning the knowledge and skills we teach. Learning styles do, however, affect our responses to learning activities. Learning in some situations seems natural and comes easily; in others, it feels awkward, requires concentration, and takes more time—like writing with the hand we do not normally use.

Knowing about learning styles, like knowing about student developmental patterns, helps us design instruction and provide support for diverse learners. To these ends, we outline the dimensions and findings of research using four well-established learning style inventories.

Witkin's Field Independence

Field independence, one of the earliest dimensions of learning styles to be studied, was initially identified by Herman A. Witkin in the late 1940s. Although several tests of field independence exist, all of them measure the extent to which people are "able to deal with a part of a field separately from the field as a whole, or the extent to which [they are] able to disembed items from organized context" (Witkin, 1976, pp. 41–42). For example, in the Embedded Figures Test, subjects must be able to identify a simple geometric figure embedded in a more complex geometric pattern. Those who quickly recognize the simple figure, presumably because they are relatively uninfluenced by the surrounding field, are called *field-independent*. Those who have difficulty locating the figure in the allotted time, presumably because they are heavily influenced by the surrounding field, are usually referred to as *field-dependent*. Because of its more neutral connotation, we use the term *field-sensitive* to designate this orientation (see Claxton and Murrell, 1987, for discussion of this issue).

Early investigation found that a tendency toward field independence or field sensitivity was related to a variety of other learning characteristics (Chickering, 1976; Claxton and Murrell, 1987; Fincher, 1985; Messick and Associates, 1986; Witkin, 1976; Witkin, Oltman, Raskin, and Karp, 1971). Field-independent students tend to approach learning tasks analytically. They identify parts of a whole or individual aspects of a situation, consider them independent of context, and impose their own organization on them. When they listen to a lecture, for example, they extract information, organize it, and record notes in outline format even if the instructor does not present an organizational framework (Frank, 1984). Accustomed to considering information separate from its surroundings, these students have little problem with tasks that require pulling some element out of context and using it in another, or relating it to some other element. Tasks that require attention to context, particularly human or social context, require more concentration from field-independent students. They tend to focus less on people than on things or abstractions; they are more comfortable working alone and often prefer doing so.

Field-sensitive students approach learning tasks more globally. They see ideas, issues, and problems in context. Because everything seems interrelated, breaking problems into parts, isolating ideas, or restructuring problem situations are not natural acts for field-sensitive students and require their concentration. Frank (1984) found that when students took notes from lectures in which no organizational framework was furnished, all recorded about the same amount of information in their notes. Field-sensitive students, however, were less likely than field-independent students to use an outline format and did not perform as well on a follow-up test. The difference in test scores vanished when the lecturer presented an outline. Field-sensitive students seem more attuned to the human and social aspects of the environment than their field-independent peers do. Field-sensitive students, for example, show better memory for information that has social content and for people's faces. They want others around when they are learning and prefer courses that emphasize student discussion, small groups, and collaborative learning.

Although tests of field independence are not prominent in current research on learning styles, many of the characteristics associated with the field independence–field sensitivity dimension also surface in investigations using other learning style assessment instruments. Collectively, this research tells us, for instance, that students differ in their tendencies to see the whole or analyze into parts, to attend to problems in a human context or in the abstract, to prefer working alone or with others.

What does all this mean for teaching first-year courses? We address this at some length later in this chapter and throughout Part Two, but it is not too early to begin thinking about some of the implications. We might want to give field-independent students opportunities to work alone and study in their own ways. But we may need to give more explicit cues or directions when tasks demand attention to social issues or interpersonal skills and allow them more time when considering context is important. For field-sensitive students, we need group work and collaborative learning, outlines or study questions to help them organize information from a lecture or reading, and more time when a problem or task requires breaking things into parts or taking something out of its original context.

Kolb's Learning Style Inventory

David A. Kolb's identification of learning styles is grounded in an experiential model of learning, which he calls a learning cycle (Kolb, 1984, 1985). The learning cycle includes four phases, each requiring its own process to acquire information and learn skills.

Concrete Experience

Students experience things directly by immersing themselves in hands-on activity such as field work, a laboratory, simulation, or role playing. Activities might also include vicarious experiences such as reading a firsthand narrative or viewing a film.

Reflective Observation

Students look back on their experiences; identify significant aspects, events, or reactions; and think about their meaning. Journal writing and other writing-to-learn assignments, study group assignments that emphasize sharing and comparing experiences, and discussion inviting reflection on experience are among the activities that prompt reflective observation.

Abstract Conceptualization

Students compare their observations to conceptual or theoretical material and seek to develop an explanation or hypothesis that can be generalized for their experience. Reading and attending lectures are ways to obtain theoretical material, but discussion, written assignments, group projects, and tasks that invite students to use theoretical information to explain what they have observed are the key activities during this phase of the learning cycle.

Active Experimentation

Students extend and elaborate their understanding of concepts and theories by experimenting with them in new or more complex situations. Activities during this phase might find students developing a proposal, designing a project, or identifying another context or problem in which concepts or theories might apply. Carrying out their proposal or plan takes them full circle to concrete experience, and they begin the cycle anew.

Learning styles come into play in Kolb's model because each of us is more comfortable and more skilled in some phases of the learning cycle than in others. As Kolb (1981) points out, two dimensions figure prominently in this model of learning, each requiring "abilities that are polar opposites" (p. 238). In one dimension, *concrete experience* and *abstract thinking* represent opposites. In the other dimension *reflection* and *action* are opposites. Because most of us lean toward one end of each dimension, we feel more at home in certain phases of the learning cycle than in others.

Some students easily immerse themselves in direct experience and understand abstractions better when they consider them in terms of their own experience. They may, however, have to work at thinking beyond it. For other students, direct experience feels awkward, often because it involves social interaction; they are more comfortable thinking about things in the abstract and sometimes need a reminder that theories must fit reality. In terms of the active–reflective dimension, some students prefer doing things, experimenting, and participating; they may need prompting to stop and think about what they are doing. Others are accustomed to observing, listening, and thinking about things; they may need prodding to test their ideas in action.

Drawing on an extensive experiential learning research and theory base, Kolb (1981, 1984) maintains that learning is more meaningful and retained longer if we work through all four phases of the learning cycle. James E. Stice (1987) reports that retention increased from 20 percent when only abstract conceptualization was emphasized to 90 percent when all four phases were incorporated. Marilla Svinicki and Nancy Dixon (1987) illustrate how various disciplines might sequence the activities we have suggested (and some others as well) to establish learning cycles.

Although Kolb identifies four learning styles on the basis of the four possible combinations of polar opposites, we do not review them here. If we take the learning cycle as a guide for planning instruction—and we think it offers a good working model—it is enough to know that students will feel more accustomed to some phases of our courses and with some of our assignments, while at other times what we ask them to do will require more concentration on their part and more support on ours.

The Myers-Briggs Type Indicator

The most complex assessment of learning styles considered here, the Myers-Briggs Type Indicator (MBTI), measures preferences on four bipolar dimensions and identifies sixteen personality types, each with its own preferences for learning (Consulting Psychologists Press, 1990; Myers, 1987; Jensen, 1987). Describing all sixteen types goes beyond our purposes, and perhaps beyond the descriptive power of the MBTI (an issue we address in the concluding section of this chapter). We think the MBTI identifies four dimensions that probably matter in instruction, raises issues to consider when planning courses, and can help us accommodate diverse learners.

Extraversion–Introversion

This dimension focuses on preferences for either the "outer world of people and things" or "the inner world of ideas" (Consulting Psychologists Press, 1990). Extraverts rely on activity, learn by talking things through, like to work with others, need an active break when reading or writing, and tend to jump right into an assignment or task.

Introverts need quiet time for concentration, learn by thinking things through before participating or acting, like to work alone, are comfortable with a long stretch of solitary study, and like to plan before starting an assignment or task.

At a given moment, our instructional activities will likely favor students on one or the other end of the extraversion–introversion continuum, but there are some things we can do to strike a long-term balance. In Chapters Six and Seven, for example, we describe activities for getting students more actively involved during class. Small-group discussion techniques are well suited to extraverts; writing-to-learn activities favor introverts. If we employ both and alternate their order, we can avoid favoring one learning style all the time.

We can vary assignments similarly. Extraverts take well to group projects, group assignments, study groups, and the like. To support more introverted students as they undertake such assignments, we might encourage groups to set an agenda, write questions for discussion before meetings, and make time during meetings for students to sit quietly and collect their thoughts. In contrast, reading and other individual assignments play to introverts' preferences. To support extraverts in activities of this kind, we might encourage them to form study groups in which they talk through a reading, perhaps even to read the assignment in the company of a classmate with the explicit purpose of pausing now and then to discuss the reading.

Sensing–Intuition

This dimension indicates preference for perceiving the world through the reality of experience or for intuiting meaning and possibility. Sensing students focus on the concrete and the here and now, prefer an inductive approach that moves from the concrete to the abstract, like to be able to put what they learn to use, prefer an established way of doing things and clear instructions, and tend to reach conclusions in step-by-step fashion. Intuiting students look for general impressions or trends, prefer deductive approaches that move from the abstract to the concrete, like to learn new skills but are less concerned about using them, follow an inspiration or hunch, become impatient with doing the same thing repeatedly or checking facts, and prefer open-ended assignments.

We appeal to the motivation of sensing learners when we introduce instruction with a concrete example, a case study, a data set, a laboratory experiment, or an experiential learning assignment, and when we suggest they use well-established procedures to interpret, analyze, or resolve an issue. For intuiting students, we might introduce the same examples, cases, data sets, and so on but ask students to select among procedures they have studied or come up with a procedure for interpreting and analyzing results. Alternatively, we might present theory or research and invite students to propose examples, applications, or further experimentation. Again, if we alternate our approach, we avoid systematically giving students with one style an advantage.

Thinking–Feeling

This aspect of the indicator points to a preference for making decisions on the basis of logic and objective analysis or on values and what is likely to benefit people. Thinking students are interested in learning principles that govern how systems work, tend to anticipate logical outcomes of various choices, and make decisions by considering logical consequences. Feeling students are interested in learning things that might serve people or personally held values, tend to think about the effects choice has on people, and make decisions by considering what they and others value.

Although it might seem that disciplines tend to line up on the thinking or feeling side of things, this is not so inevitable as first appears. Science, technology, engineering, and mathematics (STEM) disciplines, which tend to emphasize the thinking end of the continuum, might engage a feeling style by using a social or human problem to introduce concepts, by placing practice problems in a social context, or by highlighting the contribution of their discipline to solving problems of particular concern to humanity. Courses and disciplines that seem naturally to lean toward the feeling dimension might point out that there is a *logic* for thinking about people and values, pose examples and articulate what that logic is, and highlight proposals, answers, and solutions that embody the logic. We have found the distinction between and suggestions for dealing with separate and connected knowing identified by Belenky, Clinchy, Goldberger, and Tarule (1986) especially useful in thinking about the thinking-feeling dimension of the MBTI.

Judging–Perceiving

The judging-perceiving dimension indicates preference for a planned, orderly approach or for a flexible, spontaneous one. Judging students work best when they can plan and follow the plan, like clear goals and deadlines, and must finish or accomplish things to feel they are learning. Perceiving students depend less on finishing things to feel they are learning, prefer to keep options open, tend to feel constrained in a highly structured situation, and may start too many things and have trouble finishing any.

A detailed syllabus with clearly stated goals, structured assignments, definite due dates, and detailed evaluation rubrics supports students on the judging end of the continuum. What about students on the perceiving end of this dimension? Although we might not want to accommodate their inclination to start too many things and not finish any, neither do we want to curtail their exploration. Indeed, many faculty score high on perceiving and identify with the preferences and constraints these students feel. Offering options may allow us to have it both ways. Here are some possibilities:

- Clearly state goals, but ask students to identify those they wish to emphasize

- Carefully structure assignments, but offer choices or invite students to substitute their own proposals

- Outline evaluation procedures, but ask students to determine how much weight they wish to give each one or invite them to propose alternatives

Do we really have a significant number of students with these various preferences in our classes, such that we should concern ourselves with these differences? Writing about research using the MBTI, Thomas Carskadon (1994) notes that the frequency of preferences varies dramatically for individual groups but reports these estimates for the general population: "Extraversion is probably preferred by about two-thirds of the population, introversion by one-third. Sensing is probably preferred by two-thirds to three-quarters of the population; but among college students, sensing and intuition are usually closer to 50–50. Thinking and feeling are close to 50–50 overall, but gender plays a role: about two-thirds of women are feeling types, while at least 60 percent of men appear to be thinking types. . . . Finally, judging is probably preferred by about 55 to 60 percent of the population, perceiving by 40 to 45 percent" (p. 72). Variation is, of course, most evident in courses for first-year students.

Felder-Silverman Learning Style Model

Working primarily with faculty and students in science, math, engineering, and technical disciplines, Richard Felder has researched and written extensively about how learning styles affect study in these fields. The *Index of Learning Styles,* developed in collaboration with Barbara Soloman, assesses four dimensions of learning style. We synthesize their discussion in summaries here (Felder, 1993, 1996; Felder and Soloman, n.d.).

Active-Reflective

Active learners understand better if they do something with the material they're studying: try it out, talk about it, explain it to someone else, apply it in a problem. Reflective learners prefer to think about things before participating in discussion or working on applications.

Sensing-Intuitive

Sensing learners prefer dealing with factual information and real-life situations, are careful with detail, and would rather learn tried-and-true procedures than come up with a new way to do things. Intuitive learners prefer dealing with abstractions and theories, and they enjoy coming up with new ways to do things. They tend to dislike "plug and chug" problem solving and find checking details or calculations tiresome.

Visual-Verbal

Visual learners remember best what they see; they prefer lectures and texts that present information in pictures, diagrams, graphs, maps, and demonstrations. Verbal learners are more attuned to words. When a lecture or text includes visual representation, verbal learners say they are more likely to remember the text summarizing results or what the instructor said rather than the visual presentation itself.

Sequential-Global

Sequential learners tend to focus on one thing at a time and then to put it all together to see the big picture. They prefer instruction that lays out material in clear, sequential steps, and they approach problems one step at a time. Global learners understand in spurts. They tend to flounder until they see the big picture, but once they do, they get it. These students prefer the sort of instruction that gives an overall picture before going into detail.

The *Index of Learning Styles* assesses dimensions similar to those underlying the instruments discussed earlier and uses a question format similar to the MBTI. The index is unique, however, in asking about activities and approaches specific to science, mathematics, engineering, and technical disciplines (for example, "When I am doing long calculations, I tend to . . ." "When someone is showing me data, . . ." "In a book with pictures and charts, . . ." "When I solve math problems, . . ."). The *Index of Learning Styles,* scoring instructions, and interpretation guidelines are available at www.ncsu.edu/felder-public.

Concluding Thoughts

"I've not been inclined," a colleague told us, "to use discussions even in my smaller classes. I stop to answer questions, of course, and sometimes a discussion results. But I never really got much out of discussions—the kind where you sat in a circle and the professor didn't say much—when I was a student." The impulse to teach as we were taught, or as we thought we were best taught, is powerful. We forget that most of our classmates reacted much differently to the courses we took. Most did not go on to major in our discipline, and only a few went on to graduate study. The majority were less successful academically. Clearly those courses that worked so well for us worked less well for many of our classmates.

Nowhere in the undergraduate curriculum will we find so many students who differ from us and from one another in so many ways as in first-year courses. To succeed in teaching to such diversity, we must look beyond our own experiences and reactions, try to understand how our students learn, and find methods and practices that suit their learning styles as well as our own. We think research and discussion of learning styles can help us do that.

In our work with faculty, we caution against making too much or too little of the literature on learning styles. Common sense tells us to be skeptical of claims that a twelve-item inventory such as Kolb's LSI can identify four distinct learning styles or that the MBTI, even with ninety-two items in the self-scoring version, can accurately identify sixteen distinct personality types. Indeed, a 1993 review of literature and research on the MBTI concluded, "Although the test does appear to measure several common personality traits, the patterns of data do not suggest that there is reason to believe that there are 16 unique types of personality" (Pittenger, 1993, p. 483). The MBTI is probably the most widely used and most thoroughly researched inventory discussed here. We would not be surprised to learn that other inventories, were they subjected to such close scrutiny, might raise similar doubts. When we administer and discuss these inventories with faculty or students, our first follow-up question is always, "How well do you think this style description fits you?"

To caution that these inventories might not identify distinct styles or types is not to say that they do not assess preferences on dimensions important in an instructional context. Even David Pittenger's very critical review (1993) of the utility of the MBTI acknowledges that it measures several important personality traits and does not challenge their relationship to learning approaches. Our summaries of learning style inventories focused on their underlying dimensions rather than the particular styles they claim to identify. To the extent that reflection on those dimensions helps us think about how students in our courses might differ and about the support they might need, discussion of learning styles can help us think beyond what worked for us to what might work for the many and differing students in our classes.

Discussing learning styles with students can also help them reflect on their approaches to learning. We do not advocate administering batteries of learning style inventories to students, although administering one or two that seem particularly relevant to a course or discipline can be a powerful entrée to discussing how to succeed in a program. An alternative to using published inventories asks students to respond to a series of questions:

- How do you think you learn best?
- What kind of activity or assignment do you find especially challenging?
- After reading the syllabus and attending the first class, which aspects of this course especially appeal to you?
- What are you unsure about?
- What do you dread, and why?
- How might I help you succeed in this course?

Chapter Eleven offers suggestions for student self-reflection exercises and Chapter Fifteen includes a discussion of study strategy questionnaires as well as activities for initiating reflection and discussion with students.

How we find out about student differences—whether it be using one of the dozens of learning style inventories, a course-specific survey, or relying on published research—is less important than recognizing that differences exist. Even more important is trying to respond to those differences with reasonable rigor and appropriate support. Suggestions on how we might do that constitute Part Two.

For Further Exploration _____

- Evans, N. J., Forney, D. S., and Guido-DiBrito, F. *Student Development in College: Theory, Research, and Practice*. San Francisco: Jossey-Bass, 1998.

  Student Development in College is a comprehensive overview of student development research and theory, including both the learning style issues discussed in this chapter and the cognitive-structural themes discussed in Chapter Two. Although written primarily for student affairs practitioners, the discussion addresses classroom applications and other issues of interest to faculty.

- Silverman, S. L., and Casazza, M. E. *Learning and Development: Making Connections to Enhance Teaching.* San Francisco: Jossey-Bass, 2000.

  The chapters "Ways of Knowing" and "Learning Styles" contain especially useful discussion of the research on these topics as well as practical suggestions to guide course design and classroom instruction.

PART TWO

Effective Instruction for First-Year Students

Part Two presents an extensive catalogue of teaching strategies and practices that are especially effective for first-year students. Chapter Four lays the foundation for the remainder of the section with its discussion of the intellectual goals for first-year courses and how they can be communicated effectively to students. Chapter Five begins our discussion of classroom practice with guidelines for the first-year course syllabus and discussion of the importance of the organization and conduct of students' initial encounter with college coursework, the first day of class. Lecturing (or, as we prefer, presenting and explaining) remains the dominant mode of instruction for first-year students; Chapter Six is a review of good presenting practice with emphasis on those techniques that involve students actively.

The emphasis on active student involvement continues in the four subsequent chapters. Chapter Seven contains an inventory of active learning practices designed for classroom use. Chapter Eight devotes attention to perhaps the most difficult challenge first-year students confront: learning from reading. We offer advice for constructing assignments that encourage and support active reading on the part of first-year students. Chapter Nine continues our discussion of active engagement outside class, focusing on a collection of individual and collaborative assignments that support active study practices. Chapter Ten explores several ways to reconceive courses to engage students. We discuss problem-based learning, learning communities, and service learning as instructional strategies that can have a powerful positive impact on first-year students.

Part Two concludes with chapters on evaluation and grading. Chapter Eleven explores a variety of methods for evaluating first-year student performance and offers suggestions to make evaluation fairer and more accurate. In Chapter Twelve, we address several questions faculty who teach first-year students have about grading. We also address the important issue of academic integrity and make some suggestions to faculty for dealing with cheating and plagiarism.

CHAPTER 4

Knowing, Understanding, Thinking, and Learning How to Learn

The Goals of First-Year Instruction

Effective instruction demands consistency among course goals, instructional activities, and evaluation procedures. Because it makes no sense to talk about teaching practices without a clear vision of the goals to which those practices are aimed, we begin by considering what we hope first-year students will learn in our courses.

When we are asked to identify the most important goals for instruction, getting students to think is high on everyone's list, and knowing and understanding the subject matter are not far behind. What we have in mind when we use these phrases, however, is not so clear. Definitions are not shared, and important distinctions are often blurred. For example, *knowing, understanding,* and *thinking* do not clearly distinguish the different intellectual activities required to answer these questions.

- Summarize how Utilitarians and Retributionists justify punishment.
- A student is dismissed from the university for cheating on a quiz. The student admits cheating on the quiz but argues that dismissal is an extreme measure for a relatively minor offense. With which philosophical theory is the student's argument most consistent? Explain why you think so.
- Consider these observations. Criminals are deprived of their liberties when they are imprisoned. Carriers of infectious diseases are deprived of their liberties when they are quarantined. Would a Utilitarian view these practices as justifiable or unjustifiable, and on what grounds? How would a Retributionist respond to the same questions?

Stating goals in the form of behavioral objectives, as educational psychologists urged us to do for years, did not seem to improve communication with students or guide course planning. The insistence that objectives describe *observable* behaviors too often resulted in objectives that emphasized the trivial because it was observable and neglected important goals because they did not lend themselves to direct observation. In the end, behavioral objectives were no better at differentiating levels of intellectual activity than are the words *knowing, understanding,* or *thinking* and were pretty much banished from the college campus. That left us, however, with language for talking about instructional goals that was inadequate for communicating with one another and for planning instruction.

The assessment movement has refocused attention on defining what we want students to learn in our programs. In response to demands by accrediting agencies and others that we articulate learning outcomes and assess the extent to which students are achieving them, faculty on many campuses have participated in serious and sustained discussion about what students in their programs should know and be able to do. Anyone who has participated in an effort to define learning outcomes knows that much discussion and debate go into selecting just the right verb to convey what exactly we mean by terms such as *knowing, understanding, thinking, applying,* and so on. Such conversation, though frustrating and tedious as it may seem at the time, goes a long way toward establishing shared understanding about learning outcomes, at least at the programmatic level. Many faculty and most students, however, are not participants in the discussion and do not share definitions. Articulating and explaining instructional objectives remains an ongoing task and challenge.

In working with faculty to clarify course goals and explain them to students, a strategy we have found useful looks both at the goals that instructors articulate and at the questions they ask students. We take a similar approach here. We offer working definitions of the terms faculty and students use in everyday conversation about learning, definitions created mostly by the questions faculty ask during class, in assignments, and on exams. Along the way we preview some of the implications of these goals for teaching practices.

Knowing: Memorizing

If students are to think and to organize their thoughts, they need something to think about and to think with. Much of what goes on in introductory courses has the instructor presenting and explaining course content in the interest of providing food for thought or tools for thinking. If students are to have the information available for thinking and solving problems, they must commit it to memory and be able to recall it when needed.

The information first-year students are asked to memorize sometimes includes names, dates, definitions of terms, even a fact or two (What is Avogadro's number? When was the Renaissance? What is the current rate of unemployment?). More often in college courses, students are asked to remember complex ideas and relationships: definitions of concepts, characteristics of styles or periods, key points in an argument, theoretical constructs, principles, laws, procedures, conventions, trends, findings. Such ideas and relationships are the conceptual framework for combining and organizing course material that otherwise would exist as isolated pieces of information. Although these organizing ideas and relationships come in numerous forms, we refer to them generally as concepts. When faculty check to see whether students know important concepts, they ask questions such as these:

- So far, we have examined four approaches to critical reading: historical analysis, character analysis, thematic analysis, and analysis of narrative point of view. Describe each of these approaches, noting the questions each asks and the conventions each uses for seeking evidence.

- In the second portion of *Human Rights as Politics and Idolatry,* Michael Ignatieff identifies three "challenges" to the idea of human rights: the Islamic challenge, the challenge of Asian values, and the challenge from the West itself. Explain the nature of each of these challenges as Ignatieff sees them.

- State in your own words the Law of Conservation of Mass, the Law of Constant Composition, and the Law of Multiple Proportions.

- What are the distinguishing characteristics of each of these artistic movements: Neoclassicism, Romanticism, Impressionism, and Postimpressionism.

In most courses, students memorize basic information. In some courses, that is all they do. Following a major study of college testing practices, Ohmer Milton (1982) concluded that undergraduates are tested almost entirely for their grasp of factual information rather than their ability to understand, apply, or evaluate. Some argue that exams do not tell the whole story, but we have observed too many classes in which not much more can be said. The emphasis on memorization and the disconnect between what faculty and students report appear to have changed little over the past twenty-five years. The 2004 report on the National Survey of Student Engagement indicates that although only a third of faculty say their courses emphasize memorization, first-year students say about 70 percent of their course work stresses memorization.

Is it a problem when introductory courses place so much emphasis on memorization? We think so. We first mentioned the NSSE findings in Chapter One in our discussion of the bargain faculty feel pressured to strike when students show up with skills in memorizing far more developed than other learning and thinking skills. We urged faculty to think more deeply about support for students but not to abandon more complex intellectual challenges. Discussion of student development in Chapter Two stressed that students in early developmental positions come to see learning as more complex than memorizing facts, information, and right answers by confronting challenges that require something more than memorization. Again, we urged colleagues to think about how to support students as they confront those challenges, but we warned that ignoring or deemphasizing those challenges might delay development. Here, we introduce a third, more pragmatic line of argument for limiting the amount of material we ask students to commit to memory: if students are to remember the information they memorize beyond the next exam, then at least two conditions must be met. Both require time and attention.

First, practice is an important condition for all types of learning, including memorization. In fact, a primary consideration in selecting teaching methods or developing assignments is whether the activities under consideration include practice for the goals to be achieved. Practice that facilitates memorization and retention takes many forms: paraphrasing, summarizing, taking notes in one's own words, talking to oneself, explaining to someone else, quizzing oneself. Such activities not only involve practice in retrieving information from memory but also engage students in making ideas personally meaningful (deWinstanley and Bjork, 2002; Graesser, Person, and Hu, 2002; Halpern and Hakel, 2003).

Establishing connections between the information to be memorized and the knowledge students already possess is the second, and perhaps the more important, condition for remembering. Such connections are made by appealing to students' interests and values, by elaborating or extending things they already know, by interpreting or reinterpreting experiences they have had, and by linking those ideas that are abstract, distant, or unfamiliar with what students regard as concrete, immediate, and familiar. Forging such links goes by many names—comprehending, understanding, making material meaningful—and leads us to other categories of learning. When memorization is disconnected from these other forms of learning, as is often the case in introductory courses, the information memorized is soon forgotten.

Understanding: The Ability to Recognize

We all know students who can rattle off definitions of concepts, recite principles and rules, and summarize entire theories. They can even do so in their own words. However, if we show these same students a particular example, they cannot name the concept exemplified. If we conduct a demonstration, they cannot recognize the laws or principles that are operating. We should be concerned when this happens. It indicates that students are memorizing without understanding, and it foreshadows forgetting.

When students understand, they can see a relationship between a specific instance and a more general idea. If we ask them to think of examples that illustrate concepts or principles, they can do so. Conversely, when we pose a specific situation or example, students can explain how it relates to a broader idea. Unlike "knowing" questions that ask students to define concepts, state generalizations, or describe characteristics, the questions below require students to recognize those general ideas in specific situations. These questions assess understanding.

- Attached you will find an essay on Hawthorne's "Rappaccini's Daughter." Which approach to critical reading has the writer taken? Explain why you think so.
- When the Universal Declaration of Human Rights was adopted, the American Anthropological Association issued a statement claiming that people were more than mere individuals; they were also members of social groups that gave their lives meaning. Which of the challenges to human rights that Ignatieff identifies is most similar to the statement from the association?
- Which of these chemical equations conform to the Law of Conservation of Mass? [Samples provided]
- The slide we are viewing is a reproduction of a painting we have not discussed. Do you think this is an Impressionist painting? Why or why not?

Understanding does not come cheap. It develops gradually as students encounter new examples and illustrations. Students begin with a sketchy outline of an idea. As they encounter new examples and situations, they see other ways in which key properties and relationships are embodied or excluded, and they elaborate or revise the outline they have in mind. In the process, what might have been learned as a meaningless sequence of words or phrases becomes connected, integrated, and elaborated.

We know a good deal about how concepts are learned and about the instructional activities that promote understanding. (For a comprehensive discussion, see Bransford, Brown, and Cocking, 2000; Svinicki, 2004.) Here, we note two essential ingredients. First, examples and illustrations are critical because they contain the keys to meaning. We have more to say about selecting and discussing examples in Chapter Six. Meanwhile, suffice it to say that when we teach for understanding, we move back and forth between general ideas and specific examples.

Second, students need to practice recognizing or supplying examples and explaining how they represent the general ideas. Unfortunately, practice that leads to understanding is too often neglected. We typically introduce a concept, explain it by way of examples, perhaps even contrast them with nonexamples, and then move on to the next concept. We get a lot of practice while students watch and cheer us on. A far better use of class time would see us posing examples and *students* explaining how the examples relate to the concepts under study.

Thinking: Applying What One Has Learned

It is one thing to be able to define a concept or summarize a school of thought, and another to recognize how these ideas look in a specific situation. It is yet another to use what one has learned to solve a problem, explain cause and effect, draw a conclusion, make a recommendation, critique an argument, and a host of other things we ask students to do. These tasks require transforming, combining, or creating something beyond what currently exists. Students must, of course, be able to recall previously studied ideas and recognize how they relate to the situation or problem at hand, but the job is not done until they can fashion something new of the ideas they bring to bear and the information given by the task.

In his review of research on thinking and problem solving, Norman Frederiksen (1984) distinguished between "well-structured" and "ill-structured" problems and tasks. These terms continue to be useful in marking the ends of a continuum along which fall assignments that challenge students to think.

Thinking About Well-Structured Issues and Problems

Like questions that lead to understanding, questions that stimulate thinking present specific situations, problems, examples, data, and the like. Unlike the questions that asked students to recognize concepts or ideas embedded in a situation, these questions demand students create something beyond what is given in the situation.

- The editors of the campus literary journal have decided to devote an entire issue to critical analysis of Hawthorne's "Rappaccini's Daughter." They hope to include several articles, each reflecting a different approach to critical reading. You have been asked to write the thematic-analysis article. As a first step, outline the major points you intend to make and note the passages you will cite.

- There has been considerable debate recently about the applicability of human rights in non-Western societies. Some people argue that efforts to establish human rights are nothing more than an attempt to force others to become more like the West. Other people argue that respect for human rights is essential for any decent society. Come to a conclusion about which side in this debate is right and support your decision using Ignatieff's discussion of the challenges to human rights.

- Natural gas consists largely of methane. (A methane molecule contains one carbon atom and four hydrogen atoms.) When we light a Bunsen burner, the methane combines with oxygen in the air to form two products: liquid water and gaseous carbon dioxide. Write a balanced equation (that is, one that conforms to the Law of Conservation of Mass) for this reaction [Adapted from Masterton, Slowinski, and Stanitski, 1983, p. 66].

- Posted around the room are reproductions of twenty paintings. You have been asked to organize an exhibit that captures the spirit of Impressionism, but space limitations permit you to include only five paintings. Decide which five paintings you would select for the exhibit and explain why you would choose those five.

Questions that stimulate thinking range from easy to difficult, depending in part on the amount of structure in the problem situation and the complexity of the information that must be brought to bear. Compared to questions we will see later, these are fairly structured. They do not contain much extraneous information. They explicitly state or strongly imply the content to be applied. Finally, although the conceptual information that students are asked to apply is complex, it is easier to work with one approach, theory, assertion, or style than it is to work with several. As we increase the complexity of the information given in the question and reduce the structure and directions about how to proceed, the questions become more and more challenging.

Thinking About Ill-Structured Issues and Problems

In life outside the classroom, issues and problems do not come in neatly wrapped packages complete with directions about how to solve or resolve them. In real life, challenges to think are far less structured. More information is available than needed, and key ideas or relationships are often embedded in a morass of conflicting or irrelevant detail. We are not told how to approach a task or which ideas might illuminate the situation. Thinking through an issue or solving a problem often requires performing a series of steps or combining information studied at various times. There is usually more than one acceptable conclusion and more than one way to reach it. Although the next questions are not identical to those we might encounter outside campus boundaries, they do come closer to real-world challenges.

- The editors of the campus literary journal have decided to publish a volume on Hawthorne's short stories. They want to include one article on "Young Goodman Brown," and they've invited you to write the analysis. Note that the editors have not specified which approach to critical analysis you should use. They are leaving it to you to decide which approach or combination of approaches will produce the most illuminating and insightful analysis of the story. As a first step, outline the major points you will make in the article and note the passages you will cite.

- Singapore has been criticized by human rights activists for its harsh treatment of those found guilty of crimes. Even minor offenses are punished severely, often by flogging or a long prison sentence. Yet Singapore is a very prosperous and orderly society. Crime is infrequent, and survey data indicate the population is contented with government and its practices. A local religious group has asked you to address them on the absence of human rights in Singapore. What approach will you take in your talk, and how will you support your position on this issue?

- Benzene is reacted with nitric acid. Two products are formed, one of which is water. The other product is an oily liquid that has a molecular mass of 213. Propose a laboratory procedure for determining the composition of this unknown, and for writing a balanced equation for the reaction of benzene with nitric acid [adapted from Masterton, Slowinski, and Stanitski, 1983, p. 84].

When students confront ill-structured problems, they must do two things simultaneously. One, they have to restructure the problem by pulling key elements out of the context in which they are presented, seeing relationships that are not immediately obvious, and deciding which features of the situation merit attention. Two, they must sort through all they have learned and select what is relevant and useful in the situation at hand.

How do we teach the structuring and restructuring, the weighing and choosing, the selecting and rejecting skills required for complex thinking and problem solving? Decades of transfer of learning studies and more recent research comparing problem-solving approaches used by experts and novices have produced findings useful to those of us who wonder what we might do to foster development of thinking skills. In the next several paragraphs, we try to distill and transform those findings into practical suggestions for promoting the development of thinking skills.

First, there is little evidence that generic courses or workshops are successful in teaching thinking skills that transfer across subject-matter domains (Bransford, Brown, and Cocking, 2000; Kurfiss, 1988; Zull, 2002). Thinking—logically, critically, creatively, and otherwise—is intimately connected with the subject matter about which one is thinking: "The ability to plan a task, to notice patterns, to generate reasonable arguments and explanations, and to draw analogies to other problems are all more closely intertwined with factual knowledge than was once believed" (Bransford, Brown, and Cocking, 2000, p. 16). In his discussion of the biological processes involved in learning, James Zull (2002) suggests that efforts to teach generic, transferable thinking skills tend not to work because neuronal networks essential for recognizing patterns and connecting ideas "grow by building on existing networks, so our entrée to reasoning in one subject comes through the neuronal networks for information in that subject" (p. 192). The bottom line is that if we expect students to think in our courses, then we must give attention to both content and thinking skills.

Second, instruction that promotes thinking focuses both on the content to be learned and on "rules" for when and how to put the content to use. Svinicki (2004) offers an especially clear example of how such instruction works:

> For example, if I'm teaching several methods of analysis of variance in a statistics course, the students should be learning both the types of analysis and the rules that determine which to use when. I would want to drill into my students a list of questions that they have to ask themselves before choosing a particular form of analysis of variance: What kind of data are we looking at? Are there with-in as well as between-subject variables? How many and how independent are the individual observations? Which are the independent and which are the criterion variables? These questions determine which formula gets used in each situation, and so the first step in confronting a new situation is to run through the decision steps to decide which response to transfer [p. 104].

Third, thinking skills develop through practice over time and in a variety of situations. Unfortunately, many of us underestimate the amount of practice students need. We forget what it is like to be a novice in our field—how it felt to encounter a problem the first or second or umpteenth time. We worry about covering content, fall prey to the temptation to shortcut practice and hope for the best, and wind up feeling frustrated and disappointed when our hopes are dashed. If we are serious about getting students to think, it does not pay to cut corners on practice. In *How People Learn,* John Bransford and his colleagues do not mince words about the implications of this need to practice: "Superficial coverage of all topics in a subject area must be replaced with in-depth coverage of fewer topics that allows key concepts in that discipline to be understood" (Bransford, Brown, and Cocking, 2000, p. 20).

Fourth, in most courses it makes sense to sequence instruction so that students begin thinking about more structured issues or problems and gradually move to more complex and unstructured tasks. In some first-year courses, the initial challenge to think comes in the form of a project or paper assignment that more closely resembles questions in the ill-structured category than in the well-structured one. In other courses, students never get beyond the well-structured problems.

Neither practice encourages development of thinking skills. Students do not learn to handle complex, unstructured tasks if they never encounter them, but few students can handle complex, unstructured tasks their first time out. Although problem-based learning, service learning, and other experiential approaches may appear to contradict this recommendation in that they begin instruction by posing very complex problems or situations, successful use of these methods actually provides a good deal of structure in helping students work through and reflect on their learning. Chapter Ten discusses these methods in more detail.

Fifth, explicit emphasis on problem-solving techniques and procedures helps students develop thinking skills (McKeachie, Pintrich, Lin, and Smith, 1986; Bransford, Brown, and Cocking, 2000). When first-year students confront even a highly structured problem, they do not always distinguish what is given in the question from what is being asked. After reading a problem, many cannot state what the question is, which may explain why we often receive answers to questions other than those we asked. Highlighting problem-solving techniques and procedures might include paying explicit attention to questions such as: "What is given in the question?" "What are you being asked to do?" "What concepts or ideas are you asked to bring to bear?" "What steps will you need to take?"

The instructional task becomes more complicated as we move toward ill-structured problems. We know that students often read the problem and throw a formula at it, or read the assignment and reach for the first idea that crosses their minds. If the formula does not work or the idea does not go anywhere, they give up. Studies comparing experts and novices offer some ideas about how to help students tackle ill-structured problems. Experts, for example, report that as they read problems they jot down key ideas and information, note relationships, list assumptions, outline issues, write themselves questions, draw diagrams and pictures, break complex problems into simpler steps (Frederiksen, 1984; Kurfiss, 1988). Such activities make sense as strategies for restructuring and understanding a complex situation. We might explicitly tell students to use them.

Once they understand the problem, students must sort through all they know and decide what is relevant in the situation at hand. A mental survey of what one knows may seem an obvious step, but students often give up if an idea does not leap immediately to mind. We need to teach students how to move beyond this impasse. Some strategies might include

- Free-association techniques in which students take a few minutes to jot down everything that comes to mind when they first encounter a question

- Recalling rules of applicability

- Brainstorming ideas about a question or issue before trying to answer it

- Taking a tentative position and then arguing the opposite before committing oneself

- Imagining how several theorists or experts might answer before developing one's own answer

Although further research is needed to determine the effectiveness of particular strategies and techniques, current reviews advocate that we explicitly teach strategies for thinking and problem solving along with the subject matter content (Bransford, Brown, and Cocking, 2000; Kurfiss, 1988; McKeachie, Pintrich, Lin, and Smith, 1986; Svinicki, 2004).

Sixth, we should plan instruction so that students receive lots of guidance on early attempts but progressively less on subsequent attempts. Students often need step-by-step prompts, hints, and feedback when they first encounter a problem or situation that asks them to think. In fact, we recommend that initial practice exercises be done in small groups *in* class, where an instructor is available for such guidance. This is not the time to use the sink-or-swim approach. Many first-year students find it too frustrating, give up prematurely, and drown in their sense of failure. On the other hand, students *do* need to learn to cope with problems or situations on their own. They will not do so if we continue to lead them through analyses or solutions or critiques. Gradually, we need to withdraw prompts, hints, and step-by-step questions.

Seventh, we might prompt students to verbalize what they are doing and why they are doing it. Research on problem solving suggests that verbalizing the reason for taking a step before doing so results in improved performance, and that verbalization is most helpful during the initial stages of learning (McKeachie, Pintrich, Lin, and Smith, 1986; Svinicki, 2004).

Finally, students need to learn that thinking involves some trial and error, often pursues a random course, and usually requires hard work. More often than not, students see us discuss the final version of a solution or analysis—as if the solution or analysis emerged in polished form; as if key ideas, questions, and relationships were self-evident; as if we ourselves never felt confused, got stuck, pursued blind alleys, or had to start over from scratch. It is little wonder that students conclude they either get it or don't and give up prematurely if an answer does not spring immediately to mind.

The suggestions offered in the previous three sections of this chapter focus on what we as instructors can do—the opportunities and prompts we might make available—to help students remember, understand, and use the information and ideas taught in our courses. Although most of us are willing to incorporate those prompts into our instruction, we are also concerned that students develop habits and skills that free them from dependence on the instructor and enable them to become independent learners. This brings us to a fourth category of instructional goals for first-year courses: learning how to learn.

Learning How to Learn

We complain, often at great length, that first-year students do not know how to study. To hear many tell it, first-year students cannot read for comprehension, listen for the key ideas in a lecture, or learn from discussion. They do not know how to take notes, how to use them once they have them, how to approach or think through problems, or how to prepare for exams. Given all that we allege students do not know how to do, it is somewhat ironic that our most frequent advice to first-year students is that they should study more and learn to manage their time better. No doubt, many students could profit from following that advice, but it does not suffice.

For a long time, we in higher education assumed that first-year students would—indeed, *should*—come to our classes knowing how to study for them. When we discovered that many students seemed not to have developed the skills needed in our courses, it was tempting to blame high school teachers for not preparing students, and perhaps understandable that we might resent having to teach study skills on top of everything else. Research on learning is making it increasingly clear that neither the assumptions nor the responses are tenable.

The developmental findings summarized in Chapter Two tell us that students' views of knowledge and learning undergo transformations during the college years. With them come changes in students' readiness and willingness to engage in different strategies for studying. Research on cognition indicates that capability and motivation for using various learning strategies accumulate as students acquire more information about a subject, develop useful schemes for organizing their knowledge, and gain experience in using what they are learning in thinking and problem solving (Bransford, Brown, and Cocking, 2000; Svinicki, 2004). Adding it all up, we conclude it is less likely that learning how to learn is a prerequisite students should have mastered before admission to college, one that high schools failed to teach. Learning how to learn looks instead more like a primary goal for college students, one that can be pursued only as students gain knowledge and experience in particular subject areas.

Discussion of the conditions, challenges, and supports that promote development of independent learning ability goes by the term *metacognition.* We hesitate to use a term that triggers many faculty to sound the "jargon alarm," but the research on learning skills is now plentiful, and this is the heading under which it is typically found. Metacognition is variously defined as *thinking about thinking, learning about learning,* or *the ability to plan and monitor one's learning* (Branford, Brown, and Cocking, 2000; Svinicki, 2004; Weinstein and others, 2002). For those of us looking for something a bit more concrete, Svinicki (2004) outlines four categories of metacognition: knowledge of strategies and tactics, knowledge about task demands, knowledge about oneself as learner, and executive process knowledge.

Knowledge of strategies and tactics is what many of us have in mind when we talk about learning and study skills: outlining, paraphrasing, summarizing a reading, note-taking, quizzing oneself, brainstorming possibilities, and so on. Many students come to college knowing a fairly limited number of such strategies. They may, for example, have learned to underline or highlight ideas in the text and answer review questions at the end of a chapter. If these strategies do not lead to success, often because assessment emphasizes something beyond memorization, many students do not know what else they might do to study more effectively. Introducing students to a wider array of study strategies and tactics is one way we instructors can help them become more effective learners. This chapter mentions several such strategies; later, especially in Chapters Six and Seven, we suggest others.

Knowledge about task demands enables students to determine which study strategies and tactics are called for and when. Textbooks in mathematics and the sciences, for example, call for reading strategies different from what novels or philosophical treatises demand. Discussion and laboratory work demand different note-taking strategies than do lectures. Indeed, effective note-taking strategies often vary with the lecturing style. Helping students determine when to use various study strategies and tactics is a second way we can foster independent learning skills.

Knowledge about themselves as learners allows students to select strategies and tactics that work best for them. Talking with students about the dimensions of learning styles discussed in Chapter Two is one approach to increasing their awareness of how they learn best. An alternative approach systematically invites students to experiment and reflect on learning strategies. For example, pausing from time to time to summarize lecture or reading content in one's own words is a strategy that promotes understanding and retention, but there are several ways to go about summarizing, among them explaining the content to a study partner, writing a summary, or drawing a diagram or a concept map. When we ask faculty in workshops to try each of these tactics, most find one summarizing activity easier and more useful than the others, and they identify at least one as a real struggle. Always, there is variability in preference. Most faculty, of course, discovered long ago which study tactics work for them and almost automatically use them. First-year students are less aware of study skill options and have not given much thought to what works best for them. Systematically introducing new learning strategies for students to try and encouraging them to reflect on which work best are things we can do to help them develop knowledge about themselves as learners.

Knowledge about executive control processes enables students to manage their learning activities. This category includes such skills as setting learning goals, identifying what needs to be done to achieve a goal, planning a schedule, selecting study strategies, monitoring progress, recognizing when one is off-track or stuck, figuring out how to move forward, and knowing when one has achieved a learning goal. Such activities may seem obvious to us, but many students take a less reflective, more trial-and-error approach to studying. They jump into a reading assignment and highlight their way through without considering reading goals, often producing solid pages of highlighting. Many do not think to (or know how to) monitor their learning progress, so they finish reading the pages but cannot remember anything they have read. They use particular study techniques simply because they have always used them, not because they are suited to the task. Asking students to reflect on the effectiveness of their study practices *in a particular course or subject area* is a first step in helping them take control of their learning.

A Note on Classification of Learning Goals

We have discussed course goals in four categories. We have tried to talk about them using the everyday language of faculty and students. These categories, however, were derived from and reflect distinctions made by learning researchers and parallel major areas of learning research: memory and retention, concept formation, transfer and problem solving, and metacognition (for discussion of theory and research in these areas, see Bransford, Brown, and Cocking, 2000; Gagne, Briggs, and Wager, 1988; Svinicki, 2004).

Other schemes for classifying course goals exist. A popular alternative is Bloom's Taxonomy, developed by Benjamin Bloom and colleagues in the 1950s and recently revised (Anderson and Krathwohl, 2001). The revised Taxonomy identifies six levels of cognitive process (remember, understand, apply, analyze, evaluate, and create) on four knowledge dimensions (factual, conceptual, procedural, and metacognitive). Although close comparison between the classification we discuss and Bloom's Taxonomy might surface discrepancies in what is prerequisite for the next level of learning, the differences mainly reflect the number and kind of discriminations these schemes make. For example, our discussion of thinking encompasses the top four levels of Bloom's Taxonomy. Similarly, we group together factual, conceptual, and procedural knowledge dimensions. If faculty are willing to think about and articulate finer distinctions, we are all for it, and Bloom's Taxonomy offers a useful guide.

In *Creating Significant Learning Experiences* (2003), Dee Fink proposes another taxonomy for categorizing course goals, prompted by his observations that

> . . .individuals and organizations involved in higher education are expressing a need for important kinds of learning that do not emerge easily from the Bloom taxonomy, for example: learning how to learn, leadership and interpersonal skills, ethics, communication skills, character, tolerance, and the ability to change. My interpretation of the aforementioned statements is that they are expressing a need for new kinds of learning, kinds that go well beyond the cognitive domain of Bloom's taxonomy and even beyond cognitive learning itself. This suggests that the time may have arrived when we need a new and broader taxonomy of significant learning" [pp. 29–30].

The taxonomy Fink proposes discusses learning in six categories (foundational knowledge, application, integration, human dimension, caring, and learning how to learn). The six categories are not hierarchical as they are in Bloom's Taxonomy and in the classification system we discuss. Instead, the taxonomy assumes that the categories are interrelated and dynamic so that learning in one category enhances the possibility of learning in others. For example, if instruction enables students to see how new information and ideas (foundational knowledge) relate to themselves and others (the human dimension), they may in the process become more interested in studying the subject further (caring) and in learning how to study the subject (learning how to learn). Fink shows how to use the taxonomy to create *significant* learning experiences—that is, experiences that are engaging, prompt lasting change, and have value to students in their personal and communal lives as well as in the world of work.

We are not wedded to a particular classification scheme, but we do think using some classification system can help clarify and distinguish the various learning outcomes to be emphasized in our courses. Also, such schemes are useful as a reminder that we are interested in learning that goes beyond acquiring content, and as a deterrent to overemphasizing that form of learning. Whatever classification scheme we use to define the types or levels of learning, we need to remember that a student brings his or her own definition of learning to our courses.

Students' Definitions of Learning

In Chapter Two, we saw that students' views of knowledge and learning change during the college years, and we traced the transformations from positions of dualism to multiplicity, relativism, and commitment in relativism. What happens when students in these various positions confront the challenges we have discussed?

Students who define learning as accumulating facts and right answers (as students in positions of dualism do) are likely to understand a challenge to memorize. They may have doubt about *what* they are asked to memorize ("Why do we need to know all these different theories? Why not just learn the one that's right?"), but memorizing factual or authoritative information fits well with their views of knowledge and learning. What sense do these students make of the other forms of learning we have discussed? First-year students often talk about understanding and thinking, but many complain: "The examples on the test were not discussed in class." "How are we supposed to know what Ignatieff would say about this? It wasn't in the book." "I don't think it's fair to ask us to write essays on stories we haven't discussed." In short, students in early developmental positions take understanding and thinking to mean remembering the thoughts of others.

In contrast, we can expect students in positions of multiplicity to welcome questions that ask them to explain, interpret, analyze, critique, or otherwise think through the issues and problems we pose. They too appear to transform our questions into something other than what we intend. We expect *informed* opinions—recognition of the contribution of others, evidence, documentation. But these students say, "Who cares what Ignatieff would say? This is what I think." A student in a position of multiplicity may welcome questions that we have classified as understanding and thinking, but the response is likely to neglect the role of factual information or authoritative opinion.

Not until students reach positions of relativism are they likely to understand fully the goals we set in our courses or the assignments we give. Remember that most first-year students are in earlier developmental positions. Teaching and testing for understanding and thinking may seem a waste of time. Some faculty respond by emphasizing memorization and saving other forms of learning for more advanced courses. Two serious problems arise from this approach. First, when memorization is disconnected from other forms of learning, the forgetting curve is steep. Second, students transform their views of learning when they encounter challenges to those views. Postponing the challenge puts off transformation and retards development. Sooner or later, faculty and students will confront these developmental issues. We advocate sooner rather than later.

At the same time, if first-year students are to meet the challenges, they need support. So far, we have talked about what first-year students bring to college and what they encounter when they arrive. Now we begin to talk about what faculty can do to make those encounters productive. We start with preparing a syllabus and meeting the first class.

For Further Exploration

- Fink, L. D. *Creating Significant Learning Experiences: An Integrated Approach to Designing College Courses.* San Francisco: Jossey-Bass, 2003.

  Dee Fink suggests categories of learning that include more than cognitive outcomes and proposes a nonhierarchical scheme that emphasizes the relationships among categories. His discussion about how to use his taxonomy in creating significant learning experiences may be of special interest to faculty using, or thinking about using, the instructional activities we discuss in Chapter Ten: problem-based learning, service learning, and learning communities.

- Anderson, L. W., and Krathwohl, D. R. (eds.). *A Taxonomy for Learning, Teaching, and Assessing: A Revision of Bloom's Taxonomy of Educational Objectives (abridged ed.).* White Plains, N.Y.: Addison-Wesley Longman, 2001.

  Bloom's Taxonomy remains a popular method for clarifying and classifying learning objectives. For those interested in drawing finer distinctions than we have in this chapter, this volume is an excellent resource.

CHAPTER 5

Preparing a Syllabus and Meeting the First Class

For first-year students, the first class is a signal event, something they have been anticipating for weeks. At last, they will find out how college differs from high school. The prospects are exhilarating, but they create a good deal of anxiety as well: How much work will there be? Will I be able to do it? Are professors people? What will mine be like? What if I do something really dopey and humiliate myself in front of everyone? Am I the only one who feels in over my head?

Students have two agendas for the first class meeting. They want information about the course—the content, the requirements, the evaluation procedures, and so on. These matters constitute the explicit agenda for the first class meeting. A good syllabus helps address these issues, so we begin with suggestions for preparing the syllabus. Equally important, however, is the tacit agenda as students try to determine what the professor is like, how the class is run, and what climate will prevail. This agenda is an experiential one; students form impressions and learn the rules for class behavior more from what we *do* in the first class than from what we *say*. We address this tacit, experiential agenda and suggest a sampler of activities for the first class later in the chapter.

Preparing a Syllabus

"Why should I spend a lot of time writing a syllabus," we often hear our colleagues ask, "when students won't read it anyway?" Perhaps some do not read the syllabus and will not, no matter what we do. Others might read it if only they had not lost it, a problem easily addressed these days by posting the syllabus online. Many students do read and rely on the syllabus, and more might if prompted to do so by an assignment that requires them to read and reflect on plans for the course. In any case, not preparing a good syllabus exacerbates the problem of students not reading it.

In our view, the syllabus is a major instructional document. It is not only a form of communication to students but also a reflection of thoughtful course planning. The latter function makes syllabus preparation an increasingly prominent factor in tenure and promotion processes, a topic we address in Chapter Sixteen. Here, we outline the contents of a good syllabus, present examples of different components, and try to sample a variety of disciplines in the process.

Basic Course and Instructor Information

Given the dizzying pace of the first days in college, it is no surprise that students find themselves in the wrong place at the wrong time, forget names and numbers, and neglect writing down information they might need. It is easy enough for us to include on the syllabus the course number and title, when and where it meets, the instructor's name, office location, phone number, e-mail address, and office hours. Because many first-year students feel intimidated by the thought of meeting professors one-on-one, we might also consider including an explicit invitation to visit during office hours. Something along these lines is more inviting than simply listing office hours:

> I do hope you will visit during my office hours. Come individually or with friends. It's a chance to talk about the course, assignments, exams, study strategies, or whatever else you'd like to discuss. You don't have to have a *problem* to visit. If you find yourself having difficulty with a reading or assignment, however, I definitely want to see you; I may be able to help. If these office hours are impossible for you, please let me know so that we can make an appointment for another time.

Students with disabilities report that they feel far more comfortable about approaching faculty to request accommodation when the syllabus includes an invitation to do so, and notice of office hours is one logical place to include such an invitation:

> If you need individual accommodations to meet course objectives because of a documented disability, please make an appointment with me to discuss your needs as soon as possible so that we can ensure your full participation in class and fair assessment of your work.

Required Texts

Most of our syllabuses list required texts. Considering how much rides on whether or not students do the reading, we think it is worth the additional effort to include a paragraph or two about why texts were chosen, how they will relate to class activities, and what students might expect to gain from reading them. Here is how two colleagues discuss required texts in their syllabuses:

> The following three texts are required for Introduction to Philosophy: (1) Anthony Weston, *A Rulebook for Arguments*, 3rd edition. I picked this text to start our work in philosophy because it is extremely clear in laying out the fundamental approaches to making philosophical claims. By reading this book first, we don't just read *about* philosophy; we *do* philosophy ourselves from the start. (2) Plato, *The Phaedo*, translated by G.M.A. Grube. This is a classic text in philosophy and a good introduction to many of the issues we'll be exploring this term. It's also very imaginative and fun to read! (3) Stephen Law, *Philosophy Gym*. This is an unusual but ultimately useful introduction to the subject of philosophy, presented as a series of twenty-five "cases" that cover a great variety of puzzles and problems. Your logic training will give you the tools you need to grapple with these challenges, though we'll begin with the "warm up" levels in order to ease you into the process! [*Source:* Cheryl Foster, professor of philosophy, University of Rhode Island]

> The textbook for Introduction to Biology, *The Living World* by George B. Johnson, is up-to-date and aimed for a nonscience audience. It has useful course outlines, beautiful and informative illustrations, excellent practice and thought questions, additional reading suggestions at the end of each chapter, and a good glossary at the end of the book. Look at the figures and read the figure legends; they contain important material that may summarize key information better than the text itself [*Source:* Marian Goldsmith, professor of biological sciences, University of Rhode Island].

Introduction to the Subject Matter

Just because students have registered for a course does not mean they know what they will be studying. A course title such as General Chemistry, or Introduction to Literature, or Principles of Economics, does not say much about the content of the course, and most catalogue descriptions offer little elaboration. Students take for granted that they will find out soon enough what they are studying, but their complacency about this is not a good sign.

"What is this course about?" often leads to "Why would or should anyone want to learn this?" First-year students enroll in many of their courses to meet curricular requirements, and they bring about as much enthusiasm to the task as we might expect from people doing something that someone else has decided will be good for them. Yet there is no getting around the relationship between motivation and learning, so we may as well address motivational issues at the outset.

The reasons first-year students give for coming to college and the objectives they claim are important may not give us much to go on. Few of us can claim a direct link between our course and a better job or higher salary—and we are not convinced we should even if we could. It is also true, however, that students are just as interested in what is happening in their lives right now as they are in the good life they envision down the road. If we can find even one or two connections between our subject matter and the questions, issues, or dilemmas students encounter, their motivation will be strengthened. At the very least, we might mention why *we* find the subject matter interesting or important. Our enthusiasm may not be as contagious as we would like, but it is more motivating than the lack of it.

The excerpts here illustrate how two colleagues begin the introduction to their subjects. Both include additional paragraphs that identify and elaborate major issues to be addressed in the course. We sacrifice including a full introduction to sample different disciplines and approaches.

> BIO 104B, Introduction to Biology, is designed to introduce non-biology majors to selected areas of biology with emphasis on basic principles and recent advances in scientific research. It is a series of special topics, not a survey course. . . . My aim is to give you some exposure to a few basic areas of biology so that you can appreciate some of the central ideas in the life sciences, such as evolution, and gain some familiarity with recent developments in some related areas of research and medicine today, such as human genetics and gene technology. I also hope that you will begin to get a feel for how scientists work and what kinds of procedures they use to study the kinds of biological problems we cover in the course [*Source:* Marian Goldsmith].

> Welcome to Sociology 112, Families in Society. We're about to take a detailed and analytical look at one of our most fundamental social institutions. I hope you find this course an important part of your general education, because as we head into the twenty-first century, we find ourselves more and more worried about what's happening to families. The wide array of "life-style choices" available to us, high divorce and lower marriage rates, nonmarital partnerships, and mothers' employment all illustrate that we are living through some major changes in families that have led to much greater family diversity. The emphasis on "family values" in politics and social discourse indicates that we are concerned about how increased family diversity is affecting society. Family diversity has called into question how we define what families are, how we think about the place of families in our own lives, as well as what we expect families to do for society [*Source:* Helen Mederer, professor of sociology, University of Rhode Island].

Statement of Course Goals

Because students are more likely to accomplish course goals if they know what the goals are, a syllabus should inform students where all the reading and studying are leading. When all is said and done, what will students have gained? Knowledge, to be sure, but most courses aim for more—understanding, thinking, reasoning, problem solving, using one's knowledge somehow. If we think back to our discussion of student development in Chapter Three, how are we to explain such goals to students, many of whom assume thinking means whatever opinions one happens to hold or memorizing the thoughts of others? It is not an easy task.

Let us begin with suggestions for writing course goals that help us stay focused on student learning and that remind students they are the major actors in the learning process. Statements of course goals should

- State what students will be able to do, not what the course will do ("You will be able to . . .," not "The course will introduce you to. . . .").

- Indicate the behavior expected, not the state of mind students will be in ("You will be able to recognize a variety of issues and problems in which the material we study is relevant," not "You will have an appreciation of the importance of the subject matter").

- Identify the outcomes of instruction, not the processes we employ ("You will be able to report and explain the significance of current research about a topic of interest to you," not "You will write a term paper on a topic that interests you").

The second of these suggestions—indicate the behavior expected—is the most difficult. Educators and researchers have for decades been working on what it means to know, understand, think, create, appreciate, and so on, and how to talk about these goals. Their efforts have helped faculty and researchers design instruction and talk to one another, even across disciplines—definitely an improvement from earlier times. Still, we have no formula for stating objectives in terms *students* will understand because, as we saw in Chapter Three, students interpret our statements according to their developmental position. So why should we bother? In addition to clarifying our own thinking, efforts to define what we mean when we say we want students to know, understand, think, and so on help some of them focus their studying and perhaps prompt others to reconsider their notion of what learning is.

One approach to clarifying goals focuses on carefully selecting the verbs for these statements. Colleagues who use this approach have found Bloom's Taxonomy (Anderson and Krathwohl, 2001) a useful resource. As we noted in Chapter Four, this Taxonomy identifies six levels of cognitive process in four knowledge dimensions. Discussion of the various levels of cognitive processing suggests a selection of verbs likely to elicit each level of processing. This is a helpful feature both for articulating objectives and for developing assessment measures.

An alternative approach, one that seems to get students' attention for reading and thinking about course goals, uses a strategy similar to the one we took in Chapter Four. On the syllabus, we might list course goals in the everyday language of knowing, understanding, thinking, and the like. We then clarify what would otherwise be vague and ambiguous goal statements by giving descriptions or samples of questions to be used to assess performance on those goals. The syllabus for an introductory biological sciences course, for example, explains three major goals:

1. *Factual knowledge and scientific vocabulary.* I will test your knowledge of scientific vocabulary, structures, and their functions, by asking you to select the definition of a term in a multiple choice list.

2. *Conceptual understanding.* A somewhat harder kind of question tests your understanding of a concept. For example, I might give a term or its definition, and you will have to recognize and pick out the correct or appropriate example that applies to this term. Or vice versa: I give an example, and you pick out the correct term or definition.

3. *Solving problems.* I will also require you to use the information that you have learned in a new or different way to show that you can solve problems. For example, the genetic code is based on triplets in which three nucleotides stand for a single amino acid. To show that you really understand what this means, I might ask you to figure out how many amino acids are coded by a gene that is 993 nucleotides long [*Source:* Marian Goldsmith].

Several of the questions included in Chapter Four were actually questions faculty included on a syllabus to clarify course goals. The sample test questions included in Chapter Eleven on evaluating student learning could also be used to illustrate how major goals might be assessed. Using sample test questions or assignments to clarify course goals has much to recommend it, not least that it attracts students' attention by addressing one of the questions most on their minds: "What will exams and other evaluation activities be like?"

Description of Evaluation Procedures

Both research and experience tell us that students work for grades, and their expectations about how they will be evaluated largely determine what they study and how they study it. We can deplore and resist this motivational reality, or we can put it to constructive use. Early discussion of what students want to know about evaluation practices can go a long way toward directing their attention to appropriate study activities and patterns. Before we can answer such questions for students, of course, we must answer them for ourselves, and that is never easy. We preview some of the issues and our recommendations here and discuss them in more detail in Chapter Twelve.

First, students want to know what will count and how much. The possibilities for assessing student learning are numerous: exams, quizzes, written assignments, individual and group projects, journals, homework, field experiences, and more. In general, the greater the number and the variety of opportunities students have to show what they have learned, the more confident we can feel about the validity, reliability, and fairness of the grades we assign. In Chapter Twelve, we caution faculty about counting things such as class attendance, participation, effort, and improvement; there we discuss the issues in more detail. For now, the bottom line is that the syllabus should list whatever is going to count toward students' grades and clearly indicate the relative weight of each activity.

Second, students want to know at the outset what tests, papers, projects, and other graded assignments will be like. If the course relies heavily on exams and quizzes, students want to know what form questions will take: multiple choice, essay, matching, true-false. The syllabus should address these questions, but we would be wise to keep in mind that many students mistakenly assume that the types of tests we give dictate the level and depth of learning required. Many first-year students believe, for example, that multiple choice questions test only memorization, so they study accordingly. As we see in Chapter Eleven, multiple choice questions can test a much broader range of objectives. It is especially important for faculty who use multiple choice tests to show at the start how these questions are used to test various forms of learning.

Students also want to know what will be expected on other evaluation activities, especially if they contribute significantly to the final grade. In many cases, including a general description of the assignment and perhaps sample questions, tasks, or topics is enough to let students assess the match between the assignment and their interests, abilities, and schedules. This description includes detail that is probably enough for most students:

> Research abstracts: Twice during the semester, each student must locate a research article related to the topics we are discussing and write a 150-word abstract of the article. Each abstract should (1) state the goal or purpose of the research; (2) describe the participants or subjects of the research; (3) explain the methods (how the data were gathered, instruments used,

and the like); (4) briefly describe the findings; and (5) discuss the conclusions. To help you understand this assignment, we will do a first article and abstract in common, working from an article that I provide for you. Each abstract is worth 10 points [*Source:* W. Lynn McKinney, professor and dean of the College of Human Science and Services, University of Rhode Island].

Sometimes it makes sense to include more detailed instructions, and perhaps even a scoring guide, in the syllabus. If our course requires a major project, field experience, or service learning component, for example, or if evaluation activities are likely to be unfamiliar to many students, then students want—and need—more detail about how those activities will be evaluated. We revisit these issues and what the syllabus might usefully include in Chapters Eleven and Twelve.

Finally, students want to know up-front how final grades are determined. Will it be by comparing individual scores to predetermined standards (criterion-referenced) or by comparing individual scores to the scores of other students (norm-referenced, or grading on a curve)? Chapter Twelve discusses the pros and cons of each approach and recommends against norm-referenced grading, but it is not a black-and-white issue. The question of how final grades are determined does affect how students go about a course, however, so we should address questions about grading according to standards, grading on a curve, and scaling grades in the syllabus.

In one additional note, we suggest keeping the system for calculating grades as simple as possible. On the one hand, including a variety of assessment activities and weighting them differently (perhaps even allowing students to choose weighting systems to maximize their strengths) are practices that make some sense. On the other hand, as the grading system becomes more complicated there comes a point where it ceases being useful to students. "Keeping me informed about how I am doing" is the item on our teaching feedback questionnaire that elicits the most recommendations for improvement from students at all levels. Part of the problem is that many students cannot figure out how to estimate their grades on the basis of information included in the syllabus. There are thousands of points, scores of ways to earn them, dozens of ways to lose them, many possible combinations, and weights for everything. In most cases, a total of one hundred points works just as well as five hundred or one thousand, and the smaller total makes calculation easier.

Preview of Class Activities and Assignments

Much of the anxiety first-year students feel springs from the expectation that college will be different, without knowing just how. Information about how classes are run and what students are asked to do as preparation for class can settle their nerves and clarify their responsibilities. There is, however, another and perhaps more important reason for including such information in the syllabus. Learning to think demands active involvement in practicing whatever forms thinking takes in a course. To the extent that students view learning as transcribing and memorizing what the professor and text have said—and that is the portrayal emerging from research on secondary and early postsecondary students (see Chapters One and Three)—class activities and assignments that call for active involvement are not always greeted with enthusiasm. To many first-year students, these activities seem a waste of time that would be better spent writing down what the professor says.

By itself, the syllabus is not going to convert passive learners into active ones, but it can pave the way. At the very least, a preview of class activities tells students their instructor has given some thought to the activities and that there may be method to what some think is madness. Some faculty describe a typical class and indicate how students are expected to prepare for class. Others describe the kinds of activities they have planned for the course and indicate why students will be asked to participate in them. This example from a philosophy course takes the latter approach.

> Most students don't get a chance to study philosophy before coming to college, so I don't expect you to have any background in the areas we'll be exploring. Still, it will be helpful if you have both some ideas of what I expect from you and what, in turn, you can expect from me!
>
> *Reading*: Although the course requires no written homework as such, you are expected to complete readings from our texts in preparation for each class. Many students don't realize that doing well in college, and in philosophy particularly, takes more than simply skimming a reading and highlighting what looks important. Our readings for this course are not particularly long, but they *are* challenging; they are exercises in using your brain, in thinking through a set of issues from all sides. Don't highlight your book. Underline in pencil, write notes in the margins and later, summarize the reading in outline notes of your own. Always bring your book to class!
>
> *Writing*: We will do several short in-class essays on the required readings. These essays will not be graded. I shall use the essays to provide you with the chance to refine your skills in critical thinking and written expression.
>
> *Talking*: Most of our work in Philosophy 103 will be done in small groups to which you will be assigned shortly after the start of the term. One requirement in these groups and in open class discussion is good manners. While I expect you to question the views of others and to express your own views, I also insist upon respect and courtesy in all your interactions with your peers [*Source*: Cheryl Foster].

Course Outline

Time management is a particular challenge for many first-year students. A course outline indicating reading assignments, assignment due dates, and the examination schedule can satisfy students' needs for structure, direction, and security. Opinions differ as to how much detail should be included and how precise the schedule should be. First-year students tend to prefer more structure rather than less, but they often find deviation from the schedule unsettling. In most courses, a week-by-week schedule of topics establishes the structure students need while allowing some flexibility for responding to their needs and interests. The course outline should, however, indicate the exact dates on which exams are scheduled and on which papers or other major assignments are due. We sometimes forget that students are taking several courses and that exams fall at similar periods. Students need this information at the outset if they are to manage their time and be able to meet four or five sets of requirements.

Course Policies

One colleague calls this section of the syllabus "the fine print." The syllabus should indicate policies governing attendance, late assignments, make-up work, safety regulations, and whatever other rules we deem necessary for the course to run smoothly. A sentence or two explaining why such policies have been adopted can make them seem less harsh or arbitrary and may be one way of humanizing students' initial encounters with the details of college academic life.

Discussion of Academic Integrity

Discussion of academic integrity is a necessary part of a course syllabus, especially for first-year students. If self-reports are to be believed (and they probably underestimate the extent of the problem), violation of academic integrity—from copying a homework assignment to cheating on an examination to downloading a completed paper from a commercial Website—is rife in secondary school and on the college campus (Center for Academic Integrity, 2004). Sending a clear message about the importance of honesty in academic work early on in a student's career may not eliminate cheating and plagiarism, but it will, like the rest of a syllabus, tell the student that integrity matters in this classroom and on this campus.

How we discuss academic integrity with students depends not only on the culture and rules of our campus community (is there, for instance, an honor code?) but also on the tone and style of our own teaching. For example, these paragraphs appear prominently in a syllabus of a general education social science course especially designed for first-year students.

> Our course is an academic community that is bound together by the traditions and practice of scholarship. Honest intellectual work—on examinations and on written assignments— is essential to the success of our own community of scholars. Using classmates' responses to answer exam questions or disguising words written by others as your own undermines the trust and respect on which our course depends.
>
> The work in this course is challenging and will demand a good deal of each of you. I have every confidence that each of you can succeed. Doing your own work will enhance your sense of accomplishment when the semester comes to a close.

The tone is positive and nurturing, seeking to persuade students of the importance and value of academic integrity to the course and also to their own satisfaction. Some of our colleagues find this sort of discussion a bit too soft, preferring something more ominous and direct about the consequences of being caught. (One of them promises students that she "will make it her life's work" to see that they are "expelled" for any serious breach.) Whether we extol the virtues and rewards of honesty or outline the costs of being dishonest and getting caught, the syllabus should let students know that because we take the issue of academic integrity seriously they should as well.

Style and Tone

We need to pay some attention to style when preparing a syllabus because how we talk about course content, goals, requirements, and so forth communicates beyond the words we say about them. A poorly written syllabus full of misspellings and punctuation errors undermines our credibility in insisting that sloppy thinking and careless work will be unacceptable. A syllabus that talks about what students *should* do, *must* do, and *will* do—and what will happen if they do not do it—sets a different tone than one that talks about what students *may* do or *might want to* do. We create and convey moods through anecdote, metaphor, parenthetical comment, quotation, and even a cartoon or two. A good syllabus makes good reading, and we can see something of the person between the lines.

A good syllabus, in sum, is more than a list of topics to be covered and assignments to be completed. At its best, a syllabus introduces the subject matter, gives a rationale for learning what is to be taught, and motivates students to do their best work. It lays out an organizational framework that indicates major topics, suggests the relationships among them, and previews the order in which they will be explored. It describes how class meetings are conducted and what students need to do by way of preparation. It spells out how student progress is measured, notes the date when work is due or a test is scheduled, and indicates how final grades are assigned. It does all this in a manner reflecting our own teaching style.

Meeting the First Class

Important as the syllabus is, it is only a part of getting a course off to a good beginning. Actions speak louder than words, and most students take their cue about the course and instructor from what happens or does not happen in the first class meeting. Take Elena's encounters with a couple of opening sessions, for example:

> Early Wednesday morning, Elena arrives at her classroom just a minute or two before her first college course. After finding a seat, she waits nearly ten minutes, growing increasingly anxious (Am I in the right place? Is this my course?). Finally, an instructor appears and announces that he will sign add slips at the end of class. He distributes a syllabus, suggests students read it, and then says, "Well, we'll get started more seriously next time; I'll see you Friday." Elena closes her notebook and departs in silence, filing out with her classmates.
>
> Later in the day, she makes her way to her next course. Her instructor is already present and distributing the syllabus. The class begins. The instructor calls the roll, highlights information in the syllabus, and moves quickly into a rather fast-paced introduction to the course content that Elena struggles to keep up with. As the hour draws to a close, the instructor pauses, "Well, that's probably enough for today. Remember, the success of this course depends on your contributions to discussion, so I expect each of you to come next time ready to make some meaningful contribution."

Although this vignette may be exaggerated, it does capture the essence of many students' experiences on the opening day of classes. Elena's initial encounters with her courses give her two kinds of information. In each case, she receives a syllabus that describes the course, its content, requirements, evaluation procedures, and so on—an important place to begin. But Elena also *experiences* her instructors, her classmates, and the conduct of her courses for the first time, and we might guess that in neither case will Elena's impression of the course be what her instructor hoped to convey.

A student's experience of a first class is powerful. A first session that sets an appropriate tone and engages students in the sort of activity that will typify classroom practice can go a long way toward getting a course off on the right foot. In addition to distributing the syllabus, then, we suggest finding some way to do several additional things in the first class:

- Find out something about students enrolled in the class. Information about their background, interests, activities, and aspirations can be helpful in planning instruction. Requesting such information also suggests that the instructor is interested in students.

- Help students meet and establish a connection with other students in class. Feelings of isolation get in the way of learning.

- Get students to talk. If they speak up on the first day, they are more likely to participate in subsequent class meetings.

- Include an activity that requires students to be actively involved: a problem to solve, a question to discuss, a paragraph to write. If they sit passively through the first class, they will do the same in the next.

- Make an assignment for the second class. Some faculty are reluctant to give an assignment until enrollment settles down, but how are students to know what the course will be like without an assignment?

There are hundreds of ways to accomplish these tasks. Here we sample nine opening-day activities, in the hope they stimulate creation of other approaches.

Introductory Survey

Collecting information about students is one good way to start a course. Several of our colleagues distribute note cards and ask students to write answers to questions such as Why did you sign up for this course? What other courses are you taking this semester? In what do you intend to major? Are you working this semester? on campus or off campus? how many hours per week? What do you anticipate might be difficult for you in this course? What can I do to help you do your best in this course? Answers to such questions can be enormously helpful in figuring out how to connect course material to students' interests, in selecting meaningful examples and problems, and in knowing how to support students' efforts.

Student Introductions

Asking students to introduce themselves to one another is another good starter, one that helps students meet others and begin establishing connections with peers. In smaller classes, it is possible to ask each student to introduce himself or herself to the rest of the class. Because even the most fascinating introductions grow tedious after the twelfth or fifteenth, we need to think of alternatives for larger classes.

One variation asks students to introduce themselves in pairs first and then perhaps in fours, with students introducing their paired partner to the other pair. However we decide to approach this activity, a list of questions helps students get through the awkward moments of what to say in their introductions: Where are you from? How did you decide to come here? Next to going to classes and preparing for them, what activities take most of your time? What is one thing we probably would not find out about you unless we asked this question?

Scavenger Hunt

Several colleagues have used a variation of the scavenger hunt to help students meet and begin talking to one another. To begin, each student receives a sheet of paper that lists several activities and includes instructions such as these:

> Find other students who have done the activities listed below and write their names on the lines provided. To make things a bit more challenging (and to make sure you meet more of your classmates), a student's name can appear only once on the sheet. The first student to fill in all the blanks or the student who has the most blanks filled after fifteen minutes wins the scavenger hunt.

The activities listed can vary widely and often with purpose, whether to provide a springboard for discussion of course content and activities, facilitate connection among students outside class, lighten the mood, or increase awareness of multicultural experiences. Some examples of activities:

> Has read at least one novel in the past year
>
> Knows how to solve a quadratic equation
>
> Has visited a country on another continent
>
> Has done volunteer work
>
> Hopes to major in _____
>
> Knows who wrote "Leaves of Grass"
>
> Has acted in or directed a play
>
> Can name all the state capitals
>
> Knows a folk tale from another culture
>
> Plays a musical instrument
>
> Has already bought the text for this course

Distributing several versions of the activity list introduces additional variety. To follow up on the activity, we might collect the sheets, make a summary list of all students named for each activity, and distribute copies in the second class.

Curious Students Want to Know

Looking for something a bit different and a way to connect with students in a very large class, we developed an icebreaker that has students meeting one another but focuses their conversation on sharing curiosities and questions. After reviewing the course syllabus, students break into groups of three or four, introduce themselves to others in the group, and try to agree on one question they would like the instructor to answer—a question they write on a note card. After ten minutes, the instructor collects the note cards, reads several questions, and answers each in turn. Students become slightly bolder in groups, which is one of the advantages of this technique (even in a smaller class), so a few questions go unanswered. Simply reading the questions, however, seems to break the ice. Students ask a variety of "answerable" questions: "Where did you go to college?" "Will we be talking about _____?" "Do you have children?" From time to time, a student group will also submit a version of "If you were stranded on a deserted island, what would you most want to have with you?" This question offers a natural segue in the answer we choose: "The texts for this course! And speaking of that, your assignment is. . . ."

Learning Styles and Preferences

Discussion about learning styles generates additional possibilities for first-session activity. One approach asks students to jot down answers to questions about their learning preferences: "(1) Think about a course you've taken that really worked for you. What was it about the course that made it work? (2) Now think about a course that didn't work as well; what was it about the course that made it not work so well?" Depending on class size, students might share their answers with the whole group or in small groups; both strategies help student meet and connect with others.

Another entrée to discussion of learning styles asks students actually to complete a learning styles inventory, score results, and compare preferences. The cost of purchasing an inventory is a deterrent for some, but faculty might investigate no-cost alternatives available on the Web or ask if the "first year experience" course required on many campuses includes a learning style assessment. Time required for students to complete and score a learning style inventory also discourages some faculty from using this as a first-class activity. Instead, we might create a first assignment that asks students to complete the inventory and then reflect on the syllabus in light of their learning style.

However informal or formal our assessment of learning styles, the follow-up discussion is critical and creates an opportunity to stress several points: (1) because students have seen for themselves that they differ in their learning preferences, it is often easier to explain why the course includes a variety of activities and to invite students to be patient when a particular activity favors another learning style. (2) While acknowledging that some activities might seem unnatural and require extra time and concentration, we can assure students that they can learn from all of them and become more flexible learners in the process. (3) Asking students to read or reread the syllabus with their learning style in mind prompts many to pay closer attention to its contents. As an assignment for the second class, for example, we might ask students to read the syllabus closely, list the activities that seem more and less compatible with their learning style, and then outline a plan for making sure they have the time and support they need to benefit from the "less-compatible" activities. Such an assignment not only encourages development of the metacognitive processes described in Chapter Four but also elicits information that is useful in understanding and responding to the needs of individual students.

The Mystery Game and Variations

The Mystery Game, an activity we have used to open workshops with faculty who in turn used the activity with their students, originally appeared in the group dynamics literature as a strategy for creating group norms and developing discussion skills. In brief, the instructions tell students that each of them will receive a card or cards containing a clue to a murder mystery. If they put all the clues together, they will be able to solve the mystery—that is, to determine the victim, the murderer, the weapon, the time of the murder, where it took place, and the motive. Students may read or paraphrase their clue for the group, but they may not show their card to other members, a rule that guarantees everyone will contribute at least once.

After students solve the mystery, follow-up discussion focuses on three questions: "What happened in your group that enabled you to solve the mystery so effectively? What did your group do that sometimes got in the way of progress? On the basis of what you said, what ground rules might we establish for discussion in this course?" The activity is fun, it gets everyone talking, and a basic premise of group theory is that members are more likely to abide by the rules if they set them. (For instructions and clues for the Mystery Game, see Stanford and Stanford, 1969, pp. 23–26, or Johnson and Johnson, 1975, pp. 121–122.)

Of course, not everyone is comfortable spending class time in activities unrelated to the subject matter, and many creative first-session activities are those that faculty tailor to fit their course content. For example, Eric Schoonover, a colleague in English, developed a variation of the mystery exercise for an introductory course in poetry. Students form groups of six, and each is given a card containing one line of a six-line poem (Denise Levertov's "Leaving Forever"). Students must first reassemble the poem (students may not show their card to anyone, so they have to read the lines aloud) and then decide what the poem means to them. Follow-up discussion focuses on how easy or difficult it was to reassemble the poem, how students determined the order of the lines, and what meanings the poem conveyed. In addition to getting students to participate during the first class, the activity sets up a powerful punch line: by the end of class, students have successfully read a poem, talked about its poetic elements, and interpreted its meaning *on their own*. Colleagues in other disciplines have created similar variations. A computer scientist types programming lines on note cards and asks students to reassemble the program. A biologist lists a set of characteristics of a species and asks students to identify the species and answer several questions about its adaptations.

In addition to getting students talking to one another in the first class meeting, the Mystery Game and its variants offer an opportunity for them to consider what sort of practice makes for effective group work. If we have made group work or cooperative learning a major part of our courses, we might want to direct at least some of their attention to the group dynamics aspect of the activity. In Chapter Nine we take a closer look at these processes in the context of a short case study, which could be used as an opening-class activity.

The Seven Most Important . . .

We created the Seven Most Important activity primarily to get students in the first meeting of an introductory sociology course working together and to connect the course content to what students know and believe. To begin, we ask students to break into groups of three to five and list the seven most important events (or, alternatively, the seven most important people) in history. After ten to fifteen minutes, we poll the groups and note their responses on the board. Their lists are fairly predictable but nonetheless interesting, and especially so to students. The events or people named are almost always modern, if not recent; rarely does a group list something or someone before 1500 C.E. They are disproportionately American, occasionally European, rarely Asian or African. "Important" history is made in political or military arenas; literature, art, and music rarely make the lists. We use these lists not to scold students for what they do not know but rather as an entrée to reflections on what Americans do know, how they have come to know it, what the limits of their worldviews might be, and why the study of sociology asks them to think about other societies, other sources of information about society, and other times in history.

We have demonstrated this activity in workshops for faculty for several years, and it is one of the most widely adapted for first classes. Philosophy faculty ask what the seven most important ethical dilemmas are; pharmacy faculty ask for the seven most important drug discoveries; engineers ask about the most impressive structures. Again, the activity helps students meet at least a few classmates, gets them actively involved in discussion, and is an entrée to talking about the subject matter.

Experiments and Demonstrations

An experiment or demonstration is a natural for a first class. It can pique curiosity and make it hard to resist becoming involved in figuring out why something happens. One of our colleagues, James Fasching, performs an experiment in the first meeting of his introductory chemistry course and asks students to record data—changes in temperature, color, mass, or some other indicator of a chemical reaction. After the experiment has run, students meet in small groups to discuss their observations, formulate hypotheses about the identity of the reactants and the nature of the reaction, and propose additional experiments that would enable them to confirm or reject their hypotheses. Before class concludes, each group reports its hypotheses and proposals for further experiments. The assignment for the second class asks students to decide which experiments they would run first and why.

Case Studies

Later chapters discuss the case study as a powerful method for engaging students, and the first class is not too early to begin. Frank Heppner, another of our colleagues, uses cases throughout his introductory course in biological sciences to illustrate that the subject matter has relevance even for nonscience majors. The cases are all derived from actual events. The case for the first class (and also the last class) is drawn from a newspaper account of a rape trial in which the prosecuting attorney based his argument on positive identification by the victim and DNA fingerprinting. The defense attorney's argument turned on the high moral character of the accused, an ironclad alibi, and the fact that DNA fingerprinting is not universally accepted by the scientific community. After reading the case, students discuss two questions in small groups: (1) If, as jurors, you were permitted to ask three questions of the expert witness on DNA fingerprinting, what would they be? (2) If you were not permitted to ask questions, what is your jury's verdict? Before the end of class, the instructor polls the groups, posts their verdicts, and lists their questions. Students find it difficult to reach a verdict and their questions reflect little knowledge about DNA fingerprinting, but they leave class more eager to learn about DNA.

Conclusion

There is enormous variety in activities for a first class, and they are fertile ground for creativity. Our main point, however, is that what we ask students to do in their first meeting sets the stage for the rest of the course. Once the instructor and students assume their roles and the action begins, the plot may thicken and the characters may develop, but it is too late to alter the script dramatically. A good syllabus is an important prop in the first class meeting because it communicates details about course requirements and policies that it might otherwise take an entire class period to convey. We should avoid this practice because it assigns students to a relatively passive role and does not leave time for other action and interaction. Equally important to information about the course are activities that ask students to assume an active role, encourage them to interact with one another, get them over the hurdle of making a first contribution in class, and sample how classes will be conducted—the experiential agenda.

For Further Exploration

- "Syllabus Tutorial" (http://www1.umn.edu/ohr/teachlearn/syllabus/index.html; retrieved Jan. 2006).

  The University of Minnesota's Center for Teaching and Learning Services has created an online "Syllabus Tutorial" that outlines major components of the syllabus and gives examples of syllabuses from several disciplines. Excerpts from exemplary syllabuses are plentiful.

CHAPTER 6

Presenting and Explaining

For most of our students and for many of us, teaching is lecturing. That equation makes sense if the aim is to transmit information that students are to remember for an exam; research indicates that the lecture is about as effective as other teaching methods when recall of information is tested. The lecture, however, turns out to be less effective than other methods when instructional goals include retention of information beyond the end of the course, application of information, development of thinking skills, modification of attitude, or motivation for further learning (Bligh, 2000; McKeachie, Pintrich, Lin, and Smith, 1986). In short, there is more to effective teaching than lecturing.

We titled this chapter "Presenting and Explaining" to put the lecture in its proper place as a method for presenting information that students are to remember, explaining by way of example, and demonstrating how one might use the information to solve a problem or think through a variety of situations. Presenting and explaining are rarely sufficient if the goals call for understanding or thinking, but a clear explanation or demonstration is often a good place to start instruction.

Before suggesting some things we might do to improve our presentations, we explore briefly how the mind works—or at least how psychologists currently think the mind works. A passing acquaintance with the research on cognition sheds some light on what our students are doing (or should be doing) while we are presenting, and it lays the foundation for recommendations to follow. Because our discussion is necessarily brief, we suggest consulting other sources for additional information (J. R. Davis, 1993; Leamnson, 1999; McKeachie, 2002; McKeachie, Pintrich, Lin, and Smith, 1986; Norman, 1982; Zull, 2002).

How We Process Information and Construct Meaning _____

We do not see things as they are or hear things as they are said. Instead, we catch bits and pieces, work them over, and reassemble what registers on our senses. To use the metaphors that currently dominate discussion of learning, we *process information* and *construct meaning*, and apparently we do so in stages. We will talk about the process in three stages, an oversimplification but one our colleagues have found useful in planning their classes.

Our first encounter with new information occurs through the senses. Zull (2002) opens his discussion of the biological processes involved in interpreting sensory information by proclaiming "How sense-luscious the world is!" (p. 135). We are talking metaphorically rather than biologically, but the idea of a sense-luscious world is a good reminder that at any moment we experience many more sights, sounds, and sensations than we are capable of interpreting. Learning requires that we ignore some of these stimuli, and how we do that has been the focus of much research. In brief, it appears we have complex filtering systems that enable us to ignore stimuli unrelated to our immediate concern and focus only on relevant information. Students are largely in charge of what they focus on, but we can help them by directing their attention to goals, stressing relevance, minimizing distraction, and presenting the same information via multiple sensory registers.

If we can get students to attend to our presentation, our next concern is with the processes that enable students to remember. Here, a distinction between short-term memory and long-term memory is helpful. Short-term memory, or working memory as it is sometimes called, keeps information temporarily in mind while we try to make sense of it and decide what to do with it. Short-term memory, however, is severely limited in the amount of information it can hold—usually not more than seven-plus-or-minus-two pieces of information. Also, information cannot be stored there for long; we have only a few seconds to make some sense of it before we lose it.

A simple experiment illustrates both the limits and the possibilities for short-term memory. Show this sequence of thirteen letters to a few colleagues: SATIQGPAABCDF. Let them look at it for a few seconds, and then ask them to recite the sequence. Chances are good that they will not be able to repeat the sequence accurately. Then, repeat the experiment, but present the letters in this way: SAT IQ GPA ABCDF. Most faculty will exhibit perfect recall of the sequence because the information is organized into "chunks" that are meaningful to them.

By presenting the information in chunks, we reduce the load on short-term memory from thirteen pieces of information to four. Because the chunks already have meaning for most faculty, it takes only a few seconds to make sense of them. A word of caution is in order here because we sometimes forget that meaning does not reside in the content itself. Those of us schooled in American education systems quickly make sense of SAT and GPA, but those sequences of letters may have little or no meaning to faculty in other educational systems. The same is true for students. Meaning resides in the *relationship* between new material and what they already know.

If new information in short-term memory has meaning or can be made meaningful, it is transferred to long-term memory. Long-term memory is somewhat like the filing system many of us use. We collect ideas and information, put them in a file, and affix a label indicating the file's contents. Barring flood, fire, or a compulsion to clean, those files and their contents are there forever. In theory, we should be able to pull out their contents whenever we need them, months or even years later. In practice, however, we do not label our files very well and rarely cross-reference the content, so often we cannot find information when we want it. Eventually, we may forget it is even there. Information in long-term memory may suffer the same fate. If it is "filed" in isolated bits, chances of remembering it are not good. Worse, if we never or seldom use what we learned, whatever tenuous connections exist in long-term memory tend to weaken further and make access to information even more difficult.

To illustrate what this looks like in instruction, think about an all-too-typical class week. We present and explain new information or ideas in one class, include several good examples to demonstrate processes and importance, and give a summary at the end of class. In the next class, we pose a question or problem intended to review the content of the previous class, a good practice before moving on to new content. Unfortunately, students respond as if it is the first time they have encountered such a task. They seem not to know where to start. Prompts and hints appear not to help. If our review takes the form of a quiz, some students complain we never taught them how to answer such questions or solve such problems. These are not good signs; they suggest students may be storing information and ideas in isolated files that can only be accessed if a new task, problem, or question is identical to or closely resembles those presented during instruction.

In contrast, if the information in long-term memory is organized around meaningful concepts and if those concepts are connected, the chances of remembering information and procedures substantially increase. When we encounter a new problem or question, we recognize some cue that prompts us to recall one of those interconnected concepts. The concept we initially retrieve may not be the one we need, but one thought leads to another and eventually we find the needed information. In short, our ability to think and solve problems depends a great deal on whether the information and ideas in long-term memory are interconnected.

How, then, can we prompt students to make those connections? Here, the research that distinguishes between surface processing and deep processing is helpful. Ideally, students are actively involved in *deep processing* of new material. They integrate, elaborate, and extend new ideas by connecting them to what they already know, considering them in other contexts, thinking of new examples and applications, noting similarities and differences. Along the way, students reconsider previous experience and prior learning, see new meaning in those events and ideas, and revise how they have interpreted or connected them. Students who engage in these activities are more likely to see the need for and remember information across a variety of contexts and problems.

Unfortunately, students—and this may be especially true of first-year students—often take a *surface processing* approach to learning instead. They set out to learn information exactly as it is presented. They memorize phrases and definitions verbatim. They consider only those examples and problems that the instructor happens to present. They do little to elaborate and extend the meaning of ideas or to relate them to what they already know. Some students take this approach because it is the only one they know; others make a conscious or quasi-conscious decision to do so. They explain: "I'm not interested in this subject; just tell me what I need to do to pass"; "I'm overwhelmed this semester, so I need to focus on courses that are important and do the minimum in others"; "It's impossible to learn everything in this course, so I just try to get what I think will be on the test." Whatever the reason, students who adopt a surface learning approach store information in long-term memory, but the information is inaccessible unless the prompt to retrieve it—the question, problem, or context—closely resembles that presented during discussion. (For more detail on surface and deep approaches to learning, see Marton and Säljö, 1984.)

In the end, students determine how involved they will be in elaborating the meaning of ideas and connecting them with other information stored in long-term memory. We cannot do these things for them, no matter how good our lectures. As we present material, however, we can inhibit or encourage students to process information at these deeper levels.

Suggestions for Presenting and Explaining _____

Many of our suggestions for presenting and explaining boil down to two connected pieces of advice: avoid practices that lead to surface processing, and adopt practices that promote and support deep processing.

Abandon the Nonstop Fifty-Minute Lecture

This may be the most important thing we can do to improve learning, but even the most well-intentioned of us find it hard to give up the nonstop lecture. Our content is important, and we can cover a lot of it in class if we are not interrupted. Most of us will, of course, acknowledge that it makes no sense to cover material if students do not understand it and do not remember it. Nevertheless, covering content is a powerful drive, and it often rules the day—usually at the expense of activities that would result in greater learning.

Compulsion to cover so much material in class is usually counterproductive, but it is especially destructive in a course with first-year students. Lecturing without pause tends to reinforce the passive-listening, verbatim note-taking, and superficial information-processing strategies that many students bring to college. Students must learn course content, to be sure, but first-year students also need to be weaned from their conviction that material cannot be important if it is not covered in class. For our part, we must give up the belief that students cannot learn it unless we say it. Once students develop the deep-processing strategies noted earlier, they are able to get more from reading and process information faster during a lecture. Meanwhile, we should restrain our inclination to cover everything in class and abandon those nonstop lectures.

We make more productive use of class time if our presentation lasts no more than ten or fifteen minutes before we allow time for students to work with the ideas presented. Wilbert McKeachie (2002) reports research indicating that attention increases during the first few minutes of a lecture but students' minds begin to wander after about ten minutes. Daydreaming is sometimes the lure, but students often tune out because the information is coming too fast and there is no time to think. Indeed, most of us have found ourselves not hearing what a speaker is saying because we were thinking about an idea presented earlier.

Ten minutes is usually enough time to introduce a concept or procedure and give an example or two. Then students need time to think about the ideas—to summarize the material in their own words, come up with their own examples, or try using the ideas to solve a problem or analyze a situation. Once students have tried their hand at working with the material, we can come back to elaborate and extend or move on to the next topic.

Define Objectives

After identifying two or three topics to be explained in class, we need to decide what students should be able to do with the information. Do they merely need to remember definitions, procedures, factual information? Should they be able to recognize new examples or illustrations? Will they be asked to use the information somehow? A clear vision of what students should be able to do with information presented indicates what the presentation itself must include and points to the questions, problems, or tasks that should follow.

Plan an Introduction

A good introduction captures students' attention and focuses it on the objectives, usually in that order. Getting students' attention is no small challenge, but the problem with many lectures is that they do not play to curiosity. They jump to a conclusion, solution, or resolution before raising the issues, posing the problem, or identifying the conflicts. Students have no time to become curious or see how course material relates to things about which they are already curious. If they did, students would pay more attention.

Opening with a problem, question, quandary, or dilemma is one way to capture attention. If the problem is grounded in student experience, all the better. There are a variety of ways to do this. For example, start with something students take for granted and confront them with information or observations indicating things are not so obvious or certain as they initially appear. Present a list of incongruous facts or statistics, and ask, "How can this be?" Show an experiment or a film clip and ask, "What is going on here?" Remind students of a campus incident or current event and promise that the day's material will shed some light on it.

The first order of business is to get students' attention; the second is to focus it on the objectives. Knowing what they are expected to do with information presented in class influences how students listen to a presentation. Most first-year students assume that they will be asked to recall the information, so they go to great lengths to get it all down in their notes, and they memorize every definition, example, and detail presented. Many students assume this is all there is to it. They do not attend to our instructions on how to recognize or use the information in a new context, nor do they engage in the thinking activities—extending, elaborating, relating—that we have developed to help prepare them to cope with new problems or situations. If we tell students what the objectives are for each class, what they should know and what they will be asked to *do* with what they know, we take a first step toward transforming how they listen to the lecture and think about the ideas presented.

Highlight the Major Points

Key ideas may be obvious to those of us who have worked with the material for years, but they are not obvious to beginning students. At least once, we all should try asking students at the end of class to jot down the main ideas discussed that day. The results may be shocking, but they are instructive. Students have trouble distinguishing generalization from example, conclusion from evidence, trend from isolated event, the main idea from the details that surround it. If the examples, evidence, isolated events, and details are vivid and compelling, as they should be, students are even more likely to forget what is being exemplified. The ability to sort out these things comes with experience with the subject matter. In the meantime, students lament after an exam that they "studied the wrong things." Outlining key ideas on the board or in presentation software, reviewing them periodically, and summarizing them at the end of class are all good strategies for highlighting major points. It also helps to label explicitly the various parts of a presentation: generalization, examples, conclusion, evidence, and so forth.

Select Appropriate Examples

Much of what we learn is by way of example, illustration, or demonstration. Indeed, some evidence suggests that what we retrieve from memory is not the description of a concept or principle. Rather, we recall some prototypical example or image and use it to reconstruct the appropriate definitions and relationships (Norman, 1982; Park, 1984; Zull, 2002). Good teachers know the power of a telling example, and they go to great lengths to find one. Several things merit consideration in selecting examples.

First, it is crucial that the examples and illustrations in fact embody the key ideas students are to remember. Examples should clearly depict the characteristics that define a concept; demonstration should clearly show how principles or laws look in action; models for problem solving or reasoning should clearly indicate critical considerations and procedural steps. We cannot afford to settle for examples, illustrations, or demonstrations that miss or muddy some critical point; our students are using these examples to construct the prototypes they store in memory.

Second, explanation should begin with relatively clear-cut examples and gradually introduce more complex and subtler illustrations. Our first task is to show the key properties or relationships. If the early examples are too complicated, abstract, or unfamiliar, students get lost in the complexities and lose sight of the key ideas. On the other hand, if all the examples and problems are simple ones, students will not learn to handle more complex situations.

Third, examples, illustrations, and problems should come from a variety of situations and settings. Our hope here is that if students see a few good examples or illustrations, they will be able to transfer their learning to new situations and problems. It is an optimistic hope because the research shows that not much transfer of learning occurs even in the best instructional circumstances. It appears, however, that students' ability to transfer their learning improves if the examples and problems used during instruction sample the range of contexts in which we expect them eventually to use the information.

Fourth, most of us underestimate the number of examples and illustrations that students require. The concepts and relationships we teach are highly complex, abstract, and usually unfamiliar to our students. Yet we often assume our students will understand them after seeing two or three examples. Eventually, when we give an assignment or an exam, we discover how foolhardy those assumptions are. How many examples and illustrations do students require? Obviously, the answer depends on the nature of the material, and it differs from student to student. One way to find out if students have seen enough is to pose one more example and ask them to explain how it illustrates a concept or how they would solve the problem. If they cannot do it, they need more illustrations and practice.

Finally, we should have available in our notes a few more good examples than we anticipate using. Many of the best instructors tell us they spend much, if not most, of their preparation time on examples. Having a sufficient number of good examples avoids the embarrassment of being unable to produce one on the spur of the moment if needed or of creating one that confuses or misleads rather than clarifies.

Discuss Examples

It is important for us to state explicitly how examples, illustrations, and demonstrations relate to the broader generalizations they are intended to exemplify. Students need help in recognizing how particular examples embody the characteristics of conceptual categories—what features of a painting make it an example of Impressionist art, what specifics exist in a novel that lead us to call it an initiation story, why we classify a chemical reaction as oxidation-reduction. In the absence of these explicit cues, students may attend to other details in the example, mistakenly take them as the characteristics that define the concept, and miss entirely the points we regard as important. Similarly, our students often get so caught up in watching us solve particular problems that they miss the problem-solving procedures and steps that we intend to demonstrate. Presenting the example, illustration, or demonstration is an important step. Explaining how the particular relates to the general increases the likelihood that students will get the point.

Use Visual Aids

Many of us have learned from experience that audiovisual aids are helpful both in holding student attention and in explaining difficult material. Neuroscience research underscores the importance of such aids. Zull (2002) recommends that whenever possible we convert ideas into images because they are the easiest thing for the human brain to remember. Further, he suggests that playing to multiple senses helps strengthen the interconnection in long-term memory. Current technology offers many more practical options for audiovisual aids than were available a decade ago, but not all of us need to be producers of high-tech multimedia. Simple outlines, diagrams, flow charts, and concept maps help to highlight key ideas and show their relationships. Slides, videotapes, and films present examples far more vividly than does verbal description alone. A single slide can lend visual focus in defining a concept; a series of four or five can trace a course of events. Videotape, DVDs, and film offer ways to bring life outside the classroom into it, magnify the microscopic, quicken or slow the pace of time. Students learn more from watching an experiment run than from hearing it described. We know, of course, that searching for visual aids is time-consuming, and there is often a significant initial investment in preparing them for classroom use. Many, however, can be used for several semesters, and given their impact on students it is usually worth our trouble.

Guide Note Taking

By and large, first-year students are not good note takers. They furiously try to get down every word spoken and are so desperate to have an exact transcript that they often ask us to repeat relatively unimportant details. Yet if we ask them about an important point just made, they often cannot answer. If we chance to look at their notebooks, the errors and omissions are disturbing. The only thing more depressing than their lack of skill in taking notes is their belief in them. Some students measure learning by the number of pages filled in their notebooks. Comments such as "The course was good; she gave a lot of notes" are not infrequent on course evaluations. Because people do not generally abandon bad habits until they have better ones to replace them, telling students to stop taking verbatim notes is likely to go unheeded. We will have more success if we think in terms of weaning first-year students from verbatim note-taking habits. To that end, here are some things to try.

First, present a skeletal outline of the main points covered (point by point as you come to them, or all at once at the outset) and allow time for students to get the outline in their notes. The outline supplies the basic structure first-year students need.

Second, pause from time to time and ask students to paraphrase what they have written in their notes in their own words, as if they were telling a friend—to rewrite a definition, restate a relationship, retell an example. First-year students often find this difficult to do, and they will need more time for it in the beginning. However, the time is well spent. Paraphrasing is a step toward making material meaningful, and developing this skill increases understanding and retention.

Third, encourage students to elaborate their notes by completing thoughts such as "Another example of this might be . . ."; "The last time I saw a problem like this was . . ."; "I remember talking about this issue with . . ."; "This information might explain why. . . ." When we prompt students in these ways, we encourage them to forge a connection between new material and what they already know—another step toward meaning, understanding, and retention. Several of the writing-to-learn techniques discussed in the next chapter are also useful in helping students develop better note-taking strategies.

Attention to how students take notes is important not so much because students need to have good notes. They do, but if that were all then we could simply hand out copies of *our* notes—a practice we do *not* recommend (except for students with specific disabilities) because it promotes even more passivity on the part of students. Our primary interest in student note taking is that the activity is a means to engage them in processing information more deeply. (For a more detailed review of the research on student note taking and additional suggestions, see DeZure, Kaplan, and Deerman, 2001.)

Check for Understanding

Because our aim in presenting and explaining is to develop better understanding, it makes sense for us to stop now and then to see whether or not students *are* understanding. Pausing to ask, "Are there any questions?" is better than nothing, but not much. For students to respond to this invitation, they must both recognize that they have not fully understood and also be able to formulate a question quickly. Our carefully planned and smoothly presented explanations tend to lull students into complacency. Not until later, when they review their notes or try an assignment, do they realize that they have missed or misunderstood something critical. Students and the instructor lose time and energy in having to go back over material explained two days or two months earlier.

Instead of asking, "Are there any questions?" we might better assess students' understanding if *we* ask the questions. For example, to determine how well students understand a concept, we might say: "We have gone over several examples. Look at one more and tell me whether it illustrates this concept and why." If we want to know how ready students are for independent practice in problem solving, the check for understanding might begin: "We have worked through several problems. Now you try one just to make sure you understand." When students try to answer questions on their own, they frequently discover that things are not so simple or so obvious as they thought and that they do not fully understand after all. At that point, they may be ready to respond to our traditional invitation, "Are there any questions?"

Summarize Often

Sometimes a lecture tailored for a particular class of students is clearer and more understandable than a text, but only if we compensate for what is lost as students listen to rather than read an explanation. In reading, students control the pace of ideas, stopping often to retrace their steps—to look more closely at an idea passed by quickly, to reassure themselves that they read it right the first time. In listening to a lecture, however, students do not control the pacing or retracing. They may stop to think (at least the best ones do) but the presentation continues. Students miss a phrase here, a sentence there, and sometimes even a whole paragraph. They need to go over it again, but in a lecture they cannot scan a paragraph or turn back to a page. They can only hope that we will repeat the information and review the important points. Frequent repetition and periodic summaries throughout a presentation help compensate for not having pages to turn back.

Summarizing at the end of class is also important. Although time seems to pass more quickly as the class session draws to a close, we cannot afford to run out of time before drawing things to a conclusion. If we do not supply a concluding summary, we can probably expect to hear students say "The class was interesting, but I didn't see the point" or "There was a lot of discussion, but we didn't really learn anything." A strong conclusion does three things. First and most obviously, it reviews key points, issues, and ideas—the scaffolding for organizing more detailed information and ideas. Second, a concluding summary reminds students what they should be able to *do* with the information now that they have heard it. Finally, a strong conclusion includes an assignment designed to give students practice in doing whatever it is they should be able to do.

In *Learner-Centered Teaching,* Maryellen Weimer (2002) makes a good case for asking students to take over learning tasks such as summarizing a lecture or other instructional activity. Though acknowledging that many students are not very skilled at summarizing, she reminds us that this is an important learning skill that students need to develop if they are to be lifelong learners, and she warns that students are not likely to develop the skill simply by watching their instructor summarize. We agree and think first-year courses can be a good training ground for practicing and developing such skills.

We might, for example, use the last five or ten minutes of class to ask students to review their notes and list the main ideas discussed that day. Earlier we noted that instructors who ask students to identify the main ideas are often shocked to discover how student lists differ from one another's and from the instructor's. Building in feedback on students' attempts at summarizing is important, at least at first. Asking students to compare their lists with those of one or two people sitting next to them is a way to provide feedback and a correction mechanism. Collecting a sample of student summaries, presenting them at the beginning of the next class, and asking students to compare the summaries in their notes with those presented can work both as feedback on students' summaries and as a review of the previous class.

Assess Learning and Request Feedback Frequently

Students can be of great help to us in determining what is working in class and what might merit more of our attention. Taking five minutes at the end of class to ask students to summarize the ideas presented, solve a sample problem, or apply information to a new situation is a good strategy for finding out what students understood and what they did not. We do not need to do it every class, but collecting such feedback from time to time is useful in tracking student learning.

Similarly, asking students to take five minutes to write their reaction to the day's class and doing so several times during the semester can help us determine what we might do to strengthen our instruction for a particular class of students. Exhibit 6.1 presents a questionnaire that our colleagues have found useful in collecting feedback from students. They like this questionnaire for several reasons: it focuses on a single class, it takes only five minutes to complete, it can be used several times during the semester, and it elicits feedback about several of the issues discussed in this chapter.

A Look Back and Ahead

This chapter offers suggestions for presenting course material in ways that are likely to enhance student understanding and ability to recall information. Our suggestions are grounded in research on learning, which we summarized in metaphorical terms at the beginning of the chapter with a note acknowledging that the biological processes involved in learning are far more complex than our discussion revealed. Many of our colleagues have found this metaphorical discussion

Exhibit 6.1. Class Reaction Survey

I would like to know your reactions to today's class. Please read each of the statements below and circle the letter corresponding to the response that best matches your reaction in today's class. Your choices are:

a. No improvement is needed. (Terrific! This works for me. Keep it up.)
b. Little improvement is needed. (Maybe a ragged edge or two, but don't lose any sleep over it.)
c. Improvement is needed. (Not awful, but this merits some attention.)
d. Considerable improvement is needed. (This is causing me problems. Please help.)

Today, the instructor

a   b   c   d   1. Limited what was covered to a manageable amount of material

a   b   c   d   2. Made it clear why the material might be important

a   b   c   d   3. Told us what we would be expected to do with the material (memorize it, use it to solve problems, or whatever)

a   b   c   d   4. Highlighted key ideas or questions

a   b   c   d   5. Presented plenty of good examples to clarify difficult material

a   b   c   d   6. Provided enough variety to keep us reasonably alert

a   b   c   d   7. Found ways to let us know whether we were understanding the material

a   b   c   d   8. Helped us summarize the main ideas we were supposed to take away from class

a   b   c   d   9. Let us know how we might be tested on the material

a   b   c   d   10. Provided exercises or an assignment so that we could practice using the material

11. What is your overall rating of today's class?

    A Excellent   B Good   C Satisfactory   D Fair   E Poor

12. What made you rate today's class as high as you did?

13. What kept you from rating today's class higher?

helpful in designing instruction, and it suited our purpose for discussing effective lecture practices. As we look ahead to several chapters devoted to additional strategies for engaging students actively, we need to discuss more concretely the biological processes involved in learning.

Learning involves physical changes in the brain. To discuss those changes, we need to talk about *neurons,* the basic cellular unit in the brain. In the process of learning, neurons bud and grow *axons,* which connect to other neurons and form connections or *synapses.* Offering a glimpse of how amazing all this is, Robert Leamnson (1999) notes that "neurons in the embryonic brain are crudely programmed . . . to divide and spread out in rough patterns until there are a hundred billion of them, more or less" and that in the normal adult "one neuron has a thousand connections to other neurons" (p. 12).

Initially, the connections between neurons are tenuous, and they degenerate if not used. If those connections are used repeatedly and in a variety of situations, however, they become familiar and almost automatic pathways—the neural rendition of "one thought leads to another" and the neural argument for "practice makes perfect." This process does not occur quickly. As Leamnson points out, "Even with the best of intentions, students cannot produce in one pass the hardwired circuitry that makes a concept familiar" (p. 16). This is the rub. Too often, first-year courses proceed at a pace that permits only a brief encounter with the concepts and theories of a discipline.

The biological changes involved in learning that endures require students to repeatedly practice recalling ideas, their connections, and their many applications. These activities are so important for learning that we devote our next several chapters to the discussion of strategies for engaging first-year students in those critical practices.

For Further Exploration

- Bligh, D. A. *What's the Use of Lectures?* San Francisco: Jossey-Bass, 2000.

  Donald Bligh presents perhaps the most comprehensive and detailed discussion of lecturing tasks and techniques. Topics include lecture organization, making a point, providing reasons and explanations, student note taking, preparing and using handouts, obtaining feedback, and incorporating other methods when lecturing is not enough.

- Svinicki, M. D. *Learning and Motivation in the Postsecondary Classroom.* Bolton, Mass.: Anker, 2004.

  Marilla Svinicki summarizes current research and theory about learning and motivation and discusses implications for college teaching and learning. The book is organized around the kinds of learning emphasized in college and draws on several theoretical perspectives to inform recommendations for teaching.

- Zull, J. E. *The Art of Changing the Brain: Enriching the Practice of Teaching by Exploring the Biology of Learning.* Sterling, Va.: Stylus, 2002.

  James Zull, a biologist, states at the outset that learning alters the brain and suggests that understanding the biological processes involved in learning can aid selection and understanding of best practices. Zull describes the brain and the biological processes involved in learning in clear, nontechnical language.

CHAPTER 7

Creating Involvement
in the Classroom

Although we have much yet to learn about how understanding and the ability to think develop, one thing is clear: practice is an essential ingredient. On the basis of an extensive review of theory and research in problem solving and creativity, Norman Frederiksen (1984) concluded:

> The theory and research reviewed shows that it is possible after much practice to perform remarkable feats of problem solving. Such skill is developed primarily through a great deal of practice and it is specific to a relatively narrow area of expertise, such as algebra, mechanics, or chess. There appears to be little if any transfer from one domain to another, being an expert in chess apparently does not transfer to *go*, and skill in solving physics problems does not transfer to politics or economics. However, a given individual may acquire such skill in a number of domains [p. 391].

More recent discussions of learning research (Bransford, Brown, and Cocking, 2000; Leamnson, 1999; Zull, 2002) reach similar conclusions. Instruction for thinking and problem solving must take place within a subject-matter domain and must engage students in practice. Useful practice activities vary according to the phase of the instructional cycle. Reviewing and connecting ideas help stabilize neural pathways and promote fluent recall; considering and using ideas in different contexts promote transfer; determining when, where, and how ideas apply (metacognitive skills) helps students deal with increasingly complex problems.

In suggesting methods and techniques for getting students involved during class meetings, we have in mind the variety of practice activities needed to promote deep and lasting learning. At the same time, we recognize the expectations and assumptions about teaching and learning that first-year students bring to their courses (see Chapter Two), and their particular needs prompt many of our suggestions about how to use these methods in introductory courses.

Small-Group Discussion Methods

When we think about class discussion, we often imagine a spirited exchange of ideas involving most, if not all, students in the class. In practice, this rarely happens even in a small class. More often, a few students participate in the discussion while most sit quietly, perhaps listening and thinking about what is said, perhaps not. Simple arithmetic reveals one reason this is so. If we have twenty-five students (a small class for many who teach first-year students) in a fifty-minute class and we want all students to participate, each student will be able to speak for two minutes—not much time to express an idea, never mind pursue it. Subtract from that whatever time students need to reflect on what their peers contribute and to formulate a response. Also, the two-minutes-per-student allotment assumes that the instructor says nothing during class, an assumption that is neither likely nor a good idea. We can vary the numbers to fit a variety of instructional situations, but if we do the math, getting all students actively involved in a spirited whole-class discussion is not a realistic instructional goal for many introductory courses.

We need not and should not give up discussions in first-year courses, however, because discussions offer powerful practice and feedback opportunities. Small-group discussion is an especially versatile option because it works in classes of any size and can be designed to engage students in practicing a range of skills.

To use small-group discussions, we begin by posing a question or task, divide the class into groups of three to five, and ask students to prepare a group response. While students discuss the task, we move from group to group, to monitor progress, offer help when needed, and note areas of confusion for later review. When time is up, we reconvene the class and ask the groups (or a sample of them) to report their answers or conclusions. Group reports may stand as given, call for feedback or comment from us, spark discussion in the larger group, or stimulate another round of small-group discussions.

Small-group discussions can serve a variety of instructional purposes depending on the questions or tasks posed. The sample here illustrates how we can prompt the deep processing activities mentioned in Chapter Six as well as create opportunity for students to practice using new knowledge.

- To review the previous class: "compare your notes from last class with the notes of others in your group. Then as a group, list the most important ideas discussed last time."

- To introduce a new topic or unit: "Before we start talking about this topic, put your heads together and list everything you already know about _____."

- To warm up before a whole-class discussion: "Before we start today, break into groups and take five minutes to share your reactions to the assignment. Talk about whatever thoughts, opinions, feelings, questions come to mind."

- To generate questions for class discussion: "On the basis of the readings for today, formulate one or two questions that members of your group agree we should discuss in class."

- To promote understanding of concepts: "In your group, define [name a concept]. Then think of an example we've not discussed and explain how it illustrates the concept."

- To encourage application of ideas in new contexts: "Think about the situation portrayed in the videotape [or reported in a paper, etc.]. In your group, imagine what [theorist X] would say about the situation. Prepare a two-minute summary."

- To offer practice in problem solving: "Here is a problem slightly more challenging than the one we just did but more like those you'll encounter later. Work the problem in your group. Remember, talking about why you take each step helps develop problem-solving skills."

- To encourage consideration of multiple perspectives: "In your group, take one position on this issue and list all the arguments for that position. Then take a different position on the issue and list all the arguments for that position."

- To discuss a case study: "In your group, identify the problem or issues raised in this case. Then try to agree on the course of action you would take in this situation. In fifteen minutes, we'll poll the groups and compare answers."

- To do a role-playing exercise: "In your group, assign one student to be the consultant, another to play the client, and a third to serve as observer whose job will be to summarize the interaction afterward. To begin the action, the client calls the consultant and poses this question. . . ."

- To summarize periodically during class or at the end of class: "In a small group, compare the notes you've taken and list the most important ideas from the discussion so far."

As a strategy for engaging students during class, the small-group discussion has several advantages. First, it is more likely to engage all students in discussion, not just those few who are verbally assertive. Second, a small-group discussion allows students to collect their thoughts and talk them over with peers before venturing a contribution to the whole class, an advantage not only for shy students but also for the extravert learning styles discussed in Chapter Three. Third, small-group methods enable us to interact if not with individual students then at least with small groups of them. We may not be able to visit every small group in every class meeting, but over time we can talk to most of the small groups. Because of these advantages, many faculty use small-group discussion in combination with other methods, either as a warm-up or as a follow-up activity.

Writing-to-Learn Activities

"Ask first-year students to write? Do I look crazy?!" Because we are often greeted with this response when we suggest writing as a learning activity, we stress at the outset that we are not talking about the writing assignments that strike terror in the hearts of faculty—those that elicit pages and pages of sometimes dreadful prose that must be carried home, marked up, and returned within the week. Traditionally, we assign papers or reports in order to assess what students *have* learned. Writing *to* learn is an altogether different enterprise.

Typically, writing-to-learn exercises are short; students write a few sentences, perhaps a paragraph or two. Although we might want to look at what students write in order to see what is on their minds, writing-to-learn exercises need not be graded. Students write to and for themselves in the interest of collecting their thoughts and getting them down on paper, where they can be inspected, extended, organized, and revised.

We can use writing-to-learn activities to accomplish a variety of purposes. In Chapter Six, we mentioned paraphrasing, summarizing, and sentence-completion exercises—three forms of writing to learn—as strategies for helping students develop note-taking skills. This sample of tasks illustrates some additional ways to use writing-to-learn activities to encourage deeper processing of new information and practice in thinking and problem solving.

- To review the previous class material: "Look back over your notes from last time and write a one-paragraph summary of the most important ideas discussed."
- To introduce a topic or unit: "Before we start, take a couple minutes to jot down what you already know about _____."

- To warm up for a discussion: "Before we begin our discussion, take ten minutes to collect your thoughts in a 'free write.' Write whatever thoughts, ideas, or questions you have about today's topic and readings."

- To summarize during discussion: "We've heard several different ideas, and we should keep track of them. Let's pause for a few minutes so that you can get these ideas into your notes. List what you think are key ideas, issues, and questions. Then we'll resume."

- To prompt students to connect ideas: "Look back over the topics we've discussed this week and draw a concept map—a diagram that identifies the key ideas and shows the relationships among them. Draw lines between the ideas that are related and then label the lines to indicate the nature of the relationships (for example, cause and effect, concept and example, conclusion and evidence)."

- To encourage practice in applying ideas: "The question on the screen was included in last year's final exam to test students' ability to use the ideas we've studied in analyzing stories in the news. For practice, take ten minutes and outline an answer."

- To cool a heated discussion: "These are controversial issues about which many feel passionately. Let's take a short time-out from discussion and collect our thoughts in writing. What are the issues? What opinions have been voiced so far? Where do we agree? disagree?"

- To ask students to reflect on their learning: "Please take a note card and write your answers to two questions: (1) What are the two or three most important things you learned in today's class? (2) What is one thing you are not sure you understand?"

- To encourage active reading of assignments: "After you've read the assignment for next time, imagine that a friend sends an e-mail message asking, 'What's this chapter about?' Write a brief (half a page or so) summary of the reading as if you were replying to your friend."

- To prepare for an exam: "Before we begin our review, propose three exam questions that you think would allow you to show what you've learned in this section of the course."

As a form of practice, writing-to-learn activities have some unique advantages. In small-group discussion, students who sit back and wait for others to do their thinking often go unnoticed. In a writing-to-learn exercise, an idle pencil is conspicuous and flags a student who needs our attention. Further, a written response is tangible. When students look at what they have written, they confront what they can and cannot do. Writing may not correct misconceptions or fill gaps in understanding, but it can expose them and give impetus and direction for additional study. When used in combination with small-group discussion, writing-to-learn activities allow students with an introvert learning style time to think quietly before they must participate.

Case Study Methods

A case study tells a story, complete with characters and action, tension and conflict, ambiguity and dilemma, problems, and questions. When used as a focus for discussion, case studies often bridge the gap between theory and practice, between the abstract and concrete, between the classroom and the world beyond.

Case study discussions can vary enormously, but two dimensions of this variation are noteworthy in using case methods with first-year students. First, the cases themselves can range in length and complexity. Some are short—a paragraph or two presenting a fairly well-defined problem in its barest outline. Other cases are quite long, often several pages, telling a complicated story rich in the details that make for the ambiguity and confusion of real life.

Second, case study discussions may differ in the amount of structure and guidance we offer. At one extreme, we might pose a series of questions that lead students step by step through analysis of the case. At the other, we might simply ask students to "analyze the case," and our opening question might be something like "What do you want to say about this case?" Students are on their own to identify the issues and structure the discussion, making this a useful strategy for practice in dealing with the kind of ill-structured situations described in Chapter Four.

Room exists for a full range of case study discussions in a college curriculum, and perhaps even in an introductory course. When working with first-year students, however, we should probably be cautious. Students do not learn to handle real-life situations by being overwhelmed by detail, totally confused about what they are supposed to do, and without a clue about where to start. That is a formula for flight, not insight, and we should be alert for signs of it. On the other hand, it is unlikely that students will develop skills for dealing with complex situations independently if we assign only structured cases with step-by-step guidance for analysis. We recommend starting with simpler cases that have more explicit directions for analyses and then moving gradually to more complex cases with less guidance. The examples given here illustrate simpler, more structured cases that challenged but did not overwhelm students.

Watch this clip from the film *Lone Star* [the clip shows a fictional encounter between parents and teachers arguing about the manner in which Texas history is taught in the schools], listening carefully to the dialogue so that you understand what is being disputed and what is at stake in this scene. Then do two things: (1) write an analysis of the scene using the ideas we have developed over the last several days. What do the ideas of recognition and equal moral consideration have to do with this scene? (2) Come to some conclusion about how you might resolve the dispute in the scene. The principal suggests that it's best not to talk about "winners and losers," but is it possible to resolve the dispute so that there are no winners and no losers? [*Source:* Calvin B. Peters]

The manager of a high-volume discount store has just received a huge shipment of cheap iPyd music players. The manufacturer who shipped them sometimes tries to unload a batch of "factory seconds"; that is, 45 percent of the iPyds are defective in some way. A normal shipment contains only 22 percent defectives. The manufacturer will allow the discount store to return any shipment, no questions asked, as long as the discount store pays the relatively small shipping charge. Testing iPyds is pretty expensive, so the manager doesn't want to test every one, but she does want to take a small sample and test them. If less than 30 percent of them are defective, she will accept the shipment. Otherwise, she will pay the shipping charges and send them back. What is the smallest number of iPyds she can sample and be 99.75 percent certain not to accept a shipment of factory seconds? [*Source:* John Montgomery, professor of mathematics, University of Rhode Island]

Limited space prevents inclusion of longer, less structured cases here, but the National Center for Case Study Teaching in Science, a Website hosted by the State University of New York at Buffalo, is a rich resource for cases of varying complexity in a variety of disciplines (http://ublib .buffalo.edu/libraries/projects/cases/case.html). Clyde Herreid (1998) offers helpful suggestions for faculty who wish to write their own cases. Samuel Zeakes (1989) describes an interesting variation in which *students* create cases, which then become the focus for class discussion or additional homework practice.

Role-Playing Methods

Like the case study, a role-playing exercise poses a real-life situation or problem. Role-playing methods differ, however, in that they place students *in* the situation and ask them to assume the role of a character in the story. We set the stage for a role-playing activity by presenting a situation—the setting, characters, and some action that has led or might lead to a conflict, problem, or dilemma. Students then assume the role of a character and act out the rest of the drama knowing what their character would know, thinking as their character would think, and acting and interacting as their character would act and interact. After the role play, students discuss the issues, actions, feelings, or interaction depicted.

One variation of role playing especially lends itself to courses in which students explore various theoretical perspectives and their implications or applications. Instead of talking *about* how two (or more) theorists would interpret or respond to particular situations, students assume the roles of those theorists and talk to one another or to some neutral character. McKeachie (1986), for example, describes a role-playing activity designed to involve students in comparing and contrasting the views of B. F. Skinner and Sigmund Freud. The activity asks students to imagine that Skinner, Freud, and a student are talking about a newspaper report that a baseball player punched his manager. The student notes that the player has been in trouble for fighting before and asks what should be done about him. The stage is set for the role play.

We developed and have used a variation of "role-play a theoretical perspective" to engage both students and faculty in thinking about multicultural issues. After reading an article outlining perspectives on multiculturalism in America, students assume roles as advocates of the four perspectives (assimilationism, pluralist unionism, pluralist separatism, and nationalism) to discuss and try to resolve the conflict in this situation:

> Some years ago, the University built a new Multicultural Center located symbolically in the center of campus. Shortly after the Center opened its doors, controversy developed over use of its rooms. That controversy has been resolved *ad hoc* each year, but it simmers and periodically resurfaces. To some, rooms in the Multicultural Center seem ideal places for scheduling meetings, seminars, colloquia, and a variety of other public programs to explore issues of diversity. To others, space in the Multicultural Center should be assigned to the various student organizations that would determine how their rooms are to be used. They argue: "We demand to be recognized as a distinctive and important collection of students. We face unique challenges and have unique interests. We need a 'place to call our own.'"

Other strategies for conducting role-play activities create additional variations in this method. One strategy has a few students participating in the role playing while the rest of the class observe. This approach focuses everyone's attention on one way to deal with a situation at a time and establishes common ground for discussion afterward, but it makes most students observers, a role that easily becomes passive.

As an alternative, we might divide students into groups, assign each student one of the roles, and run concurrent role-playing exercises. On the positive side, this approach involves more students more actively in coping with the role-play situation, and it often elicits a richer variety of responses for discussion afterward. The follow-up discussions can be more difficult to orchestrate, however, because the groups have somewhat differing experiences.

A third strategy for staging role-play activities asks all students to assume essentially the same role, such as a task force, a committee of advisers, members of a consulting firm, or some other collection of "experts." They then interact with the instructor, who assumes the role of the "novice." Yngve Ramstad, one of our colleagues in economics, regularly breaks his class into small groups and asks the groups to imagine they are "economic advisory committees" to the governor. Drawing on newspaper reports of economic events or trends, he creates scenarios in which the governor must make decisions or comment publicly on the reports but first wants advice from the economic advisory committees. The committees have ten or fifteen minutes to decide what they will advise, before the instructor (playing the role of governor) asks for their recommendations. This approach resolves the problem of getting all students involved without having several role plays going on at the same time. The approach also reduces any anxiety students may have about their acting ability or about being put on the spot for a cameo appearance.

In still another variation, students do not actually act out a scene or situation but during discussion assume the role of someone whose opinions differ from their own. Such role-taking encourages students to look more closely at and give more serious consideration to alternative points of view. A colleague in English, for example, tells how she struggled for years to get students to consider the possibility that Bertolt Brecht's "Mother Courage" might have been a good mother. Most students thought not, which always put her in the position of arguing the other side, while they went to work to prove their original opinions, ignored evidence to the contrary, and paid little attention to the ambiguities or nuances in the play. Now she opens discussion with the same question, "Was Mother Courage a good mother?" After a show of hands, she asks students to pretend they hold the opposite view and to try to defend it with evidence from the text. The role-taking technique removes her from the discussion except as recorder; students look much more closely at the text, produce more compelling evidence for both possibilities, and reach stronger conclusions for having considered the alternatives.

The difference between talking *about* a situation and being *in* the situation, even when it is make-believe, is subtle but powerful. By taking the role of another, students can gain expertise that they otherwise might have little motivation to acquire, consider positions and points of view that they might otherwise dismiss quickly, recognize and acknowledge emotions that otherwise would be suppressed, and try out behavior that otherwise would seem too out of character.

General Suggestions

Small-group discussion, writing to learn, case study, and role playing are not, of course, the only techniques for getting students involved during class, but they constitute a good beginning repertoire for those of us who teach first-year students. These methods incorporate the conditions research identifies for learning: students' active involvement in thinking and problem solving, practice in retrieving information from long-term memory and using it in varied contexts, discussion of different views, and reflection on learning processes. They are flexible methods that can be tailored to fit most disciplines, class sizes, and objectives. Taken together, they offer a varied menu of activities, one likely to sustain interest and appeal to a variety of learning styles. Success in using these methods is not automatic, however, especially not with beginning students. We conclude this chapter by reflecting on some things to keep in mind while working with first-year students.

When thinking about activities to get students involved, begin with a clear notion of learning objectives.   Any teaching method, including those discussed here, is effective only insofar as it promotes achievement of objectives. Sometimes those who press for getting students involved sound as if it matters little what students are involved *in*, so long as they are involved. It does matter. If these methods are to promote achievement of our course objectives, then they must pose challenges and call for practice geared to those objectives.

The more we learn about cognition, the clearer it becomes that incorporating several kinds of practice tasks is important.   During early encounters with new information, activities that require paraphrasing, summarizing, and explaining how ideas are connected help build and stabilize major pathways in long-term memory. Activities that ask students to consider new ideas in a variety of examples prompt them to extend and elaborate their understanding. Further down the road, activities that involve students in applying what they have learned in increasingly complex situations promote development of thinking and problem-solving abilities.

We are *not* suggesting, as colleagues sometimes ask, that we devote introductory courses to learning basic information, assign intermediate courses the tasks of elaboration and structured problem solving, and focus upper-division courses on more complex thinking and problem solving. Research does not support the idea that students should spend a huge chunk of time acquiring new information before they are asked to do more. Deep learning is far more cyclical, and instruction is more effective if students extend, elaborate, and apply new ideas as they encounter them.

Planning instruction to involve students requires both creativity and time—more so, we think, than planning a straight lecture. We need to anticipate this in order to make time for preparation; chairpersons and other administrators need to understand what is involved so that they do not underestimate the challenges or undervalue faculty efforts to meet them. Most of the activities discussed in this chapter have two parts. They begin by posing a situation—a problem, a demonstration, a case, a scene and some characters, some form of specific example. Where do we find these situations and examples? Popular media (newspapers, magazines, television, films) are good sources; they often contain data, conflict, dilemmas, characters, and story lines that we can transform into case studies, role-playing scenes, or problems for small groups to consider. Faculty engaged in community service or professional consulting might also look to their professional experiences for real-life questions and problems.

Creating the problem situation is only the first step in designing a practice activity. The key to whether these methods provide *appropriate* practice lies in the questions we ask about the situation. A case study, for example, can focus the practice for most of the types of learning outlined in Chapter Four if we simply alter the questions we ask about the case. We can turn a potentially good case study activity into a disaster, however, if we ask students simply to recall information or recognize an example when they are ready to apply ideas and theories, and vice versa. The questions accompanying these activities direct students' thinking. We must plan them carefully, with one eye on the goals we want to accomplish and the other on where students are in the learning cycle.

Prepare to help students deal with challenges that might be beyond their developmental level. As we have mentioned several times, not all students greet opportunities for active involvement with enthusiasm. Some consider such activity a complete waste of class time. They cannot imagine what can be learned from small-group discussion if faculty are not leading them. They see no point in writing if we are not going to read and grade what they write. Case studies and role-playing exercises are, after all, only make-believe. These students think we would make better use of class time if we lectured more, went over material in the text, worked more problems (especially those that will be on the test), and gave more notes.

Such reactions are not surprising to faculty aware of the research on development (see Chapter Two), but anticipating resistance does not reduce it or make it easier to address. Abandoning efforts to involve students is obviously not the answer. To do so would be to give up our best hope for promoting understanding or thinking, reinforce passive learning, and deprive first-year students of challenges that might lead to transformation in how they view learning. We need instead to support students as they confront those challenges; our remaining suggestions highlight some of the things first-year students are likely to find supportive.

When introducing activities designed to involve students, explain why it is important that they participate. This may start to feel redundant and unnecessary, but many first-year students are undergoing transformation in their views of learning that requires reminders and reassurance that we have valid reasons for asking them to be involved. To avoid ritualistic introductions, we might alternately mention research on learning, report data on how former students succeeded in our courses, refer students back to the syllabus or to earlier explanation, or point to important issues or contributions that came up in a previous activity. Explanation on an intermittent schedule may be more powerful a few weeks into a course. Eventually, such explanation might not be needed at all. The moment arrives when students no longer say "These activities waste class time"; "We could cover more in class if the professor just lectured"; "Class discussion was interesting but we didn't learn anything."

Structure is a major source of support for beginning students, and explicit instruction about what students are to do when "actively involved" is one way we can offer it. Early in the course, ask not only for an end product (an explanation, recommendation, or solution) but also outline what students should consider along the way (particular theories, issues, or questions). We hope students will eventually learn to think through these situations without so many prompts, but students need them initially to guide their thinking.

Once students become engaged in an activity, help them take notes and structure discussions. The more involved students are, the less likely it is that their ideas and contributions come in orderly fashion. It is easy to lose track. To help students record and organize ideas, some faculty list key questions or issues on the board and record students' ideas under appropriate headings. Others record student contributions in the order in which they are offered but stop from time to time to ask students to try organizing the ideas. However we do it, both the recording and the organizing are important. Recording students' ideas acknowledges that we take them seriously and offers a concrete response to students who want "notes." Helping students organize their contributions facilitates chunking and storing ideas in long-term memory.

Look for ways to make personal contact with students, especially when class activities and tasks are likely to challenge students' epistemological views. Enrollment in first-year courses often makes personal contact difficult, but the importance students attach to this suggests it is worth the effort (see Chapters Fourteen and Fifteen). We encourage the use of in-class small-group activities in part because they permits us to interact with students on more personal terms. Follow-up meetings with individual students to discuss class activities may not be possible, but informal discussion with groups of four or five during office hours or over lunch may be. These encounters go a long way toward humanizing both our courses and us, and that is particularly beneficial to first-year students.

Interestingly, technology that seemed at first blush to be terribly impersonal turns out to be a major medium for faculty-student interaction. E-mail, class chat rooms, course listservs, and the like have exponentially increased the options for connecting students with one another, with course materials, and with faculty. Although the increased access is probably a good thing, it can create an unrealistic expectation for immediate response, and it may encourage students to think that a personal visit to an office (or even a classroom) is no longer necessary. We say a bit more about this in Chapter Fourteen.

Allow enough time for students to get involved and complete the task. Few things are more frustrating to students (and to us) than an instructional task that we have seriously undertimed. Students need time to consider a problem, read a case, prepare for a role play. Sometimes, it makes sense to assign the case, the roles, or the problem as homework so students can give them some thought outside class. Most of these activities call for follow-up discussion, and a working rule of thumb is to allow at least as much time for follow-up as for the activity itself.

Following an involvement activity, take time (and save time) to review and summarize. At one level, a review answers the question, "What have we gained from this discussion or activity?" Some students prefer having an answer to a question or resolution of an issue, but many will settle for realizing they have explored the dimensions of a problem, looked at the situation from several perspectives, clarified how to approach and think through a problem, or identified questions and issues for further consideration, so long as the dimensions, perspectives, problem-solving steps, and issues for further study are clear and recorded in their notes. If not, many first-year students return to that familiar mantra, "Class was interesting, but we didn't learn anything."

In Chapter Six, we discussed advantages and outlined techniques for engaging students in creating a summary in a lecture situation. Asking students to summarize what they gained from an activity in which they were actively involved—small-group discussion, writing-to-learn activity, case study, role-playing exercise, and the like—has similar and perhaps even more powerful benefits. Again, because many first-year students are not practiced in summarizing, they may need more specific prompts: "What was the main question or issue? What approaches or perspectives did we consider? What evidence did we bring to bear? Where do we agree and disagree? What else might we consider?"

At a second level, our review addresses the student question, "Why did we go to all that trouble to make these points when the instructor could have explained it and saved a lot of time?" Once the activity is introduced with an explanation of why students are asked to participate, reviewing the virtues of active involvement may seem redundant. The distinction between learning *what* to think and learning *how* to think is, however, a subtle one for first-year students, and it takes some time to become comfortable with it. When we review what students gain by participating in the exercises we design, we at least remind them that we have a clear purpose in mind and that we are willing to aid and support their learning.

Lastly, getting students involved in class often depends on our success in getting them involved outside class. Many of the best classroom activities succeed only when students do their homework. We turn to that topic now.

For Further Exploration _____

- Barkley, E. F., Cross, K. P., and Major, C. H. *Collaborative Learning Techniques: A Handbook for College Faculty.* San Francisco: Jossey-Bass, 2005.

  After synthesizing the research on collaborative learning in higher education, the authors present detailed procedures and variations (including online implementation) for thirty basic collaborative learning techniques. Small-group activities, writing-to-learn exercises, case studies, and role playing are represented along with several activities not discussed in this chapter.

- Bean, J. C. *Engaging Ideas: The Professor's Guide to Integrating Writing, Critical Thinking, and Active Learning in the Classroom.* San Francisco: Jossey-Bass, 1996.

  This extremely useful guide is packed with practical ideas for using writing, small-group discussions, and other active learning techniques to promote development of critical-thinking skills.

- Nilson, L. B. *Teaching at Its Best: A Research-Based Resource for College Instructors* (2nd ed.). Bolton, Mass.: Anker, 2003.

  This is another good source of practical ideas for engaging students actively. Nilson's discussion ranges widely, including chapters on small-group work, cases, writing to learn, and more.

CHAPTER 8

Encouraging
Active Reading

It is not humanly possible to do all the work. Professors should realize that students have other courses, not just theirs. Also this professor should stop thinking we're smarter than we are and get a textbook that we can understand. (first-year student)

It's the passivity of freshmen that gets to me. They don't do the reading; they want me to explain it. If they don't understand, they blame me. It does not seem to occur to them that they might have to work at understanding, that it might involve some effort on their part. (faculty member)

What can we reasonably expect students to learn and do outside class? Few questions elicit greater differences of opinion between students and faculty. Students say they have never worked harder in their lives; they frequently feel overwhelmed by the work expected, and their professors seem neither to notice nor care whether or not they learn. Faculty complain about students' lack of motivation, their unwillingness to work at learning, and their refusal to spend time doing it. All things considered (including courses that *do* demand too much), we suspect most first-year students study more than they ever imagined they would but less than we can reasonably expect.

Students' reports of the kind and amount of studying they do explain why college assignments often come as a shock. As we saw in Chapter One, first-year students report studying very little in their last year in high school, and although they say they expect to study more in college we know our assignments face stiff competition for their attention. There are people to meet, things to try, relationships to negotiate and renegotiate, hours to work, and identities to form. Academic

119

matters easily pale in comparison, especially in the short run. Perhaps we should not be surprised that students study less than we expect, yet few of them are capable of keeping pace with their courses if they spend only an hour or so preparing for class. What we expect from first-year students, and what seems necessary if they are to flourish, is more, often much more.

Studying more does little good, of course, unless students know how to study productively. Entering students anticipate needing help in basic study skills, and our initial assignments frequently confirm this expectation. Where they exist, Learning Assistance Centers can be busy places. We tend to expect miracles from these programs, however, and we seem to forget that all students, even highly capable ones, need to practice general skills in the context of the discipline if transfer is to occur. In the end, if we want students to study more, on a more regular schedule, and more productively, we need to reconsider some traditional college assignments and create others better suited to those goals.

Assignments to Reconsider

In reconsidering how to support first-year students, we should probably start with the most traditional of college practices: term papers and term projects. No matter how well intentioned, it is difficult to dispute charges that these assignments elicit lackluster work, invite plagiarism, underwrite those who peddle prepared term papers, distract students from more fruitful study, and sometimes require students to complete four or five major projects in one term—something we ourselves cannot do. Term papers and projects seem especially ill suited for first-year students, asking those who know little about a subject to identify a topic of special interest prematurely and requiring in-depth study before they know what resources could or should be consulted. Attempting to provide the direction and guidance first-year students need turns into an impossible task because we cannot supervise what are essentially independent study projects for twenty, thirty, or more students. Our most serious reservation about these assignments, however, is that they do not encourage students to study on a regular basis.

Day-to-day assignments that take the form of "read the following pages for next time" also merit our rethinking. Too often, next time comes and the students cannot answer questions about the reading; we conclude they have not read it. No doubt some students ignore these assignments, but most say they at least try to keep up. Many first-year students are passive readers, however. They highlight their way through an assignment and assume they are done. They tend not to use strategies that lead to understanding, such as paraphrasing, summarizing, questioning the text, and testing themselves, unless an assignment asks them to do so. Simply telling students to read the chapter does not give the support many of them need to become active readers.

If term papers and projects ask too much and "read the following pages" assignments ask too little, what assignments *are* appropriate for first-year students? Because reading plays such an important role in many college courses, we begin our discussion with assignments designed to help students learn from reading.

Assignments to Help Students Learn from Reading

"How can I get students to do the reading and to read for understanding?" is the question faculty most frequently ask—and in an increasingly desperate tone—in our workshops and seminars. Meanwhile, students complain in an equally desperate voice that the amount and difficulty of their assigned reading make it impossible to keep up. Many of us suspect that students' reading skills have declined, but the evidence is murky and difficult to interpret with confidence. Most research on reading focuses on learning to read in early grades, and the handful of studies of reading at the secondary and postsecondary levels raise as many questions as they answer. The 2002 National Assessment of Educational Progress found that although average reading scores for fourth and eighth graders increased over the last decade, average reading scores for twelfth graders were lower in 2002 than in the previous two assessments in 1992 and 1998 (National Center for Education Statistics, 2003). The differences in scores are statistically significant, but we are not altogether certain that they are practically significant for thinking about what we can expect students to learn from reading.

Perhaps more informative for our purposes is research on reading practices of students in college or about to enter. In their review of research, Suzanne Wade and Elizabeth Moje (2000) reported that students at the secondary level engaged in little content area reading of any kind. The conclusion may startle some and trouble many, but the more interesting findings were the reasons secondary students read so little—the development of a distinctive teacher-student dynamic. From the studies they reviewed, Wade and Moje (2000) reported that secondary teachers tended not to emphasize reading because they (1) doubted that students would be able to understand the readings on their own, (2) believed their "oral texts" (teacher explanation) were a more efficient way to deliver content; and (3) questioned the value of reading, preferring instead experienced-based instructional activities. Not surprisingly, when students figure out that they can rely on their teachers' oral texts and handouts to learn content, they see little need to read and come to regard texts—even primary source texts—as supplemental, tangential, a source to skim for answers to study questions. The less students read, of course, the less practiced they become in learning from reading.

As we discussed in Chapter One, we suspect similar dynamics occur in many first-year college courses. Faculty plan a course assuming the readings will be a major learning resource, and most give careful thought to the texts they select. First-year students, more or less accustomed to relying on an instructor's oral text or "gloss" of assigned readings, arrive and soon begin to feel overwhelmed by what they are expected to learn from the readings. "The instructor doesn't teach us what we need to know" and "Exams ask for things not covered in class" are common complaints from those who do not do well on quizzes or exams. In response, some faculty dig in and complain ever more loudly about students' lack of preparation for college. Others, reasoning that getting the information to students is the important thing, resort to presenting oral texts. Unfortunately, covering content by way of oral text all too often leads to the fast-paced, nonstop lectures and surface learning strategies Chapter Six advised against.

Neither complaining about students' lack of preparation for college nor succumbing to their proclaimed helplessness in learning from reading seem productive responses in the long run. Instead, we advocate stressing the importance and empowerment of being able to learn from reading, acknowledging that first-year students are still learning the study skills and habits they will need for lifelong learning, and offering instruction and assignments that help them develop their reading skills. The outside class assignments in this chapter focus on helping students learn from reading.

Direct Instruction on How to Read Assigned Readings

Many undergraduates, and first-year students especially, are unaware that one might approach readings in philosophy and chemistry differently; nor do they realize genres within a discipline—textbooks versus primary sources, research articles versus reviews of research, literature versus literary criticism, for example—call for distinctive reading strategies. Direct instruction on "how to get the most from assigned readings" is useful at any level of instruction, particularly so for first-year students.

A colleague in philosophy, for example, takes a few minutes during the first or second class meeting to demonstrate how active readers would read the first section of the assignment for the next class. Her demonstration points out where students might pause to think or take notes and suggests what those notes might be—a question, a summary, a reaction. She then asks students to use similar active reading strategies to complete the reading assignment and bring tangible results (books marked up, notes taken, written summaries, questions listed) to class. At the beginning of the next class, students compare their reading notes in small groups while she moves from group to group to get a sense of what students have done and to provide feedback. The activity does not require much time, can be repeated often, and conveys the message that active reading is expected in the course.

Paraphrase, Summarize, Draw a Concept Map

Chapter Six stressed that getting students to paraphrase, summarize, and visualize lecture content leads to deeper processing and better retention of information and ideas presented. The same can be said for readings. Some students have learned and use such strategies automatically, but many first-year students require a reminder:

- After you finish the reading, write a note to your roommate or to another friend recounting each of these events (or explaining each of these ideas).
- Write a one-paragraph summary of each section in this chapter (or write a one-page summary of the reading).
- Draw a diagram or picture that depicts what is presented in this chapter.

Students' paraphrases, summaries, or concept maps are often a good starting point for class discussions so we might occasionally wish to collect and skim their work in order to monitor what they are getting from the reading.

What It Says *and* What It Does *Statements*

John Bean (1996) suggests asking students to write *what it says* and *what it does* statements for each paragraph or section of a reading. A *what it says* statement summarizes the content of a paragraph or section. A *what it does* statement describes the purpose or function— that is, it poses the issue, states the main point, provides evidence pro and con, gives an example of something. Because this sort of assignment demands careful reading and focuses attention on the structure of the text, it seems especially useful for helping first-year students read difficult and complex texts.

Double Entry Note Taking

Another type of assignment asks students to divide their reading notes into two columns, record summaries of *what they read* in one column, and note *reactions to their reading* in a parallel column. Depending on the reading, it may be useful to designate intervals when students should enter notes (after the first paragraph, at the end of a section, at the end of an article) or to leave the double entries open to students ("whenever an idea strikes you as important, interesting, or personally relevant"). Thomas Angelo and Patricia Cross (1993) discuss a variation of this assignment as a "classroom assessment technique" for monitoring how students read, analyze, and respond to texts.

Guided Question Writing

Asking students to generate questions from their reading can encourage them to process it more deeply, but left to their own devices beginning students often write questions that require only lower-order thinking skills such as remembering definitions, factual information, and what the text said. To encourage students to write questions that elicit a higher level of thinking, Alison King (1993) suggests using generic question stems such as "What is the main idea of . . .?" "What is a new example of . . .?" "Explain how. . . ." "Explain why. . . ." "What if . . .?" "What are the similarities or differences between . . . and . . . .?"

Alternatively, we might ask students to write questions about the readings that elicit the levels of learning emphasized in the course. Using the categories discussed in Chapter Four, for example, assignments might ask students to develop questions in these categories:

- Knowing: questions that ask for recall of important information or ideas
- Understanding: questions that ask people to explain something in their own words or that ask them to supply or consider additional examples
- Thinking: questions that pose new problems or contexts and ask people to apply information or ideas

Whether using the category system we suggest, Bloom's Taxonomy, or an even simpler assignment to write "lower-order" and "higher-order" questions, faculty can use the guided-questioning assignment not only to promote deeper processing of the readings but also to strengthen the connections among objectives, readings, and (hopefully) evaluation procedures. Asking students to ask and answer each other's questions in pairs or small groups can be a fruitful follow-up activity, and some research suggests question answering is equal in importance to question asking (King, 1993; Nist and Simpson, 2000).

Reading Journals

Assignments to keep a reading journal take a variety of forms. An open-ended reading journal asks students to write regularly (a specified number of entries or pages per week) but does not specify what the entries should include. The general instructions invite students to summarize, react, question, argue, provide additional examples, or write about what the readings mean to them personally. When working with first-year students, many faculty prefer more structured reading journal assignments, at least initially, so that they can design specific assignments to elicit deep processing of the readings and coordinate them with planned class activities. The journal assignment may be described in general terms in the syllabus, possibly including a sample journal entry, along with an estimate of how much we expect students to write. We could then make specific journal writing assignments in each class or once a week. (For additional suggestions on using reading journals, see Bean, 1996; and Seshachari, 1994.)

In an interesting variation on reading journals, David Parkyn (1999) describes an electronic collaborative journal assignment that assigns students to small groups and asks them to write a collective weekly journal on the reading assignments. The instructions specify that each student must write two to three paragraphs. The first paragraph should comment on one or more prior entries in the journal; the others should add something new—initiate a new topic, support or disagree with a position in the reading, raise questions, or invite others to respond.

Parkyn suggests several ideas for linking the electronic journal assignments to class activities depending on the class and the nature of the entries. He notes that he always takes class time after the second or third journal entry for a structured reflection and discussion of the journal assignment. During this class discussion, students meet in their electronic journal groups to identify key issues in their journals, note patterns in their responses, identify especially effective or provocative contributions, and list ideas for making the journals more productive. The structure of the electronic journal assignment, the possibilities for linking with class activities, and the opportunities for periodic reflection on the journal assignment make this assignment especially well suited for first-year students.

One Sentence Plus Three Pieces of Evidence

One of the most widely adapted assignments to support closer reading of texts on our campus was developed by a colleague in English (Cuddy, 1985). The assignment poses an open-ended question (for instance, "In Washington Irving's *Rip Van Winkle,* is Rip or his wife responsible for the quality of their marital relationship?"), asks students to answer the question in one sentence, and requires that they include three quotations from the text to support their answers. The questions invite differences of opinion; restricting support to direct quotations demands attention to the text, which some first-year students (especially those in a position of multiplicity) tend to ignore.

Variations of this assignment in the social sciences ask students to state an opinion about an issue or policy and quote three statistics to support (or contradict) the opinion. An assignment in philosophy asks students: "In one sentence identify the type of ethical reasoning the author uses in this article and quote three passages that reveal this type of ethical reasoning." In art history, the assignment asks students to write one interpretive sentence about a painting and list three features of the painting that contribute to that interpretation. The number of statistics, passages, features, and so on is arbitrary; the idea is to focus students' attention on locating evidence.

Microthemes

These assignments ask students to write an essay of two hundred or three hundred words on some question based on readings. Bean, Drenk, and Lee (1982), early proponents of these assignments, outlined four types of microtheme:

- *A summary-writing microtheme* asks students to give an accurate and balanced account of the main ideas in a reading.

- *A thesis-support microtheme,* like Cuddy's one-sentence assignment, asks students to state a position and support it with evidence. The microtheme form demands, however, that students go a step further and explicitly state the relationship between the thesis and the evidence, a skill that many first-year students need to practice.

- *A data-provided microtheme* presents data and asks students to draw conclusions. A sociologist on our campus, for example, gives students the results of a survey and assigns them to "write a paragraph in which you discuss one survey 'finding' in light of your reading." Faculty in the sciences use experimental observations and ask students to explain the results using concepts discussed in the reading.

- A fourth variety of microtheme presents a problem or task and asks students to explain their solution in nontechnical language. Bean, Drenk, and Lee include one example that asks students to explain a physics problem, writing in "Dear Abby" style. Katherine Martin's discussion of microthemes in a general-education biology course (1989) presents some novel variations on these assignments. One asks students to "describe the white cells of the blood using an analogy of military defenders" (p. 118). Another asks them to "develop a campaign to convince teenagers that loud music permanently damages their hearing" and requires that they explain "how the ear converts sound waves of rock music to nerve impulses" (p. 119). The examples, thirty-six in all, are rich in ideas for getting students to write about material in nontechnical language, to extend meaning by way of analogy or metaphor, and to expand the contexts in which students think about course material.

Reading in Math and Science

Problem sets continue to be the mainstay in science and mathematics courses, but there is growing concern about how students approach these assignments. Although many faculty assume students read the chapter and then test their understanding by working problems, research is beginning to challenge those assumptions. A decade-long investigation at Ohio State University, for example, found similarities in approaches to studying among students who failed their first calculus exam (Allen, 1999). Their primary goal was to finish the problem sets, so they started with the problems instead of first reading the chapter. When they confronted an unfamiliar problem or became stuck, they searched the chapter for a similar example that could be used as a template. If that did not work, most of them abandoned the effort, preferring to wait for instruction in a lecture or recitation instead of reading the text more closely.

Such reports echo the findings of Wade and Moje (2000) that students at the secondary level view their math and science textbooks as a source of homework problems, but not as a resource for new learning. Many scientists and mathematicians are reluctant to give up expectations that students learn from texts, however, because doing so would require a significant increase in class time or substantial change in curricula.

Several faculty and programs have experimented with writing-to-learn activities designed to encourage closer attention and deeper learning from texts (Connolly and Vilardi, 1989). One type of assignment asks students to choose a problem from each problem set and write "step-by-step instructions for solving this type of problem." Another asks students to "select a problem for which you are not absolutely certain your solution is correct. Write about your questions or doubts. What are you not sure about, and why?"

Asking students to *explain* answers to problems and their implications is another strategy for encouraging them to think more deeply about the problems they solve. Abdullah Shibli (1992) describes interpretation and problem-solving assignments that could serve as models in several disciplines. A short housing market scenario, for example, presents contrasting dollar amounts for the mean and median prices of a single family home and asks students to explain in writing why the prices differ and why the mean is higher than the median. Another assignment presents a simple regression equation showing the relationship between the price of single family homes and the number of bedrooms and asks students to interpret the relationship and, for example, to discuss the policy implications for a homeowner considering adding a bedroom.

Just-in-Time Teaching (JiTT)

Originally developed for physics instruction, JiTT combines learning from reading, Web-based assignments, and classroom activities. In brief, students respond electronically to a Web-based assignment that is due a few hours before class. The Web-based assignment is on material not yet discussed in class, so students must do the readings in order to answer. The instructor reads student submissions "just in time" to adjust class content or activities to suit students' needs.

Because they guide students' reading and shape class activities, the Web-based assignments are a crucial component of this strategy. Unlike many of the problem set assignments in the sciences, JiTT Web-based assignments pose only three or four questions at a time. The idea is to get students to read and reflect on a manageable amount of material and repeat the process between classes. A sample assignment used in a JiTT physics course might include four question types: an essay question asking students to apply physics concepts to real-world problems; an estimation question in which key information is missing to practice working with ill-defined problems; a multiple choice question to encourage consideration of an array of possibilities, including those that play to misconceptions; and a fourth question inviting students to share their thoughts on the assignment ("What seemed impossible? What reading didn't make sense? What should we spend class time on? What was cool? and so on). The class following the assignment typically begins by reading (or projecting) a sample of student responses to the questions, which are the starting point for clarification, elaboration, or extension.

The JiTT Website reports experimentation in twenty-five disciplines and makes available sample materials in several of them. All in all, this strategy seems to be creative use of available technology and shows promise as a means to support first-year student reading. For additional information and examples, visit http://www.jitt.org.

Conclusion

If reading assignments in first-year courses are to elicit the practices that are productive of deep learning, we need to attend to them more intentionally than we do in our upper-division classes. There, we might succeed with simple directions to read according to a published schedule, trusting that our students have developed sufficient skills to do so productively. Things are different for first-year students. Most need more structure to guide their reading and more direction about how to engage it actively. Unless we specifically prompt students to read more deeply, they are unlikely to develop the habits of reading or of mind so essential to success in college.

For Further Exploration

- Bean, J. C. *Engaging Ideas: The Professor's Guide to Integrating Writing, Critical Thinking, and Active Learning in the Classroom.* San Francisco: Jossey-Bass, 1996.

  Bean's chapter "Helping Students Read Difficult Texts" contains a selection of ideas for encouraging thoughtful and active engagement with reading. The techniques are varied and adaptable across most disciplines.

CHAPTER 9

Supporting Active Study Practices

There is more to first-year course work than reading. We want students to read, but more than that we want them to take what we have covered in class, integrate it with what they have gleaned from their reading, and then use the information to think about the issues and problems that form the substance of our discipline. Our desire to have students actually think about philosophy or economics or psychology or chemistry is frequently frustrated by our failure to provide sufficient guidance for what they should do in addition to their reading. Without at least some structure in this regard, first-year students are unlikely to do what we hope, no matter how earnest our appeals. Students' willingness to invest time in our courses—and many first-year students begin classes with eagerness and enthusiasm—is often eroded by their own frustration at not knowing what to do other than highlight their reading when they get ready to study.

If we want students to see connections and use what they are learning, then we need to create assignments that prompt them to do such things. Although we discuss these assignments separately from reading assignments, we see both as part of an integrated instructional practice. On the one hand, activities designed to encourage learning from reading should lead students to engage in other active study practices. On the other, assignments that ask students individually or collaboratively to move beyond memorization should lead them back to their reading, perhaps even piquing their interest in a text that once seemed rather dry. The assignments do not need to be long or complex, nor do they necessarily have to be graded. They do need to point students in the directions we want them to go by giving them some reasonably well-defined tasks that help them draw connections among what they have learned in class, what they have read, and the world outside the classroom. We sample here a potpourri of individual and group assignments that introduce ways to engage studying actively but still emphasize day-to-day preparation for class.

Assignments for Individual Student Work

Assignments for individual student work are a staple of education in the United States. Completing workbook sections, solving problems at the end of a chapter, or submitting answers to questions distributed by instructors are things first-year students are (all too) used to doing. Of course, there is some merit in these activities. They do get students to *do* something, and that is a plus. Many of them, however, engage students only in surface learning where material is transferred from the assigned reading to the appropriate place on the form to be handed in.

A Sampler of Individual Assignments

We want to focus on individual assignments that encourage students to attend to course materials in ways that foster deeper learning. We have included five types of assignments that are especially effective in this regard.

Peer surveys. To engage students when a topic is introduced, some faculty create a short attitude or opinion survey, distribute copies to students, and ask them to get two or three of their peers to complete the survey before the next class. For example, students might ask questions about the circumstances in which the death penalty ought to be imposed, if at all. Or they might quickly assess their acquaintances' views on the reality, causes, and consequences of global warming. In class, students can introduce their results and augment them with their own views. Those who have used this technique report that first-year students seem keenly interested in what other students think and pay close attention when survey responses are reported during class. Students' heightened interest, in turn, makes it easier to engage them in thinking more deeply about supporting or conflicting data or views presented in lectures and readings.

Peer interviews. Like the peer survey, a peer interview assignment plays to students' interest in what their peers think. In brief, the assignment asks each student to interview another student not enrolled in the course about some issue discussed in the readings or to be discussed in class. For example, in an introductory education course a student might interview a friend about experience in secondary school and how well the course work prepared him or her for college. To help students get beyond generalities and platitudes, some faculty distribute specific interview questions. Others offer or work with students to develop case studies or scenarios, or to find news stories or letters to the editor so that interviews can begin with the questions "What would you do in this situation?" or "How would you respond to this and why?"

Student observations. Asking students to conduct observations generates data of a different sort but serves a similar purpose. A colleague in political science, for example, gives students an observation guide, asks them to observe a public meeting, and tells them to record examples of behavior related to certain leadership styles. Students' observation notes become illustrations when the class meets to discuss leadership styles. Chet Meyers (1986) describes an assignment that asks students to observe a conversation and record interaction patterns. A professor in communication studies asked students to conduct a simple experiment: find a friend willing to carry on a conversation for ten minutes at a distance closer than that of normal conversation, and record reactions.

Popular media assignments. The popular media are rich sources of examples and problems for many courses. A colleague teaching environmental geology, for example, relies heavily on newspaper articles and editorials as a focus for homework assignments. One asks students to rebut an editorial claiming that the victims of a volcanic mudslide could not have known the dangers. Another asks them to identify important issues not addressed in a news article about a proposed coastal development. In a given semester, he explains, dozens of newspaper articles or editorials are printed about topics related to his course, and few resources are better in helping students see the relevance of course material.

Information literacy assignments. Most of us want first-year students to learn to use the library and become discerning consumers of the vast universe of information (and misinformation) that is available on the Internet. Frequently, this desire creates a powerful temptation to assign term papers as the best (or at least the most familiar) way to develop these skills in students. As we noted earlier, the term paper, whatever its strengths, has deep flaws, especially for first-year students. More than that, however, we think there are other, more effective and more manageable ways to teach students the materials and methods of library and Internet research.

For instance, Farber (1984) describes alternatives to the term paper that were developed collaboratively by faculty and librarians at Earlham College. One example from an introductory philosophy course focusing on ethics asks students to find several articles on affirmative action, annotate two that take opposing stances, and relate them to their own views on the matter. Another in U.S. history asks students to examine primary materials on slave life or the abolition movement, compare them with their text's treatment of the subjects, and write their own brief account of the issues or events.

Another colleague has developed a series of assignments that ask students to navigate the Internet, first to locate instructor-selected articles that are relevant to the topics currently being discussed in the course. Follow-up assignments ask students to locate sites relevant to other course material on their own. In each instance, the instructor asks students to complete a form that not only assesses the content on the site but also evaluates the reliability of the site, the likelihood of bias, and its usefulness as an academic reference. Both these assignments are focused on topics and issues discussed in class, and both link the research students do to the reading they have been assigned. In addition, of course, the library and Internet assignments encourage first-year students to prepare for class and help them hone their research skills at the same time.

Commercially prepared materials. Most commercially published textbooks available for adoption in first-year courses come packaged with a variety of supplemental materials. There remain, of course, the questions at the conclusion of each chapter, but many include a much broader array of options for actively engaging students outside class. Publisher-produced Websites containing databases, document archives, and video and audio clips keyed to particular portions of a text can be a good source of raw materials for constructing assignments. Textbooks themselves often include such assignments. Our advice here is to investigate what is available and use these assignments whenever possible. As is the case with publisher-supplied test item banks, some reflective caution is in order. We want to be sure the prepared assignments reflect our emphases and that they invite students to engage in the kind and level of learning we think is appropriate.

Suggestions for Effective Individual Assignments

There are obviously many more ways to create individual assignments that supplement a student's required reading but effective assignments for first-year courses share some general characteristics. Before we turn to group assignments, we pause to highlight some crucial features of the individual assignments we have surveyed.

First, these assignments are less ambitious than the papers and projects found in many undergraduate courses. From time to time, we might ask first-year students to synthesize and integrate their learning in a four-or-five-page paper, especially if a series of shorter assignments lead to it. But if we want first-year students to study regularly rather than intermittently, we need shorter and more frequent assignments.

Second, these assignments are more focused than the usual "Think about this for next time." They are explicit in what they ask students to do: summarize, solve a problem, find an example, state a position, and so on. Focused tasks and explicit instructions furnish the direction and structure many first-year students need.

Third, these assignments ask students to produce something tangible, whether it is a simple list, a clipping from a newspaper, or more complex such as a paragraph or two stating and defending a position. Asking students to locate or produce something tangible not only helps them organize their thoughts but also tells them when they are (or are not) done studying. They may have read and even highlighted the reading assignment, but if the paragraph is not written or the newspaper example has not been found, they know there is more to do.

Fourth, to reiterate our suggestion for getting students involved during class (Chapter Seven), research on cognition can guide us in creating and sequencing out-of-class assignments. Asking students to explain ideas in nontechnical language, summarize, or connect new ideas to what they already know are useful beginning tasks. Assignments that ask students to consider ideas in diverse contexts— to find examples in the popular media, conduct observations, survey others' views—prompt students to process information more deeply and are essential to developing understanding and thinking skills.

Fifth, we need to create variety in our assignments if we are to accommodate the range of learning styles first-year students bring to our courses. No single type of assignment is suited to all the learning styles outlined in Chapter Three. By varying the type of assignment we make and giving choices whenever possible, we have a better chance of reaching all students at least some of the time.

Finally, although we recommend frequent, short assignments to help first-year students keep up with their work and study productively, we do not assume that faculty must review all or even most of these assignments. We distinguish between assignments that help students *to learn* from those that assess what students *have learned*. Although many assignments described here could with some modification be used as assessment devices, we view them primarily as assignments *to* learn. We might use some as a focus for class discussion, scan others for signs of understanding or misconception, and even designate a few as practice tests or essays and give written feedback. But none of this argues for reviewing, much less grading, every assignment.

In theory, that is. In practice, first-year students generally do not make a clear distinction between assignments designed to help them learn and those designed to assess their learning. Accustomed to receiving grades on homework, most first-year students expect us to collect assignments, mark them, and record them in grade books. If we do not grade them, it seems, students see little reason to do the work. We are not enthusiastic about incorporating the marks earned on assignments such as those in this chapter in the calculation of a course grade (we say more about this from a measurement perspective in Chapter Eleven). First-year students need the support of assignments if they are to make the most of their study time. If we must grade each of them, we are inevitably able to give fewer and less frequent assignments. Having said that, we also recognize that having more, and more frequent, assignments does little good if students do not do them or do them only haphazardly because they are not graded.

We have not found a good solution to this dilemma, but there are some practices that can help make it seem less like a lose-lose situation. Some faculty quickly scan assignments and record who did them in their grade book. These records do not affect a student's final grade, but they may prompt an invitation for an office visit or a comment reminding the student she or he is falling behind. Other faculty "grade" daily assignments using a plus-check-zero grading scheme. At the end of the term, they convert the pluses and checks to points and factor the totals into the final grade. Although this can be done fairly quickly and seems to help, the recordkeeping is no small task and grows larger with class size. An alternative is to select a smaller sample of assignments each time. In one class, a subset of students determined by some random process submits their work for review; in another, a different subset, and so on. Establishing the groups randomly (but taking care to ensure the sampling is fair) and not announcing them until the day of the assignment is due prompts students to do more of the assignments. They may even appreciate the extra "encouragement" to get their assignment done.

As a last resort, faculty might consider the weekly quiz. Although we have reservations about this strategy and would prefer to wean students from their preoccupation with grades, weekly quizzes do seem to work in getting students' attention. In fact, many first-year students actually welcome regularly scheduled quizzes because they "force you to keep up with the reading."

Assignments for Collaborative Student Work _____

Collaborative learning is a broad term that refers to a variety of activities in which students work together in small groups to achieve learning objectives. Although we may be familiar with the collaborative work of students during classroom discussion, we are less likely to think about it as a way to structure their study time. We are used to the idea that students should do their own work, and we are also well practiced in creating assignments designed to get them to do just that. We should, however, think seriously about collaborative learning as the basis for at least some of our out-of-class assignments. The approach is well grounded in learning theory and strongly supported by research. Literally hundreds of studies and several meta-analyses have shown the effectiveness of collaborative learning methods on measures of academic achievement (including knowledge acquisition as well as higher-level reasoning and creative problem solving), attitude toward learning, and adjustment to and persistence in college (Johnson, Johnson, and Smith, 1991a, 1991b, 1998; Springer, Stanne, and Donovan, 1999).

A Sampler of Collaborative Learning Assignments

Many of the activities described in Chapter Seven—small-group discussions, writing-to-learn activities, case studies, and role playing—are or can be transformed into in-class collaborative learning activities. Here we focus on collaborative learning assignments that require much or all of the work to be completed outside class. Because students have more time to devote to an assignment, we can make the tasks a bit more complex, and because students will work in groups, we can partition the tasks to ensure that each student has something to contribute to the final product.

Study groups. The study group is perhaps the most familiar of all collaborative techniques. Generally with little or no urging from us, students arrange to meet outside class to work on a problem or assignment and to study for an exam. Study groups are the stuff of college memories, and on today's high-tech campus thinking about them may seem a bit quaint. Yet recent research indicates the study group remains a valuable tool for first-year courses. The Harvard Assessment Seminars, for example, found that students who participate in small study groups of four to six members do better academically, are more engaged and more satisfied, and persist longer than those who study alone (Light, 1992). Further investigation concluded participation in a study group was especially important in the sciences;

whether or not students worked together in small study groups outside class was the best predictor of how many science courses they took (Light, 2001). Although some will question whether or not what happens at Harvard applies to most institutions, encouraging first-year students to form study groups seems unlikely to do harm and may reap significant learning gains.

Creating study groups is not so simple as it might first appear. Students' academic schedules, work responsibilities, and extracurricular activities can make the task of finding a common time for meeting daunting indeed. In light of this fact, merely encouraging students to work together or letting them form study groups "if they want" is unlikely to be effective. Many first-year students, especially first-semester students, need help in forming study groups.

Circulating a study group sign-up sheet is one way to help students form groups. The sheet might ask students to sign up for preferred meeting times or for preferred meeting places (a particular dormitory, commuter lounge, or off-campus venue). We might also encourage students to form groups by incorporating early in-class activities in which students work in the same groups over several class meetings. A follow-up exam or quiz may encourage students who have worked together in class to study together outside of class. Additionally, if those initial groups are formed with an eye toward diversity, we might be able to help students establish lasting connections across lines of difference (for more discussion of this, see Chapter Thirteen).

Alternatively, it may make sense in some courses to try to organize study groups on the basis of the combination of courses students are taking. In many institutions, curricular requirements for particular programs lead students, even in their first year, to enroll in the same combination of courses. Helping students form groups to support their study in two, three, or more courses has bonus benefits, a topic to which we return in our discussion of learning communities in Chapter Ten.

Making study groups work is also more difficult with first-year students than with more advanced undergraduates. Telling students in their study groups to go off and talk about issues and ideas raised in the reading or in class is probably not going to produce results that will make any of us happy. As we have said many times, first-year students require more support and direction. At the beginning of the term, some faculty distribute a guide for study groups including a list of things students might do in their groups. Most, however, find they still need to pose specific questions or tasks, at least initially. Other faculty give study questions to the groups weekly. Still others vary the study group assignments from week to week. A group assignment one week may ask students to submit answers to questions that are based on readings or solutions to problem sets. The next week's assignment might require analysis of a case study. The third week's assignment might be to work through a practice exam from a previous semester in preparation for an upcoming exam. Week four might ask study groups to reflect on an exam just given and to discuss group study strategies to help individual members of the group in their learning.

Study groups function best when each student becomes an active participant in the group's work. In spite of our best efforts, the generic study group often develops a pattern in which some students are active participants while others are not, a circumstance that tempts us to abandon group work in favor of individual assignments. There are, however, some techniques to structure group work in ways that makes it more likely that every student will be actively engaged in the process.

Jigsaw. In Jigsaw, each student in a collaborative learning group assumes responsibility for becoming "expert" on one part of an assignment and then for teaching his or her part to other members. The structure of the assignment is a key aspect: it must have clearly delineated parts. For example, the assignment might ask students to consider several articles or perspectives on an issue and then compare, contrast, integrate, or synthesize them. Alternatively, the assignment presents a multifaceted problem or task that can be broken into parts or phases of investigation.

Jigsaw typically proceeds in stages. To begin, students form learning groups of four or five members. The learning group's first task is to divide the assignment and determine which students will be responsible for which parts. When working with first-year students especially, many faculty prefer to prescribe how assignments should be divided. For example, the assignment may involve comparing the perspectives of four books, with each group member reading one of the four. Or the assignment might require groups to conduct an experiment with multiple samples and ask each group member to assume responsibility for one of them.

In the second phase of a Jigsaw assignment, students temporarily leave their study groups to meet with classmates from other study groups who are working the same piece of the assignment. Depending on the complexity of the assignment, these expert teams may meet once or several times at different phases of the assignment. If the assignment requires reading an article and teaching the content to other students, the expert team might meet only once to agree on key ideas, clear up any confusion, and discuss how best to present the material to others. More complex assignments may require an initial meeting to determine how to approach the task, one or more follow-up meetings to review progress and discuss findings, and another meeting or two to plan instructional strategies.

Arranging for the expert teams to meet can pose a problem. Some students may not have much space in their schedules, and working out a time when all the experts can gather may not be possible. There are a couple of ways faculty have dealt with this issue. First, some instructors use class time for the meetings of expert groups. This approach has the advantage of tying what study groups are doing directly to what is happening in class, and because of the implicit faculty supervision it encourages students to do what is necessary to become an expert. Other faculty encourage use of e-mail, text messaging, or the chat room function of various course management software programs if face-to-face expert meetings cannot be arranged. This approach preserves the outside-of-class aspect of the assignment, but it may permit passive lurking and produce less expertise unless faculty build in some monitoring strategies.

In the final phase of the Jigsaw, students return to their original learning groups to teach their part, learn from others in their group, and integrate the pieces. Because students tend to be more invested and interested in the areas in which they have spent time acquiring expertise, it is probably a good idea to remind them of the importance of learning what their peers have to teach and that they will be held responsible for understanding all the pieces of the assignment. Additionally, we might develop a follow-up assignment that builds on what groups have done during the Jigsaw phase.

Jigsaw assignments are both powerful and flexible. They allow an instructor to develop fairly sophisticated tasks that can be integrated into in-class and out-of-class work. They can be grafted onto existing study groups, or the Jigsaw groups can be formed as the assignment is made. The real strength of this approach, however, is its capacity to create a structure in which all students are engaged actively. (For additional information and ideas on using Jigsaw assignments, see Cottell and Millis, 1994; Johnson, Johnson, and Smith, 1991a, 1991b.)

Structured controversies. The structured-controversy collaborative learning technique is built on the assumptions that intellectual controversy is both an important motivator and a key mechanism for higher-order learning, considering multiple views, weighing arguments, and reasoning to best conclusions in a complex situation (Johnson, Johnson, and Smith, 1991a, 1991b, 1997). Controversy over explanations, theories, and even what constitute the facts of particular cases often occur naturally in the context of our courses, but we can enhance instruction by deliberately structuring some of our assignments around these intellectual disputes.

Structured controversy assignments work best with small groups of four to six students. These groups might be ongoing study groups, or groups might be created and recreated for these assignments. We begin the process by posing a controversial question on which informed parties might disagree, then assign readings that present two or more views on the issue, and ask pairs or trios of students in each group to prepare initially to present the arguments in support of one side. It may be helpful at this point to alert students that they will also be asked to argue other sides of the issue, so they should attend to those readings as well.

When students come to the next class, they meet first with the students in their small group assigned to the same initial position; that is, the "pros" in their small group huddle to prepare their presentation, while the "cons" do the same. After pros and cons have had time to agree on major points and a presentation strategy, they rejoin other members of their small groups. Once the groups are reformed, each side presents its position and arguments while students on the other side record the main arguments. This process might be modified a bit if our groups are more permanent study groups. We might then ask the pros from one group to make a presentation to the cons from another group, while first-group cons listen to the second group pros.

In the next phase of a structured controversy activity, students in each small group switch sides and repeat the presentation cycle. "Once-pro-now-con" students huddle to identify their main points and plan presentation strategy, while once-con-now-pro students do the same. After they have had time to prepare, they rejoin their small groups, each side presents its position and arguments, and other students in the group record. Again, it is relatively easy to adjust this portion of the activity if we are using durable study groups.

How much time does a structured controversy assignment take? David Bredehoft (1991) suggests readings can be assigned in one class and remaining phases completed in the next. Of course, a good deal depends on how complex the issue and the readings are, but first-year students may need time between classes to switch pro-and-con positions, reread assignments, and consider what their peers have presented. Also, a follow-up assignment asking students individually or in their study groups to summarize multiple viewpoints, take a tentative position, or suggest additional information needed to reach a decision may prompt deeper consideration and more integration of the views they have examined.

Group projects. Although we earlier advised against individual term paper and project assignments for first-year students (see Chapter Eight), collaborative group projects offer viable alternatives worth considering. Such projects can be highly motivating, engaging, and enriching, especially those that are short-term and correspond to or complement what students are focusing on in class and in their readings. Because students complete their projects in groups, the time required for us to advise, guide, monitor, and grade such projects is far less daunting.

For example, in a social problems course, a colleague assigned a group project to engage students in exploring issues of poverty. She divided the class into "families" of four students, gave each group a description of what its family looked like, and provided each family a budget for food, rent, car payments, and so on. Over the next several weeks, student families were to find ways to spend their budget—actual rental properties available in the area, budgeting food purchases from local markets, and so on. Because the tasks could be divided, each student was assigned to attend to a particular aspect of the family's needs. As a final product, each family was required to submit its budget, complete with expenditures and commentary about what life would have been like had they been compelled to live within the confines of officially defined poverty. In addition, each family was asked to make some policy recommendations on the basis of their experiences.

Because students worked in groups, there were fewer final projects to assess, and because class work and the assigned readings during the project dealt with poverty in the United States, there was a close correspondence between the group projects and the ongoing content of the course. Obviously, there are a multitude of ways to use group project across a variety of disciplines. In art history, for instance, we might create teams of curators and charge them with designing an exhibition of a particular genre or theme. In an economics course, teams of students might be charged with preparing a presentation for a community group on various proposals for altering property taxes or social security.

In general, those projects we often think about as "term" assignments can be adapted to group work in a way that enhances students experiences without overwhelming our capacity to provide necessary support and feedback. When developing group project assignments for first-year students, two additional issues merit attention. Creating an assignment that has an identifiable task is important if groups of first-year students are to function effectively. In the interest of fairness, the tasks need to be reasonably comparable in terms of difficulty and time involved. Using group projects for a limited period rather than for the entire term makes it more likely that projects enrich and not distract from day-to-day preparation for class.

Suggestions for Effective Collaborative Learning Assignments

Advocates of collaborative learning caution that putting students in groups and telling them to work together does not by itself promote greater learning. Throwing students together and hoping for the best can create considerable dissatisfaction for our students and for us. We need to attend carefully to the issues of interdependence and accountability in assignments we construct, to the process of group formation, and to the dynamics of the collaborative process itself. First-year students can reap considerable benefits from collaborative work that is properly designed and conducted.

Interdependence and accountability. There are two fundamental principles that underlie any successful collaborative learning assignment. First, the assignment and the process by which it is completed must create *positive interdependence.* Bluntly stated, positive interdependence means students sink or swim together. An assignment must be complex enough so students cannot complete it individually and insistently collaborative so that students can succeed only if other members of the group succeed. Typically, an assignment builds in positive interdependence by assigning more work than we could reasonably expect from an individual student or by tying individual achievement to that of group members (for example, no individual passes unless all members of the group pass, or we add points to individual scores if all members of a group score above specified level).

Second, effective collaborative learning assignments require *individual accountability.* If assessment is based only on a group project, there is potential for individual students to freeload on the work of others. To avoid this, effective collaborative learning assignments assess both the learning of individual members and their contribution to the group project. Individual questioning, quizzes, and exams are strategies for assessing the learning of each group member. Assessing individual student contributions to a group project usually involves asking group members to assess the contribution of each member of the group. Chapter Eleven includes a sample "Peer Review of Contributions to Group Work" form.

Forming groups. At the center of any collaborative learning activity is the group of students who will work together until the task is accomplished, sometimes throughout the term. Although we are adept at asking students to form ad hoc groups for quick in-class discussions, we often fret over forming groups that will work together outside class. We may spend considerable time agonizing over the structure of those groups that we want to persist for the duration of our course. To resolve these issues, we often take the path of least resistance: we let students form their own groups, perhaps intervening when we see a shy or marginalized student being left out.

This laissez-faire approach is the one preferred by many students, but we do not recommend it on instructional grounds. Students in groups with their best friends are easily distracted by their other shared interests and may devote much of their time to thinking about parties or dormitory life and not working on the substance of our assignment. Far more serious is the fact that the practice tends to marginalize or isolate students in courses where they are underrepresented by race or gender (Rosser, 1998). The consensus emerging from research and practice points clearly to intentional creation of heterogeneous groups or to groups formed by random assignment (say, numbering off). Even those techniques, however, are not foolproof. Rosser (1998) advises vigilance to be sure those practices do not isolate students underrepresented in a class.

It is probably not reasonable to expect that a random process, or even our direct intervention, will always produce groups that are integrated along race, gender, and other lines and logistically feasible as well. Busy student schedules may force us to relax some of our desires about group formation, but we should not give up at the first sign of complications. First-year students are skilled at a variety of communications techniques (e-mail, cell phones, and text messaging among them) that can be used to overcome both time and distance barriers to group work. Our best advice is to work with students to create groups that are inclusive and intellectually productive. Using group assignments at several junctures during a course and creating new groupings of students for each one may be a way of satisfying these conflicting demands. We might begin with a couple of randomly assigned groups and then let students self-select for the next collaborative activity. By monitoring how students self-select at this point, we can adjust future group formation processes to obtain the sort of groups we desire (we readdress this issue in the context of classroom diversity in Chapter Thirteen).

Group dynamics. Early adopters of collaborative learning techniques stressed the importance of initial instruction in group dynamics and group work skills. Given the widespread use of group work in elementary and secondary settings, extensive instruction at the college level is probably less urgently needed now than it once was. Some even object to taking time for such instruction, arguing that fewer faculty will use group techniques if instructional time that could be devoted to content is instead given over to procedural issues (Michaelson, 1999).

Not every course needs to have a short course on group dynamics, but asking students to have a conversation about how they will make their group work is time well spent, in college and elsewhere.

Exhibit 9.1. A Group Gone Wrong

Jason, Amy, Brian, and Jessica are scheduled to meet for the sixth and last time to complete a three-week group project for one of their courses. In brief, the project assignment asked them to select a topic related to the course material, to find and annotate 12 to 15 articles on the topic, and to prepare a 3- to 5-page report that integrates the major issues and perspectives addressed in the annotated articles. We are there for the beginning of their final meeting.

"Well, Amy, once again we're here on time," Jason says somewhat irritably. "Where do you suppose Brian and Jessica are?"

"You're not going to believe this." Amy pauses and then continues. "Brian called and left me a voice mail saying he can't make it. He said..."

"Oh, let me guess!" Jason interrupts. "He forgot about an exam and he has to study? He has to fill in for someone at work? His girlfriend is stressed? His dog is sick? Is there any excuse he hasn't used for missing our meetings? He's been here, what, two out of five times?"

"Well, today's meeting will make two out of six," Amy says, shaking her head. "At least Brian gave us the annotations of his four articles, and they weren't bad."

Nodding agreement, Jason replies, "Unlike Jessica. Could you believe her response when we told her that the two she did weren't enough, that we'd each agreed to do four?"

"Don't remind me!" Amy retorts, slamming her notepad on the table in disgust. "Telling us that she was too busy and that the worst that could happen would be we'd get a few points taken off? Yeah, right! Like none of us are busy?! Like points off for no good reason wouldn't matter to the rest of us?! She drives me crazy!" Pausing a moment to calm down, Amy continues in a resigned tone, "I suppose we should have known in the beginning when she rejected our ideas for topics because she thought they'd be too much work. Anyway, I found two more articles and wrote annotations.

The door opens and Jessica breezes in. "Hi, guys, sorry I'm late." Glancing at her watch, she adds, "Oops! Even later than I thought I'd be because I need to leave in about half an hour. Sorry. Something's come up." Silence. "But the good news is I did one more annotation. That should beef up the research part." Longer silence with glaring expressions from Amy and Jason.

It's Jason who finally breaks the silence. "Look, Jessica, Amy and I are hacked off about the way this group has worked...or not, as the case may be. The project is due in two days. This is our last meeting. We haven't talked about how to integrate the articles we've annotated, never mind how we're going to write a 5-page report. So the bottom line is we need a miracle to finish this. And you're going to leave in half an hour! And what about the evaluation we're supposed to provide of other group members' contributions?"

Discussion Questions

1. What problems occurred in this group?

2. How does your group plan to avoid these problems or deal with them should they occur?

3. Thinking back on your own experiences with group work, what characterized groups that worked well? What made groups not work as well as they might?

This is most important when the groups are reasonably durable, working on an assignment that lasts, say, a week or more. One strategy for stimulating such discussion asks students in their group to share positive and negative experiences with group work, identify behaviors that inhibit and contribute to an effective group, and make ground rules for their group.

An alternative strategy, particularly useful for long-term groups, poses a case study of a dysfunctional group. In their groups, students identify what went wrong in the case and discuss how they will avoid making the same mistakes, again as a way to establish ground rules. In Exhibit 9.1 we present a short case we have used to spark discussion among faculty; they in turn have used it with students.

Either approach—asking students to discuss their past experiences with group work or inviting them to consider a case study— could be conducted in class or formulated as the first outside-of-class assignment the group is asked to complete.

Conclusion

The assignments and classroom activities we have suggested in these last three chapters are relatively easy to incorporate into the existing structures of our course. We can still lecture, but we need to make time for students to process actively what we present. We can still assign reading, but we need to provide a more structured set of instructions and activities to make it meaningful. We can still rely on assignments, but we need to think about which will truly engage students with our material and with each other.

There are, however, other and more transformative ways to think about engaging first-year students. Rather than being plug-ins to our existing course architecture, these methods ask us to change our basic conception about how a course should be constructed and conducted. We turn our attention to these promising methods in the next chapter.

For Further Exploration

- Barkley, E. F., Cross, K. P., and Major, C. H. *Collaborative Learning Techniques: A Handbook for College Faculty.* San Francisco: Jossey-Bass, 2005.

  This handbook contains thirty specific collaborative learning techniques (CoLTs) as well as some discussion of group formation and other issues. Although many activities included here are framed in terms of classroom use, they are easily adapted to out-of-class settings.

CHAPTER 10

Trying Transformed
Teaching

In the 1990s, several major reports attacked colleges and universities for disconnected curricula, instructional approaches that failed to engage students, high student attrition, lack of faculty involvement in undergraduate education, and failure to fulfill civic mission. These criticisms were far-reaching, and institutions scrambled to respond. Universities paid more attention to their curricula and launched a number of initiatives to improve retention. In addition, faculty members began to pay more attention to undergraduate education and to the processes of classroom instruction. The academy's response was not, however, confined merely to attending to things that had been neglected. There was also a sense that some things should be done differently. The most prominent products of this realization affecting the instruction of first-year students are practices that move the idea of active learning to the center of course design and curricular designs that enhance the opportunity for first-year students to engage their courses, faculty, and each other in a sustained way.

This chapter focuses on three of these outcomes: problem-based learning, learning communities, and service learning. Problem-based learning and service learning can be used by individual faculty to reconceive their courses and assignments. Learning communities generally require some institutional commitment to be put in place. Each strategy, however, can have a profound and positive effect on first-year students.

Problem-Based Learning

In problem-based learning (PBL), students work in groups to confront a real-world problem, identify what they need to know to address the problem, and locate the resources and acquire the knowledge they need to address it. Although PBL incorporates many of the active learning, group work, and problem-solving activities discussed in previous chapters, it is a dramatically different approach to teaching and learning. A key difference lies in the role that problems play. In contrast to other approaches that assign problems after instruction and ask students to apply new knowledge, PBL *begins* instruction with a problem that serves to initiate, motivate, and direct learning.

In a typical PBL sequence, the instructor poses a complex problem before presenting any relevant concepts or information and before assigning any readings. Students meet in their working groups to discuss the problem. Initial discussion is often freewheeling; students speculate, propose hypotheses, think creatively. In the end, the initial phase asks groups to identify (1) what they know that is relevant to the problem, (2) what else they might need to know (the "learning issues") in order to address the problem, and (3) who in the group will research each of the learning issues. Students then carry out the research they have agreed to conduct and return to class ready to teach other members of their group what they have learned. So begins a new round of discussion on "what we know," "new learning issues," and "who in the group will research these new issues."

The success of PBL approaches is critically dependent on the problems posed. Experienced PBL instructors emphasize four characteristics that are essential to good problems (Duch, Groh, and Allen, 2001). First, PBL works best with real-world problems because they are more likely to engage students and motivate them to want to learn more. Second, good problems are ill defined in the sense discussed in Chapter Four; they require students to decide what is relevant in the problem, what is not, and what additional information is needed. To add complexity but in measured doses, some PBL problems are "multistage, multipage"; students receive new information or new challenges at successive stages of the PBL process. Third, PBL problems must embed the content objectives; students should not be able to solve the problem without learning essential content for the course. Some PBL users state content objectives at the end of a PBL sequence so that students can reassure themselves that they have learned essential content. Finally, PBL problems must be complex enough to require teamwork.

Exhibit 10.1 describes a PBL activity from a first-year writing course to illustrate both the nature of the problem employed and the processes students worked through in order to solve it.

Exhibit 10.1. Problem-Based Learning in a First-Year Writing Course

The problem that opens the course places students in an imaginary internship team working for James Langevin, who was Rhode Island's Second District Congressman at the time of the assignment. Introduced in class, Phase One of the assignment tells students they will be writing campaign materials for Langevin's re-election campaign. Student teams meet to discuss what they know about Langevin, what more they need to know, where they might go to learn more, and who will pursue each line of inquiry. The assignment before the second class asks each "intern" to post a one-page fact sheet about Langevin to other members of their intern teams. In the second PBL class discussion, interns meet to synthesize their individual fact sheets into one two-page fact sheet, which they then post to the rest of the class.

Phase Two of the PBL assignment begins in the third class meeting. The problem sheet places students "on the job, loaded with good information about who Jim Langevin is." A Langevin aide meets with intern teams and tells them they are to work on "the embryonic stem cell controversy." In class, students meet to share what they know about the controversy and Langevin's position, what more they need to know, where they might find the information, and who will do the research. The assignment requires each student to post a one-page "Langevin on stem cells" fact sheet before the next class. In the next class each group combines, compiles and designs a fuller "Langevin on Stem Cells" fact sheet suitable for public consumption.

Phase Three of the problem is introduced in the fifth class meeting. Internship teams learn of a backlash following their Web posting of "Langevin on Stem Cells." Some of Langevin's strong supporters assumed he was strictly pro-life and feel betrayed by his public statements; others didn't know he was a "pro-life" Catholic and regret supporting him. To repair the damage, campaign managers announce a new plan to deploy intern teams as "Langevin Liaisons" to visit four different constituent groups. In a variation of the jigsaw strategy described in last chapter, interns are re-assigned to a new Langevin Liaison team and given one of four constituent groups to work with. Teams go to work identifying what they know, what they need to learn, what resources they'll consult, and who will do the research. In the following class, each liaison group drafts an informal report summarizing what they've learned and recommending responses.

In Phase Four (class meeting seven) of the problem, students return to their original intern teams, share what they've learned about the constituent groups, and create a plan of action that takes all four perspectives into consideration. The final task is to revise the information and design of the "Langevin on Stem Cells" posted on the Website to reflect the team's new plan of action.

Source: adapted from Elizabeth Miles, College Writing Program, University of Rhode Island.

Evaluations of PBL

PBL methodologies are relatively new in higher education, and few systematic evaluation studies have been done. The most comprehensive studies, including two meta-analyses, were conducted in medical education, where the PBL approach originated. Gradually, however, research in other disciplines is confirming many of the findings from earlier studies in medical education.

On the positive side, compared to students in more traditional instruction, PBL students report they are more satisfied with their learning experiences, attend class more regularly, are more interested in understanding concepts (as opposed to memorizing information in order to pass a test), and express greater confidence in their information-seeking skills and self-directed learning skills (Banta, Black, and Kline, 2000). Although some PBL skeptics worried early on that students in a PBL approach might suffer on knowledge acquisition goals, recent reviews find they do as well on tests of content knowledge as do students in traditional instruction, and PBL students show better retention, problem-solving skills, and transfer of learning (Banta, Black, and Kline, 2000; Hung, Bailey, and Jonassen, 2003; Edens, 2000).

Evaluation research has exposed some challenges for both students and faculty using PBL approaches. Students accustomed to traditional instruction and teacher-directed learning, as most first-year students are, often have a hard time adjusting to a PBL approach. They express frustration over the ambiguity of ill-structured problems and may criticize instructors for making unclear assignments (Edens, 2000). Some studies found that students in PBL classes felt they learned less than students in traditional courses because PBL covered fewer topics; the perception existed even in courses where final exams showed no difference in content knowledge (Banta, Black, and Kline, 2000; Edens, 2000; Lieux, 2001).

Because most first-year students are accustomed to more traditional, teacher-directed instruction and because they are inclined to measure learning in the number of topics covered, faculty contemplating PBL should expect some student resistance and anxiety. PBL instructors often emphasize a strong orientation for students, including clear statements of goals, a description of the PBL process in the syllabus, and discussion of student and instructor roles. Those who work with first-year students also say they build more structure into the PBL problems and include several feedback opportunities. The PBL activity described in Exhibit 10.1, for example, presents the problem in four phases and asks students to produce a written product, which then receives instructor feedback at each phase.

Faculty too must make adjustments when using a PBL approach. The initial time investment can be high. Creating PBL problems and making sure learning objectives are embedded in them is far more complex than creating problems or case studies for students to practice applying concepts. Providing ongoing feedback and support for student groups is also time-consuming. Then too, PBL requires changed faculty roles and responsibilities, and the changes can be unsettling at first. Kellah Edens (2000) described her first experience with PBL: "Problems also were present from my perspective, for, like the students, I confronted ambiguity. For example, I was not always certain that the students were really understanding and benefiting from the PBL process. It sometimes was difficult to refrain from divulging information or dispensing advice. The syllabus could not be planned in advance and followed in a straightforward manner. In contrast to 'keeping on schedule,' class sessions evolved at an unpredictable pace" (p. 60).

In spite of the initial uncertainties and the ongoing time commitment, research indicates that most faculty who have used PBL are enthusiastic about the approach and intend to continue using it. This is a powerful approach for transforming passive learners into active ones and for facilitating development of lifelong learning skills. In addition, faculty report that interaction with students seems more meaningful. Although some of our colleagues have completely transformed their courses to a PBL format, others have started by experimenting with a unit or two. This seems to us a sensible approach for assessing PBL's potential and our ability to manage a very different classroom.

Learning Communities

When we talk about learning communities, we refer to deliberate efforts to link or integrate courses, enroll cohorts of students in linked courses, and promote collaboration among students and faculty involved in the learning community. Learning communities enrolling first-year students tend to take one of three approaches: linked or clustered courses, freshman interest groups, and to a somewhat lesser extent, coordinated studies. These approaches probably achieve somewhat different goals and each can claim its own successes. We describe these approaches and then discuss the research with an eye toward identifying what faculty who teach first-year students might reasonably expect from each one.

Linked Courses

Perhaps the simplest approach to creating a learning community links two or more individually taught courses and requires students to coregister for both or all of them. The learning community often links basic skills courses and introductory courses in the various disciplines—a writing course and an introductory sociology course; a communications course and a political science course; or a calculus course, an introductory physics course, and a first-year seminar. Linking a large class with several sections of a course taught in smaller sections—writing courses or first-year seminars, for example—is one way to reduce the anonymity and isolation students often feel in a large class.

Efforts to integrate the content and activities of linked courses vary. Some faculty work closely with learning community colleagues to coordinate content coverage and assignments. Others go it alone, viewing the learning community primarily as a structure that helps students make connections with one another. At the University of Rhode Island, where more than 90 percent of first-year students enroll in learning communities that link one or two core courses with a required one-credit first-year seminar, efforts to help students integrate content of the linked courses fall mainly to instructors of the first-year seminar. These efforts are often difficult; faculty who teach the content courses (generally to a relatively large enrollment) are already awash in attending to the needs of the first-year students in their own courses. However, when connections can be drawn, students are the beneficiaries.

Freshman Interest Groups (FIGs)

In the freshman interest group model, twenty to thirty students form a learning community by registering for a cluster of courses related to a particular interest or theme: social justice, environmental studies, or even something more open-ended, such as the arts in modern society. Most courses in a FIG are regular curricular offerings that enroll both FIG and non-FIG students, but typically there is one course in which only FIG members are enrolled. It may be a small section of one of the courses involved or a special seminar created to enable the linking function.

At the University of Oregon, where FIGs originated, a one-credit College Connections course serves as the linking mechanism for two core courses. A Human Nature FIG, for example, includes core courses in philosophy and psychology plus College Connections. The Money and Power FIG combines core courses in political science and economics plus College Connections. A whimsical Rock 'n' Science learning community combines a music course, a physics of sound course, and College Connections. The University of Oregon (http://firstyear.uoregon.edu/figs/) lists more than fifty FIG offerings that give a sense of the rich possibilities inherent in this sort of clustering.

Like their colleagues in linked course learning communities, FIG faculty are not expected to coordinate course syllabi or activities. Efforts to integrate content usually fall to the course that serves as the linking mechanism—College Connections at the University of

Oregon, a first-year seminar at other institutions, designated sections of basic skills courses in some cases.

Integrated Studies Learning Communities

In the next model, two or more faculty from different disciplines collaborate to develop and teach an interdisciplinary course organized around an overarching theme or question. Also referred to as team-taught or coordinated studies learning communities, the integrated studies learning community approach is far more complex in terms of curricular integration and faculty roles. Although programs often record credits for discrete courses in the disciplines represented in the learning community, separate course structures blur or disappear altogether as faculty seek to integrate content, instruction, and assignments. The integrated studies learning community typically constitutes all or a major portion of a student's course load, and students register for blocks of class time, so instructional activities are not constrained by what can be accomplished in a standard course time frame. Faculty are free to mix sessions designed for all members of the learning community (lectures, films, outside speakers) with smaller group activities (workshops, seminars, lab sessions, group projects), and schedules can vary from week to week.

Portland State University's learning communities are an example of the coordinated studies approach. All first-year students register for one of eight to ten yearlong Freshman Inquiry courses developed by teams of faculty around interdisciplinary themes (such as Chaos and Community, Entering the Cyborg Millennium, Forbidden Knowledge, and Pathways to Sustainability and Justice). Freshman Inquiry constitutes a student's full course load. Each learning community limits enrollment to forty students; learning communities are further divided into three smaller group *peer mentor sessions* led by upper-division students. Content and assignments are introduced and explored initially in the larger learning community meetings; further exploration takes place in the peer mentor sessions. Although the themes and content of Freshman Inquiry courses differ, the overall goals are the same: developing basic communication skills (written, oral, numeric, graphic, and visual), learning to use current information technologies, and understanding the differences and what can be gained from looking at problems from various disciplinary perspectives.

In all three models of learning community, the linking mechanism is critical. Programs vary in terms of who is responsible for the linking courses. Some insist that full-time faculty (the more senior, the better) must be in charge. Others care less about faculty rank and look more for instructors interested and willing to spend time with first-year students. Most recognize the powerful role of peers and employ advanced undergraduates to aid faculty or conduct the linking courses by themselves.

Evaluation of Learning Communities

Learning communities are popular on campuses throughout the United States, a fact that is not surprising given the relatively low cost of implementation and the reasonably clear evidence of their beneficial impact. Kathe Taylor, William Moore, Jean MacGregor, and Jerri Lindblad (2003) of the National Learning Communities Project (NLCP) compiled a summary of research on their effectiveness for first-year students. They concluded that such practices increased student retention and enhanced academic achievement. In addition, they reported that both students and faculty involved in learning communities tended to view them in a positive light. Although these results are encouraging, the NLCP report also indicated that most studies had focused on easily quantifiable factors (GPA, persistence rate, and the like), and that much less attention had been given to more direct measures of student learning. Further, the NLCP cautioned that the wide variety of learning community structures made it difficult to pinpoint which strategies and which sort of linkage were most effective in promoting first-year student success (Taylor, Moore, MacGregor, and Lindblad, 2003).

More research will, of course, settle some of those issues. For now, we should probably think that learning communities in whatever form are a good idea. They seem unlikely to thwart instructional practices that would benefit first-year students, and they just may encourage both students and faculty to get more involved in the academic enterprise.

Service Learning

Service learning refers to instructional approaches that link community service and academic study so that each strengthens the other. Service learning is not only about establishing a laboratory for students to learn skills; nor is it only about community service. What distinguishes service learning from community service and a learning laboratory or internship is a clear and conscious linkage between the intellectual opportunity to explore and the civic obligation to provide assistance to the broader community. On the one hand, service learning activities enable students to see how what they learn in the college classroom plays out in the real world, practice applying what they are learning, develop important skills, and discover what they really care about. At the same time, the communities served benefit in myriad ways—attention to issues they face, person-hours needed to address those issues, the research students conduct and the ideas they bring, and the passion some develop for continuing attention to the issues.

Programs that engage first-year students in service learning vary considerably. Many are a one-shot affair often conducted in the context of an orientation program or first-year seminar. At the University of Rhode Island, for example, all first-year students participate in a service learning project in the context of their mandatory first-year seminar, URI 101. Several nonprofit agencies, school districts, and service organizations have collaborated with the university to create service opportunities in ten focus areas, among them children and families, the environment, health care, housing, hunger, literacy. The Feinstein Center for Service Learning schedules an eight-to-ten-hour service project in one of these areas for each of the more than one hundred sections of URI 101. The center staff also support faculty in ensuring that service learning experiences are meaningful by preparing fact sheets about the focus area, collecting information from the particular agencies served, and offering examples of discussion questions for students to consider before the service experience and afterward. (For additional information, see Richmond, 2002.)

In contrast to one-day service learning projects are those that ask students to invest substantial time over a semester or a year, sometimes even two years. The University of Maryland's College Park Scholars program is an example. Designed for academically talented students, the program is a thematically based, two-year program. Each of the twelve thematic programs incorporates service learning in some form. In early 2005, the program's Web page featured two examples: the Advocates for Children program, which brings elementary school children to campus for tutoring once a week; and the Media, Self, and Society program, which developed a video to educate children about homelessness (for further information, see http://www.scholars.umd.edu).

In between the daylong and two-year programs are discipline-based courses that have a service learning component. A first-semester general education chemistry course, for example, includes a service learning project involving lead-paint analysis (Kesner and Eyring, 1999). The project asks students to develop a dissemination strategy for alerting residents in older neighborhoods to the dangers involved in remodeling homes built before federal regulations prohibited inclusion of lead in paint. Having to explain the processes and dangers to others enhances students' understanding of the chemistry involved and deepens their understanding of implications. Students also collect and prepare paint samples from some homes for atomic absorption spectroscopic analysis. Collecting and preparing samples develops their laboratory skills. The community benefits from both the laboratory testing and the information on health hazards.

Another example comes from a Lynchburg College course in ethics. In the syllabus, the instructor (Friedman, 2003) lays out the rationale for the service learning component: "Understanding moral dilemmas and being able to respond to them appropriately requires having knowledge, but also a sensitivity and imagination about the problems and those (unfortunately) involved in them. One way to achieve this goal is to participate in a service learning experience." In brief, the assigned service learning project asks students to give four hours of service to one of several specified organizations, read relevant essays in the text, and use the service learning hours to become more informed about an ethical problem. After completing the service learning hours, students write a five-page essay in which they explain the ethical dilemma they have considered, the views involved, and how their service experience informed their personal views. The syllabus for this course and several others containing service learning ideas and activities can be viewed at the American Philosophical Association's Website (www.apa.udel.edu/apa/governance/committees/teaching/viewpost.asp?submitid=59).

Service learning also plays a role in a large introductory psychology course at the University of Utah. First-year students partnered with twelve community agencies that served clients whose needs bore some relationship to course content. A carefully orchestrated series of steps led students from orientation (both in-class and onsite) through intervention to organized reflective discussion. Students augmented their work at the agencies with a series of writing assignments that linked psychological theories to the clients they had served. The preparation of the students for their service and the structured process of reflection and feedback are an example of the attentiveness that successful service learning components require.

There are many more creative uses of service learning in first-year courses. A substantial collection of them (including the University of Utah course just described) is available at Campus Compact's Website (http://compact.org/resources).

Evaluation of Service Learning

Like the other approaches discussed in this chapter, service learning programs spread rapidly during the 1990s as institutions sought to respond to criticism of higher education, particularly that aimed at the paucity of civic engagement among students. The Second Annual

Survey of First-Year Academic Practices (Barefoot, 2002) found that approximately 60 percent of the institutions surveyed offered service learning in first-year courses. In their discussion of "key findings," however, the authors noted that student participation was not high, with 37 percent of the institutions that responded saying fewer than 10 percent of their first-year students participated in service learning opportunities. Only 10 percent of institutions said more than half their first-year students participate in service learning. These numbers may change as institutions and their faculty take note of the research that chronicles the impact of service learning on students.

Janet Eyler and Dwight Giles's extensive review (1999) of the evaluation and research literature on the impact of service learning identified an impressive array of dimensions on which service learning has had a positive impact: on academic performance, including increased motivation to learn, deeper understanding of subject matter, ability to analyze problems and apply knowledge; on personal and interpersonal development, including appreciation of diverse cultures, reduction in stereotyping, self-knowledge and self-efficacy, ability to work with others, leadership skills; and on feelings of connectedness, including connections with other students, with faculty, and with community. Subsequent studies both affirm and elaborate these findings (Astin, Vogelgesang, Ikeda, and Yee, 2000; Vogelgesang, Ikeda, Gilmartin, and Keup, 2002).

This research also suggests some characteristics and issues that faculty contemplating and planning service-learning initiatives should consider. Four of them seem particularly relevant to the use of service learning in first-year courses. The first issue revolves around the quality of student placements. Will placement sites allow students to exercise initiative, take responsibility, and do important work? How will sites benefit from students' service, and are the benefits real and significant?

Second, because real-life experience does not usually come bundled in learning packages nicely paced to correspond with what students are learning in class, students may miss important connections. When we plan service learning activities, we should consider issues such as: How in-sync will the service learning project be with what happens in class? Will students need prompting and guidance to see the connections between what they are studying in a course and experiencing in their service learning projects? What questions or assignments might enable students to make those connections?

Third, all of the research points to reflection as a major predictor of successful service learning and the types of outcomes achieved. Thinking about experience, however, is not an automatic activity and not something to leave to chance. We need to do a bit of reflection in advance: What types of reflection activity will work for this class—journal writing, e-mail exchange, cooperative learning group discussion, whole-class discussion? What prompts, questions, and assignments will allow students to share feelings about their service experiences but also challenge them to think critically and creatively about the issues and problems they encounter?

Finally, if a goal of the service learning project is to promote better understanding and relationships among people who differ, then we need to consider diversity issues in our planning. What dimensions of diversity will students likely encounter at the placement site? Would students benefit from preservice conversation about unfamiliar cultural practices, communication patterns, language use, conflict management, and so forth? Eyler and Giles (1999) report that many students say they discovered the people they worked with in their service learning projects were "just like me." Students do not always take the next step of asking, "If they're just like me, why are they . . . poor, homeless, victims of domestic violence, hungry?" These questions are the sort we can and ought to prompt in our students.

Conclusion

In contrast to the involvement activities described in the previous two chapters, problem-based learning, learning communities, and service learning require substantial transformation in course design; they may also entail curricular change at a department or even institutional level. At least initially, they require more time in planning because structure and support are crucial to their success. Even with that, however, these strategies can feel risky. Students not only need to be supported; they also must be deeply involved in the problem, in the community, or in the service project. We know there are at least some first-year students who are more interested in getting a requirement out of the way than they are in getting deeply involved in any of what we offer.

Should first-year instructors take on any of this? One way to approach this issue is to think about motivation. What instructional approaches motivate students for the short run and the long haul? Which strategies permit surface learning, and which require deep learning? Which activities have the potential for transforming students who simply want to get a requirement out of the way into students who are passionately interested in the stuff of our discipline, in their connection to classmates, and to community beyond the campus? There are many possible answers to these questions, but certainly problem-based learning, learning communities, and service learning have the promise to produce the kind of student and the kind of citizen that would make any institution proud.

For Further Exploration

- Laufgraben, J. L., Shapiro, N. S., and Associates. *Sustaining and Improving Learning Communities.* San Francisco: Jossey-Bass, 2004.

  Drawing on several sustained institutional examples, Laufgraben and Shapiro explore the characteristics of successful learning communities. Their focus is primarily at the institutional level, but there are a number of suggestions that faculty working in learning communities will find helpful.

- Problem-Based Learning Clearinghouse (https://chico.nss.udel .edu/Pbl; retrieved Jan. 2006).

  Although using this site requires registration, the time it takes to fill out the online form is well worth it. There are problems posted from a variety of disciplines, ranging from accounting to women's studies.

- Zlotkowski, E. (ed.). *Service Learning and the First-Year Experience: Preparing Students for Personal Success and Civic Responsibility* (Monograph no. 34). Columbia: National Resource Center for the First-Year Experience and Students in Transition, University of South Carolina, 2002.

  The examples of successful service learning programs included in this collection cover a range of institutional sizes and types. Because each chapter focuses on first-year students or students moving from secondary school to college, the discussions are especially relevant for faculty teaching first-year courses.

CHAPTER 11

Evaluating Student Learning

If faculty were to look at the exams some of their colleagues give, they would find it hard not to sympathize with student complaints about exams and mistrust of what faculty say about assessment practices. Questions such as these do not inspire confidence that we measure significant learning or that we measure it well:

In the film series, Carol Rogers responded to Gloria with

A. Tears

B. Anger

C. A dinner invitation

D. Acceptance and caring

Long-range goals are usually achieved

A. By people with determination

B. In the distant future

C. By setting short-term goals

D. All of the above

Comment on this quote by Flaubert: "The author in his work must be like God in the universe, present everywhere and visible nowhere."

Fill in blanks with the correct word(s). (20 points)

A. The most important metaphysical idea in Taoism is _____.

B. Wei-wu-wei means _____.

C.   The Way eternal has no _____.

D.   A block of _____ untooled, though small, may still excell [*sic*] the world.

Obvious, trivial, ambiguous, and indecipherable test questions are only the tip of the iceberg, however. Beneath the surface of many evaluation policies and practices lie problems that threaten the validity of the entire process. They are all the more serious because, unlike the questions shown here, they often go undetected by otherwise competent teachers.

For starters, we claim that understanding and thinking are the most important goals in our courses, but the evidence reveals most tests require simple recall of information (Milton, Pollio, and Eison, 1986; Ratcliff, 1994). We often blame multiple choice tests for this state of affairs, but essay questions fare little better under close scrutiny. Consider, for example, this essay assignment, which appears to require fairly complex analytical skills:

> An "initiation" story dramatizes a naïve, childlike character going through a difficult, painful, or bewildering experience that initiates him or her into a view of the world that the reader perceives as more realistic or mature. Compare and contrast the initiation patterns in two of the following short stories: "Editha," "The Open Boat," "The Bride Comes to Yellow Sky," and "I Want to Know Why."

Suppose, however, students have just spent a week or two discussing the initiation patterns in each of these short stories, noting similarities and differences along the way. To write the essay, students need only remember what was said in class.

Many essay questions masquerade as tests of complex thinking skills when, in fact, they can be answered on the basis of recall. The problem, then, is not that we give too many multiple choice tests and too few essay tests but rather that neither form tests the learning outcomes we claim are most important. In measurement language, this is a *validity* problem.

A second major problem in evaluation is that we do not do enough of it. We would not think of basing scholarly conclusions on one observation in a laboratory or on one passage in a text, but we often reach a conclusion as to what students know or do not know about a topic on the basis of one test question or one paper assignment. Little wonder we lack confidence in our evaluations. *Reliability* is always in doubt when evaluation is based on too few observations.

A third problem is that assessment practices may systematically "advantage" some students and "disadvantage" others. Lewis (1997), for example, points out that a statistics exam asking students to determine the probability of a poker hand puts students who do not know how to play poker at a distinct disadvantage. To take another example, several self-evaluation schemes, including those we suggest in the final section of this chapter, pose a different challenge to students accustomed to crediting accomplishment to others than to students accustomed to claiming credit for their work. Because most of our assessment practices favor some learning styles over others, advocates of institution-wide assessment initiatives stress that we need to offer students a variety of ways to demonstrate their learning (Sedlacek, 1993; Suskie, 2000).

This chapter is no substitute for a good measurement and evaluation text, but in the space available we explore how faculty might increase the validity, reliability, and inclusiveness of their assessment practices. We begin with discussion of multiple choice questions and then turn to essay assignments, the two most common forms of assessment in an introductory course. The final section suggests alternative assessment strategies that faculty might consider in order to fill the assessment gaps or diversify assessment practices. Faculty should be aware of the strengths and weaknesses of various forms of assessment, and we spend some time on those issues, but little is to be gained from an either-or debate. Most faculty, especially those teaching first-year courses, need to combine several assessment types if their evaluation is to be valid, reliable, and fair to diverse students.

Multiple Choice Questions

Multiple choice questions are the most widely used and highly regarded form of "objective" test item. Because they have the potential to assess a variety of learning outcomes, obtain a broad sample of student work, and vary contexts in which problems might be embedded, multiple choice questions in theory can increase the validity, reliability, and inclusiveness of evaluation practices. In practice, too many multiple choice tests require nothing more than recall of memorized information, much of it trivial and the rest of it disconnected from anything important. Multiple choice questions are not to blame; the people who write them are.

At their best, multiple choice questions can test perhaps not the full range but certainly a wide range of the learning outcomes described in Chapter Four. Exhibit 11.1 includes examples of multiple choice questions that test knowledge, understanding, and application of concepts.

These examples merit study not only because they challenge the claim that multiple choice questions test only rote memorization but also because they offer patterns for creating items that test a range of

Exhibit 11.1. Multiple Choice Questions to Assess a Range of Objectives

Knowledge: Remembering important ideas

Which of the following statements best captures the meaning of Charles Taylor's statement that the development of individualism in modern societies has produced a "narrowing" of people's lives?

A. People's lives have become stressful because they are confronted with a growing number of difficult decisions.

B. People's lives have become separated from the social settings that once provided them meaning and purpose.

C. People's lives have become complicated because of the scale and scope of most contemporary societies.

D. People's lives have become lonely and isolated as a result of the time pressures created by modern society.

Understanding: Recognizing ideas in specific contexts or forms

Which of the following observations about American society is most consistent with Charles Taylor's claim that many people believe that individualism is "the finest achievement of modern civilization"?

A. The widespread belief that freedom is an essential to a good society.

B. The widespread belief that good government must be run efficiently.

C. The widespread belief that good people are no longer very common.

D   The widespread belief that part of a good life consists of helping others.

Thinking: Applying ideas in new situations

In Henrik Ibsen's play, *A Doll's House*, the following dialogue takes place:

> Helmer: First and foremost, you are a wife and a mother.
> Nora: That I don't believe anymore. I believe first and
>   foremost I am an individual just as much as you are.

Which of the following statements best summarizes how Charles Taylor would most likely respond to the tension embedded in this dialogue?

A. The tension between Helmer and Nora is evidence of the problems caused by individualism in modern societies. Nora's assertion that she is more than a wife and mother illustrates the destabilizing nature of individualism. Helmer's claim that she is first and foremost a member of a family is the sort of connectedness that is undermined by the widespread belief in self-fulfillment.

B. The tension between Helmer and Nora is really not related to the central features of modern society. Nora's assertion that she is an individual, although it seems to illustrate a commitment to individualism, is really a rejection of tradition. Helmer's claim that she is a wife and mother, although it seems to be restrictive, is really an attempt to find fulfillment through connections to others.

C. The tension between Helmer and Nora is the foundation of modern individualism. Nora's assertion that she is more than a wife and mother illustrates the liberating aspect of the modern emphasis on self-fulfillment. Helmer's claim that she is primarily defined by her social position is the sort of oppressiveness from which the modern commitment to individualism provides protection.

objectives. Faculty are, of course, well acquainted with multiple choice questions that ask students to remember information or ideas. It is worth noting, however, that the example in the "knowledge" category does not merely check attendance; it asks students to recall a key idea.

The second question illustrates one way to determine whether students see the relationship between a general idea and a specific example—one test of their understanding. The stem of the question presents an example and asks which concept or principle it illustrates; the choices present possible concepts or principles. Alternatively, the stem of the question might present a generalization and ask students to identify an example from possibilities given in the choices.

Multiple choice questions designed to test the ability to use knowledge in a variety of situations almost always present a problem or situation in the stem of the question and ask students to select the best solution, explanation, or conclusion from four or five choices. These questions tend to be longer and more complex because solutions, conclusions, and explanations do not usually come in single words or simple phrases. These questions are also more difficult to write; we must think of several plausible explanations or conclusions and we need to be sure one is better than the rest. Nonetheless, it can be done. Rejecting multiple choice questions on the grounds that they can test only memorization is neither a defensible position nor a sensible practice.

A second criticism of multiple choice questions—that students study differently for multiple choice tests than they do for essay tests (McKeachie, 2002)—is less easily reconciled. Student descriptions of their study activities indicate that in preparing for multiple choice tests they seek to memorize factual information, often exactly as it was presented. Their reports on preparing for essay tests reveal more concern for understanding and contain more references to activities such as writing summaries, drawing diagrams, working problems, and asking themselves questions. Such findings are not particularly surprising. Too many multiple choice tests require simple recall of information. If we were to write questions that called for thinking, students might learn to study differently for them. We do not change assumptions and study habits by pronouncement or overnight; therefore how students prepare for a multiple choice test merits our concern. Including at least one essay question on an exam is a way to encourage students to study more deeply for it. Handing out the stems of multiple choice questions beforehand also works to challenge students' assumptions about this type of item and to prompt the deeper processing activities typically elicited by essay exams.

To summarize our discussion so far, multiple choice questions can test a variety of learning objectives and allow the instructor to obtain a broader sample of student work. For those who use multiple choice items, our most important advice is to make sure the questions test a variety of learning outcomes. In addition, we offer these suggestions.

Suggestions for Using Multiple Choice Questions

- *Start writing multiple-choice questions during the first week of the course and try to write four or five questions each week.* A good multiple choice exam cannot be created the night before the exam. Good questions are difficult to write, and the exam requires more of them than an essay-only exam does. Writing a few questions each week makes the task more manageable.

- *Make the distracters (the wrong choices) plausible and attractive to the uninformed, but avoid trick questions.* Some multiple-choice questions fail because the distracters are obviously incorrect, while others suffer because the distracters contain errors too subtle for students at a given level to detect. Creating good distracters is the most difficult task in writing multiple choice questions. Some tactics may help: (1) think about the errors students make or the misconceptions they hold; (2) mention relevant concepts or ideas in the distracter but misstate the relationships among them; or (3) ask questions that require a conclusion *and* explanation. This last one is a particularly fruitful tactic for generating more distracters because correct conclusions can be combined with incorrect explanations. The third question in Exhibit 11.1 illustrates this tactic.

- *Make all choices approximately the same length.* In creating a correct or a best answer, we must often qualify or elaborate a statement, making the correct answer longer than the alternatives. Test-wise students can select the correct answer on the basis of its length.

- *Be careful about words such as* always, never, all, none, *or* only. Few things in a college course can be stated in absolute terms, and test-wise students automatically eliminate choices that contain them.

- *Make all choices grammatically consistent with the stem of the question.* Sometimes students select the correct answer simply on the basis of grammatical rules. Watch especially the use of singulars and plurals, subject and verb agreement, and use of the articles *a* and *an*.

- *Avoid negative wording whenever possible.* Negatives usually make a question unnecessarily complicated and confusing. When using negatives, underline them.

- *Avoid choices such as "all of the above," "none of the above," and combinations such as "both A and C" or "only A and C."* From a measurement perspective, some of these choices are more acceptable than others, but rules exist for determining which are acceptable and how they should be used. By and large, these alternatives are not worth the attention they require or the trouble they make.

- *Rotate the position of the correct answer randomly.* For some reason, faculty tend to place the correct answer in one of the two middle positions. Test-wise students know this and increase their chances of guessing correctly by selecting choice *B* or *C*.

- *Avoid reinventing the wheel by using test banks whenever possible, but be careful.* Although textbooks often have test banks for each chapter, not all items are well constructed or designed to test anything beyond memorization.

- *Take advantage of computer programs for preparing and scoring multiple choice exams.* Exam preparation software (available commercially or sometimes free from publishing houses) or common word processors make it easy to create several versions of a test by scrambling the order of questions and the order of choices—both must-do deterrents to cheating. Most campuses have optical mark readers that can quickly score multiple choice tests and produce results in a form easily pasted into an electronic grade book. Optical scanning also permits quick item analysis, which shows how many students answered each question correctly and how many selected each distracter; this information can be helpful in reviewing and revising an exam.

Essay Questions and Other Writing Assignments

Although we use the word *essay* throughout this section, most of what we say also applies to paper assignments, lab reports, and even the sort of problem one finds on exams in the sciences and mathematics. Certainly, these evaluation techniques differ, but they have one important characteristic in common: they all require students to *produce* an answer rather than *select* one. For this reason, they have similar advantages and uses, share related problems, and require attention to the same issues if they are to be used appropriately.

Perhaps the major advantage of essay questions is that they can test a range of learning outcomes, including complex thinking and problem-solving skills. In addition, essays usually permit more inspection of students' thinking processes than do multiple choice items. Last, although creating a good essay question is no simple task, most faculty find it easier to write a good essay question than to write good multiple choice items.

Relying only on essay exams and written assignments, however, creates major problems. Obtaining an adequate sample of student performance is difficult because time limits both how many essays or papers students can write and how many we can grade. Exclusive use of these assessment forms often means that evaluation is based on too small a sample of student work. Equally serious, grading of essays is notoriously unreliable. Research shows that essay grades vary, often dramatically, when two or more faculty grade the same essay or when a single instructor grades an essay at two separate times. Finally, as most faculty know, it is time-consuming to grade essays.

Despite these drawbacks, the possibilities for assessing complex learning and thinking make the essay question a useful complement to other forms of assessment. Our suggestions for effective use focus first on creating the questions themselves and then on techniques for improving the reliability and efficiency of grading.

Suggestions for Using Essay Questions and Other Written Assignments

- *Reserve essay questions and papers for assessing higher-order thinking skills.* Let multiple choice questions test recall, understanding by way of example, and application in a structured situation. Save essays and paper assignments for assessing analytic, synthetic, and creative thinking in more complex and ill-structured situations.

- *Develop clear instructions and make expectations explicit.* This is easier said than done, but the paired questions included in Exhibit 11.2 illustrate effort in the direction of clarity. Verbs such as *defend, explain, compare, argue, illustrate,* and *predict* are more precise than *discuss, comment on,* or *react to.* Listing topics to address or components to include in the essay further clarifies expectations.

Writing clear instructions for essay assignments that call for higher-order thinking skills is far more challenging than most who talk about this form of assessment acknowledge. To be sure, the second question in each pair of examples in Exhibit 11.2 is clearer than the first, but much still remains written between the lines. What are "the visual elements" to consider in a painting? What constitutes support and evidence in a sociology course? To phrase it more generally, implicit in most writing assignments are conventions governing how people within a discipline approach issues and problems, what questions they consider, what they regard as support or evidence, and how they communicate with one another. At best, un-

Exhibit 11.2. Examples of "Less Clear" and "Clearer"
Instructions for Essays and Papers

Essay exam question in an introductory Art History course

Less clear: Compare and contrast emotions or ideas conveyed in the two paintings shown on slides: Edvard Munch's *Anxiety* and Georges Seurat's *Sunday Afternoon on the Island of La Grande Jatte.*

More clear: Compare and contrast the emotions or ideas conveyed in the two paintings shown on slides: Edvard Munch's *Anxiety* and Georges Seurat's *Sunday Afternoon on the Island of La Grande Jatte.* Support and develop your interpretations by discussing the artists' *representation of the subjects*, the *visual elements*, and the *titles of the paintings*.

Opinion paper assignment in an introductory Sociology course

Less clear: I have reproduced below a piece by Nicholas D. Kristof, a columnist for the *New York Times* (the article is attached to this assignment). As you'll see, Kristof stakes out a definite position on what Ignatieff calls "the Islamic challenge" to human rights. I'd like you to compose a response to Kristof's take on the role and treatment of women in the kingdom of Saudi Arabia. In a sense, Kristof himself poses the issue I want you to address. Toward the end of his essay he asks: "Is it paternalistic of us in the West to try to liberate women who insist that they're happy as they are?"

A more clear option includes the instructions above, but adds the following explication of expectations: Your essay should state your position on this issue, provide examples or other evidence to support your position, identify alternative positions or challenges to your position, and refute the alternatives or challenges.

---

dergraduates are just beginning to learn those conventions. If instruction prior to the exam does not make those conventions explicit, it should come as no surprise when students say they spend a lot of time "trying to figure out what the instructor wants."

Students' different developmental positions also come into play in determining clarity of essay exams and paper assignments. Many disciplinary conventions for interpretation, argumentation, and analysis run counter to views held by students who are in a position of dualism or multiplicity, making it even less likely that undergraduates will think of these conventions without explicit prompting on the exam and self-conscious practice during instruction. Familiarity with the research summarized in Chapter Two can aid faculty in determining which expectations need to be emphasized, practiced during instruction, and explicated in exam questions or paper assignments.

- *Try specifying a genre other than "essay."* Colleagues in college composition programs remind us that the traditional "five-paragraph academic essay" is not used widely outside the college classroom, and an assignment to write in this genre tends not to inspire much interest among students. They advise that we try instead to create writing assignments that simulate the purpose, audience, and context in which people actually write about the questions and issues posed in our courses. Alternative genres might be a letter to the editor of a newspaper, correspondence with family or friends, a journal conversation with oneself, a review for a newspaper, a briefing for an employer or supervisor, an application for an assistantship or internship, a page of frequently asked questions, a proposal for funding, an explanation for more novice learners, or a letter to a congressperson. (For more detailed critique of traditional essay assignments and suggestions for alternatives, see Suskie, 2004.)

- *Offer students choices in essay tests.* There is debate about this recommendation. Measurement texts tend to advise against offering choices, arguing that essay options are never of equal difficulty and recommending in the interest of fairness that we ask students "to run the same race." Others argue that a single essay question is unlikely to be of equal interest or concern to all students in a class. Offering choices is the fairer approach because it tends to equalize motivational influences and has more potential for enabling students to put forward best evidence of what they have learned.

Our thinking has changed on this issue. Although we deferred to the advice of measurement texts for many years, we are now of a different mind, persuaded by those who have shown us what students achieve when they are concerned about an issue, when they are interested in a task, when they *care* beyond getting a grade. We are not to the point of advocating completely open-ended choices to first-year students. Instructions to "Write about anything you want to" or "What is your opinion on _____?" give too little structure. There are, however, ways to structure essay questions and assignments and still offer choices. We might, for example, offer a limited number of questions or topics and invite students to select one or two. Keeping the topic the same but specifying different audiences or genres is another strategy for offering choice to students.

Exhibit 11.3. Analytic Scoring Guide for an Introductory
Sociology Paper Assignment

The essay assignment is worth 10 points, to be assigned as follows:

Thesis statement: 2 points

A thesis statement clearly states the student's opinion and addresses the issue.

Arguments supporting the position: 3 points

The essay includes arguments and examples that support the position stated. Reasons and examples are original (i.e., drawn form the student's own observations of people and society) and persuasive.

Identification of alternative position(s): 2 points

The essay identifies alternative positions or counterarguments. Alternative positions are worth mentioning; they are not silly or trivial.

Arguments refuting alternative positions or counterarguments: 3 points

The essay includes arguments and examples that refute the alternative positions or counterarguments. Again, reasons and examples are original and persuasive.

- *Create and use a scoring guide—a rubric, to use current assessment language—for grading written work.* Earlier, we stressed that the unreliability of grading is a major drawback in using essay tests, papers, and similar techniques to assess learning. Eliminating the problem is unlikely, but using a scoring guide is the most important thing faculty can do (practically speaking) to control the shifting of standards that inevitably takes place when reading a collection of essays and papers.

One approach for creating a scoring guide identifies important components or traits of an essay response and defines levels or points available for each component. As faculty read an essay, they award points for each component up to the limit specified by the scoring guide and then total the points to determine the essay's grade. The example in Exhibit 11.3 illustrates this approach for one of the essay assignments presented earlier.

An approach that takes the analytic scoring guide a step further is the "primary trait analysis" (PTA) advocated by Barbara Walvoord and Virginia Johnson Anderson (1998). To transform the scoring guide in Exhibit 11.3 into a PTA, we would develop descriptive scales for each component or trait identified. The scale for "thesis statement," for example, might read:

Thesis Statement (2 Points Possible)

2.– Essay clearly states a position on the issue posed in the assignment.

1.– Student's position can be inferred, but essay does not state it explicitly.

0.– Essay does not even hint at a position on the issue, or it states a position unrelated to the issue posed in the assignment.

The PTA approach would include similar descriptive scales for each primary component. Walvoord and Anderson make a strong case for PTA, especially when assignments "count" a lot, and they present numerous examples drawn from several disciplines.

An alternative, more holistic, approach to creating scoring guides assumes that a successful essay or paper may be something other than the sum of its parts. An essay or paper containing one or two original, insightful ideas, perhaps not full-fledged and maybe supported by less-than-conclusive evidence, might nonetheless be equal or superior to an essay that presents "old-hat" ideas supported by "easy" or "safe" evidence. In such a situation, faculty say they sometimes feel trapped by more analytic scoring guides, forced into rewarding hackneyed ideas and lackluster evidence if it is abundant while prevented from rewarding a creative or novel idea supported by one or two telling examples or an intriguing line of argument. A holistic scoring guide may allow escape from such a trap because it permits some flexibility in the weighting of components.

Like the analytic scoring guides described earlier, the holistic approach begins by identifying the main components or traits that figure in evaluation of the essay or paper. Instead of assigning a range of points for each component or developing scales for individual traits, however, holistic scoring guides use the traits to describe the characteristics that distinguish excellent, good, competent, and not-so-competent essays. Exhibit 11.4 is an example.

In addition to improving the reliability of grading written work, a scoring guide has other advantages. It makes grading easier and faster. Giving students the scoring guide when making

Exhibit 11.4. Holistic Scoring Guide for an Introductory
        Sociology Paper Assignment

The essay assignment is worth 10 points, to be awarded as follows:

The 10-9 essay clearly states a position on the issue, provides support for the position, identifies at least one counterargument or alternative view, and refutes it. The evidence, both in support of the position and in refutation of counterarguments, is persuasive and original (i.e., drawn from the student's own observations or thoughts, not borrowed). The essay tackles significant alternative positions or counterarguments, not trivial ones.

The 8-7 essay states a position, supports it, raises one or more counterarguments, and refutes them. The essay contains one or more of the following ragged edges, however: evidence is not uniformly persuasive or original; counterargument is not a very serious challenge to the position; there may be one or two compelling arguments/examples, but the rest is lackluster.

The 6 essay states a position and raises counterargument, but one or both is not well developed. Also, the counterargument may lean toward the trivial. Nonetheless, the essay receives 6 points in acknowledgement of the cognitive complexity of the task. It is more difficult to consider multiple positions/perspectives than it is to find examples supporting one point of view.

The 5 essay states a position and provides original and persuasive support for the position. However, the essay does not raise or identify alternative positions or possible counterarguments, a key requirement in the assignment.

The 4-3 essay states a position and provides some support, but it does not do it very well. Evidence is scanty, general, trivial, or not original. Overall, the impression is that the essay was dashed off without much thought.

The 2-1 essay does not state the student's position or ideas. Instead, it summarizes what the text or the instructor said. The essay may include "I agree with" or "I disagree with" statements, but it contains little beyond what was said in class or in readings. The essay receives 1 or 2 points only because there may be some merit in reading the text and coming to class.

---

an assignment helps clarify expectations. Distributing the guide when returning graded essays or assignments tells students the grading criteria, reduces the need for writing extensive comments on written work, and focuses conversation with students who want to dispute a grade.

- *Once essays or papers are submitted, read a sample to see how they compare with your expectations, standards, and scoring guide.* If many students are missing the same point, confusing the same issues, or otherwise not meeting the standards, take another look at the question or assignment or the scoring guide. If the problem lies in the essay instructions or in an overly exuberant scoring guide, the time to adjust criteria or standards is *before* grading begins, not partway through.

- *If an exam includes more than one essay question, read all responses to one question before moving on to the next.* If we read one student's answers to several questions, our evaluation on any one question is likely to be influenced by the responses to other questions.

- *Grade essays and papers with the students' names hidden from view.* This practice guards against being influenced by a student's personality or our knowledge of the student's previous work.

Other Forms of Assessment

Multiple choice and essay questions offer a good beginning repertoire of assessment techniques for faculty who teach first-year students because the strengths in one form tend to compensate for the weaknesses in the other. Used in combination, multiple choice and essay questions can assess a wider range of learning outcomes and obtain more samples of student work than either could do alone.

These techniques are limited, however, even in combination. They do not, for example, generate assessment of important skills acquired through a group project, cooperative learning activity, or team learning project such as those described in Chapters Eight and Nine. They often miss and sometimes even obscure students' efforts to take intellectual risks, test new ideas or approaches, or pursue something in greater depth. They do not ask students to reflect on their learning, an activity that promotes development of metacognitive skills in addition to giving instructors useful assessment information. Assessing contributions to group work, self-reflection activities, and portfolios are three ways to fill these assessment gaps in first-year courses.

Strategies for Assessing Contribution to Group Work

If faculty want to evaluate only the disciplinary content and skills individual students acquire through group work, then traditional forms of assessment—exams, papers, oral reports—may be enough. Many faculty and students engaged in these learning activities, however, are also interested in who contributed *what* and *how much* to final projects and the learning they reflect. Colleagues tell us they have found three activities particularly helpful in assessing those contributions.

Writing minutes for group meetings. Asking groups to keep minutes of their meetings and submit them periodically is one way to monitor progress and assess individual contributions to the group. Winifred Brownell, professor of speech communications and dean of URI's College of Arts and Sciences, passed this idea on to us. She noted that, in addition to its value for assessing individual contribution to a group, the assignment to keep minutes of group meetings—more than any other strategy she had tried—reduced complaints about individuals not doing a fair share of group work.

When using the assignment with first-year students, it is probably a good idea to offer at least initially some structure for the "minutes." Instructions might ask that the minutes name group members present; report briefly on each group member's work since their last meeting and on his or her contribution to the current meeting; summarize the issues raised and topics discussed in the meeting; and outline each member's assignment for the next meeting.

Peer evaluations of individual contribution. Asking group members to evaluate each other's contributions to a group is a widely used assessment practice for group projects. The peer review form in Exhibit 11.5 is a beginning template we offer to faculty who wish to use peer evaluation forms.

Self-assessment of contribution to group work. Asking students to reflect on their own contribution to group work produces yet another perspective on individual functioning in groups. Most peer review forms are easily converted to a self-assessment form, and using the same form permits comparison between self- and peer reviews, a process that often leads to further reflection and learning. Alternatively, self-assessment forms may take the form of two or three open-ended questions:

- Overall, how would you rate your contributions to the group: more than other members, about the same as other members, less than other members?
- What do you think have been your major contributions to the group so far?
- What else might you do to increase the effectiveness of your group or improve the quality of your group's final project?

Exhibit 11.5. Peer Review of Contributions to Group Work

Group member being reviewed: _____

Listed below are some behaviors and skills that contribute to effective group work. Please rate this group member's performance of these skills by circling a letter corresponding to the following scale:

a)   Little or no improvement needed (almost always does this in really positive ways)
b)   Some improvement needed (sometimes does this, but not always or not always in positive ways)
c)   Much improvement needed (does not do this often enough or does it in ways that are not constructive.

a   b   c   1) Attended group meetings, arriving on time and staying until the end.

a   b   c   2) Came to meetings well prepared.

a   b   c   3) Helped the group be organized.

a   b   c   4) Contributed ideas and made thoughtful suggestions.

a   b   c   5) Listened to and built upon the ideas of others.

a   b   c   6) Did his/her fair share of the work.

What do you think was this person's most important contribution to the group?

What else would you like to say about this person's contributions to the group?

Student Self-Assessment

When we write about student self-assessment, we are not referring to a practice that asks students to give themselves a grade and perhaps explain why they should receive it. The activities described here begin instead by asking students to reflect on their study activities and assignments and consider how this work relates to their personal interests and motivations as well as their achievement of course goals. Self-assessment is useful both as a learning activity and as an assessment practice.

Myself as learner. Assignments that ask students to reflect on their learning styles and approaches are widely used in first-year seminars but are perhaps even more useful in content area courses. An assignment at the end of the first class, for example, might ask students to read the syllabus closely and respond to these questions:

- What did you do to study for this subject in high school?
- What seems different about this course?

- What do you think will be the most challenging aspects of this course for you?
- What do you plan to do to be sure you can meet those challenges?
- How might our teaching assistants and I help you succeed in this course?

Critical incidents. Critical-incident assignments ask students to identify and describe aspects of their learning experience that stand out for them. An example we have used asks students: "Looking back on your work during the past two weeks in this course, what discussion or activity stands out from the rest and seems like something you'll remember or think more about? In two or three paragraphs (no more than two pages), describe what happened, your thoughts about the incident, and why you think you'll remember it."

Other critical incident prompts ask students to identify and reflect on activities they found particularly relevant, meaningful, surprising, puzzling, or encouraging. Stephen Brookfield, a long-time advocate of such assignments and the one who brought the approach to our attention, offers a rich array of specific assignments and helpful discussion on how to use them (Brookfield, 1990; Brookfield and Preskill, 1999).

Postwrites. Used widely in composition courses, a postwrite assignment asks students to reflect on the process of preparing their papers or projects and on the quality of the work they are submitting. One example of a postwrite assignment (Reynolds, 1999) gives students ten minutes in class the day an assignment is due to respond to these questions:

- How did writing this assignment go? What went well and what didn't?
- State the thesis of your essay and identify your best piece of evidence to support that thesis.
- Who has read your paper or heard your ideas before me? Who was helpful, and what did that person suggest?
- How can I help you most in my response? Please be specific in identifying the sections you think still need the most work and why you think so.

Postexam reflection. Because so many introductory courses rely on exams to assess learning, asking students to reflect on their exam performance may be the most practical way to engage them in practicing metacognitive skills while producing assessment information for the instructor. A postexam reflection assignment might ask students to write a paragraph responding to the questions here:

- Does your exam performance suggest you understand some topics or chapters better than others? Looking at the questions you missed, were they focused on one or a few topic areas, or were they spread across the content covered by the exam?
- Does your exam performance show you did better on some aspects of learning than on others? How did you do on questions that asked you to remember important information or ideas? How did you do on questions that asked you to do something else, such as consider examples not discussed in class or solve new problems?
- On the basis of your analysis of this exam, what do you think you need to focus on in order to thrive in this course?
- How might our teaching assistants and I support your learning efforts?

Midterm self-assessment. Policies on many campuses require faculty to submit midterm grades for first-year students. Required or not, midterm assessment is an opportunity to ask students to reflect on their study practices for the course. A midterm self-assessment might ask students to write responses to questions such as:

- How do you study for this course on a regular (class-to-class) basis? How do you prepare for exams?
- Which of your study activities do you think are most effective and least effective? Please explain why you think so.
- Which study practices do you intend to continue for the remainder of the semester? What changes, if any, do you intend to make?

Portfolios

A portfolio is a collection of student work showing what the student has learned and accomplished over a period of time. A portfolio is not, however, simply a folder, notebook, or Web page containing everything a student has done. Three characteristics distinguish a portfolio from other collections of student work: *variety* in the work considered in evaluation processes, student *choice* in what goes into a portfolio, and student *reflection* on what the contents of a portfolio mean (Reynolds, 2000; Suskie, 2004; Walvoord and Anderson, 1998).

Variety. The emphasis in portfolio assessment on variety in work considered in evaluation processes acknowledges differences in interest and motivation among students who have mastered course content and skills. The assignment to write a five-paragraph or five-page academic essay may bore a student to tears, but he or she might really get into preparing an annotated list of "talking points" for a public debate or preparing a "frequently asked questions" brochure for future students. A course portfolio invites students to select and include those assignments in which they are most interested and that show their best work.

Most first-year students are unaware of the numerous ways in which they might show what they have learned; many are cautious about deviating from conventional evaluation practice. If we want first-year students to consider alternative ways to document their learning, we may have to begin by *requiring* them to experiment. Assignments leading up to portfolio assembly might require students to prepare an academic paper on one topic, a brochure on a second, a letter to the editor on another, and perhaps a conference poster presentation for a fourth selection. Our earlier section on essay questions suggested several genres for written work. For additional ideas about writing assignments and other ways in which students might show what they know and can do, see Maki, 2004; Suskie, 2004; Zubizarreta; 2004.

Student choice. Allowing students some flexibility in what to include is the second principle of portfolio assessment. As noted earlier, the portfolio is not a catch-all for everything students do in a course or even for every assignment they revise. Rather, portfolio assignments ask students to select and submit work that is the best documentation of their learning and accomplishments. Upper-division course and program portfolios give students considerable leeway in constructing their portfolios; first-year courses tend to include more structure and guidance about what students should include.

Faculty who use course portfolios take different approaches in providing guidance. In her first-year writing courses, Reynolds (2000) asks students to select and revise three of six assignments completed during the semester, any five additional pages that show their best work, and a reflective essay on why they selected the pieces they did and what those submissions show. Suskie (2004) describes an alternative approach that asks students to include four assignments in their portfolios: one showing their research skills, one demonstrating writing skills, a third showing their ability to use a particular concept to solve a problem, and the one from which they feel they learned the most. Other guidelines might ask students to include assignments that demonstrate their understanding of a particular topic, their mastery of a designated skill, their ability to use what they have learned in a new setting, and the type of work that they find more and less interesting.

A practice that seems especially useful in helping first-year students select what to include in a portfolio is the "time to decide" conference described by Reynolds (2000). In her introductory writing classes, individual or small-group "time-to-decide" conferences take place two or three weeks before the end of the term. Before the conference, she asks students to think about these questions:

- What do you want your portfolio to show (e.g., improvement, flexibility in writing style, creativity, steadfastness)?
- Which piece could you start working on right now, knowing you could make it better? Which do you have most energy for revisiting? Which would you dread working on again?
- In which piece do your strengths really shine?
- Which topic made you want to find more information or do some more research?

In addition to their writing folders, students must bring to the time-to-decide" conference a revision plan for at least one entry they want to include in their portfolio and possible other entries with ideas about each.

Student reflection on the portfolio. The third defining characteristic of portfolio assessment is the key to the power of the portfolio for learning and assessment. The portfolio often includes reflection on individual assignments, such as those described in the previous section of this chapter. Most portfolios go beyond such an assignment and ask students to reflect holistically on the content they have chosen to include and what the choices are meant to convey. This more holistic reflection often takes the form of a cover letter or introduction that previews what the portfolio is designed to show, what is included in the portfolio, and how each entry relates to the overall purpose; other options are possible. For example, the student's introduction might indicate what the portfolio is designed to show and preview its content; reflection before or after an individual entry might explain how each entry relates to the overall purpose; and a concluding statement might sum it all up.

The student reflection required in most forms of portfolio assessment gets directly at the development and assessment of students' metacognitive skills——the ability to think about their own thinking and learning. Earlier chapters discussed the important role of metacognition in enabling students to set learning goals, recognize the difference between surface and deep learning, monitor and regulate their study strategies, and become self-directed, lifelong learners. The reflective pieces required in portfolio assessment highlight the importance of those skills and engage students in practicing them. Student reflection also gives faculty a unique opportunity to assess the development of students' metacognitive skills.

The benefits of student reflection, both for learning and for assessment, are worth pursuing even if evaluation must rely primarily or exclusively on exam performance. It may compromise the "variety" principle of portfolio assessment, but a major component of the course portfolio might be performance on exams, especially if students write postexam reflections as described in the previous section. Imagine what students and faculty might learn if the portfolio guidelines asked students to include their exams, their postexam reflections, and a final assignment asking students to reflect on their efforts to improve exam performance—what worked and what did not, and their thoughts on how they might better show their learning.

In a final note on using portfolios, we cannot stress enough the importance of developing a scoring rubric for assessing the portfolio. Without a rubric, portfolio assessment has even more potential for challenges to validity, reliability, and fairness than any of the assessment forms discussed earlier. The basic process for developing a rubric for assessing a portfolio is similar to that described for assessing an essay: identify the primary components or traits of the portfolio, determine an assessment scale for each trait, and figure out a way to add it all up. For more specific guidelines on developing portfolio rubrics, see Maki, 2004; Suskie, 2004; Zubizaretta, 2004.

Conclusion

Our primary goal in this chapter is to help faculty think about how to make evaluation practices valid, reliable, and fair to diverse students. We focused first on creating effective multiple choice questions, showing how these questions can test a range of objectives while increasing the reliability and fairness of assessment practice. We then turned to essay questions (and other written assignments), urged faculty to reserve these questions for assessing higher-order thinking, and offered suggestions for improving the reliability of grading. Finally, we sketched some additional strategies for assessing group work, for including students' self-assessment, and for assessing metacognitive skills. Throughout, we have tried to be mindful of the unique challenges and constraints facing faculty and students in introductory courses and be practical in our suggestions. Because class size is a major constraint for many faculty, we revisit assessment issues in our discussion of large classes in Chapter Fourteen.

Of course, in the end the assessment practices we employ in our first-year courses must be converted to grades that are reported to students. Although that process is obviously connected to our assessment practices, there are some special considerations to keep in mind when we assign grades. We turn to those issues in Chapter Twelve.

For Further Exploration _____

- MacGregor, J. (ed.). *Student Self-Evaluation: Fostering Reflective Learning.* New Directions for Teaching and Learning, no. 56. San Francisco: Jossey-Bass, 1993.

  This volume gives an introduction to and rationale for student self-evaluation. The sample assignments and prompts are especially helpful in thinking about how to use student self-evaluation in practice.

- Miller, H. G., Williams, R. G., and Haladyna, T. M. *Beyond Facts: Objective Ways to Measure Thinking.* Englewood Cliffs, N.J.: Educational Technology Publications, 1978.

  Using Bloom's Taxonomy as a guide, Harry Miller, Reed Williams, and Thomas Haladyna give the most detailed instructions we have seen for creating multiple choice exams at the college level. Although the book is currently out of print, libraries may have copies.

- Stevens, D. D., and Levi, A. J. *Introduction to Rubrics: An Assessment Tool to Save Grading Time, Convey Effective Feedback, and Promote Student Learning.* Sterling, Va.: Stylus, 2005.

  Dannelle Stevens and Antonia Levi lay out a clear blueprint for constructing scoring guides at the college level, offer several examples, and suggest ways to involve students in using them.

- Walvoord, B. E., and Anderson, V. J. *Effective Grading: A Tool for Learning and Assessment.* San Francisco: Jossey-Bass, 1998.

  The chapters on "Making Assignments Worth Grading" and "Establishing Criteria and Standards for Grading" extend our discussion of creating good essay questions and scoring guides.

- Zubizarreta, J. *The Learning Portfolio: Reflective Practice for Improving Student Learning.* Bolton, Mass.: Anker, 2004.

  John Zubizarreta and other contributors present a comprehensive introduction to learning portfolios, models used in several disciplines, several examples prepared by students, and dozens of worksheets, guidelines, criteria, and other practical materials useful in developing portfolio assignments.

CHAPTER 12

Grading

What should count toward the final grade? How many exams should I give? Should I grade on a curve or set standards at the outset? Half of my class is failing; what do I do now? What are my responsibilities when it comes to cheating? What about grade inflation?

Answers to many of the questions faculty ask about grading are not to be found in research, because assumptions, beliefs, purposes, and contexts largely shape grading schemes. Faculty who believe, for example, that an introductory course should weed out students who show little promise for further study in a field use grading policies different from those who believe their courses teach content or skills important to all college graduates. Faculty who think a C is a perfectly respectable mark grade unlike those who think it not a very good one. Some place a premium on and give higher marks for getting things right the first time; others care little about how many tries it takes so long as the student eventually gets it right. Because assumptions and beliefs play such an important role in grading practices, we begin by acknowledging two that underlie our response to questions about grading.

First, we take it as a basic premise that the primary function of grades is to communicate as accurately as possible the extent to which students have learned what the course was designed to teach. This is not self-evident; faculty use grades to serve other purposes: to motivate students, provide feedback and improve learning, reward hard work, punish indifference, rank students, and maintain academic standards. Grades often do serve these purposes, regardless of intention, but they must not distort the primary one: to provide accurate information about the extent to which a student has achieved course objectives.

Second, we believe the most robust grading systems create an opportunity for students to submit their best evidence that they have achieved course goals. This belief occasionally creates a dilemma because inviting students to submit their best evidence implies permitting variety in grading opportunities, perhaps giving students a choice about what should count in grading. Such practice can create both validity and reliability problems. When faculty ask, for example, "Should we count class participation?" the measurement training in us says, "No way; assessment of that is horrifically unreliable and often based on characteristics that have little to do with learning." Our experience with diverse students tells us, "Let's talk about whether and how student participation in class might be a reasonably valid and reliable indicator of students' achievement of course objectives."

Determining Grades

Keeping in mind our assumption—that grades should communicate what students have learned in the course and should be based on their best work—we turn to the questions faculty frequently ask about grading.

What Should Count Toward the Final Grade?

There is little debate about whether tests, papers, quizzes, and lab reports should carry weight in the final grade. The question is, What *else* should count? Our answer: not much.

Class attendance and homework. Anyone who has worked with first-year students can sympathize with the temptation to factor in class attendance and timely completion of homework. First-year students are easily distracted from their studies and somewhat oblivious to the cost of not keeping up. Nonetheless, we advise against using these as factors in determining grades. Counting them is not likely to motivate students, unless they count a lot, but the more they count the less the grade can be regarded as an indication of what a student has learned. Furthermore, most faculty would agree that instruction should precede evaluation, but counting class attendance or homework makes them one and the same. Finally, if we consider these factors in determining a final grade, then we need daily attendance lists, reliable assessment of homework assignments, and accurate recordkeeping. Such is the stuff of which nightmares are made.

Class participation. We have similar reservations about factoring class participation into the final grade. Too often, assessment of student contributions in class are impressionistic and reflect a reaction to stylistic behavior as much as to substantive contribution. We remember students who contribute often or who have a good sense of humor, or on the negative side those who seem overly confrontational or critical. Because assessment of student participation tends to be unreliable and of questionable validity, most measurement experts advise against counting class participation. Yet many faculty tell us, "I have students who do not do so well on course examinations, but whose contributions in class convince me that they understand and can think clearly about what this course is about." Such reports, combined with our belief that evaluation systems should insofar as possible enable students to show their best work, lead us to put aside the "measurement hat," at least long enough to explore how assessment of class participation might be done validly and reliably. Developing a rubric for assessing class participation and a systematic plan for using it over time seem likely to minimize the validity and reliability problems. For suggestions and examples of participation rubrics, see Bean and Peterson (1998) and Stevens and Levi (2005).

Effort and improvement. We do not think it is a good idea to base a grade on the amount of effort or improvement a student appears to make. If grades are to communicate the extent to which students achieve the course objectives, then how hard they try and how much they improve merely confuse the message. Assessing these factors also poses some difficult measurement problems. On what basis do we judge effort? How do we detect improvement? Such assessment is usually impressionistic, haphazard, and unreliable. Even when faculty use pretests and posttests (and few of us base our judgments about improvement on anything so systematic), the differences observed for individual students are highly unreliable. Let effort and improvement show in successful achievement of objectives—as demonstrated, for example, on cumulative finals, test retakes, or rewritten papers.

Extra credit. "I'm not doing very well on the exams, and I really need a good grade in this course. Could I do something for extra credit?" In theory, saying yes to students who request extra-credit options might enable students to submit alternative or "best evidence" that they have achieved course objectives. We are inclined to deny such requests, however, for a couple of reasons. First, extra-credit work usually takes the form of a paper or a project, which would not be a bad idea if writing the paper or completing the project required students to demonstrate their achievement of important objectives. In practice, we rarely take time to create such an assignment, and students are left largely on their own to select a topic and complete the work. Students may learn something from such activity, but they do not necessarily learn the content or skills most central in a course. Second, this practice is not equitable unless we publicly announce that the option is available to all students.

That said, we take a different view of extra-credit options if we systematically build them into our courses and invite all students to participate. In an introductory sociology course, for example, students may earn extra-credit points by entering the Max Weber Memorial Art Contest and the Karl Marx Memorial Limerick Contest. To enter the first, students must submit a drawing expressing one of Weber's key ideas; in the second, they write a limerick about Marx's view of society.

Wendy Holmes, a professor of art history on our campus, tells students in her large introductory course that they will have opportunities during the semester to gain extra points by participating in special class events. These are writing an interpretive essay in a small group, making a collage that expresses the characteristics of some artistic movement, or submitting a drawing "in the style of" an artist they study. Extra-credit options need not be so lighthearted as these, although there is something to be said for giving students a chance to play with ideas once in a while. Beyond that, extra-credit opportunities offered to all students can build some flexibility ("forgiveness," in a sense) into grading schemes that are rarely perfect and often uncomfortably rigid. Designing extra-credit options that relate to central course objectives and inviting all students to participate ameliorate concern about validity and equity.

How Often Should We Assess Student Learning?

Our answer to faculty who teach first-year students is "The more often, the better." Grades based on several assessments are generally more reliable than grades based on fewer, but there are other reasons for testing frequently and beginning early in a first-year course. Frequent evaluations help establish the structure many first-year students need to keep up with their work. Giving frequent quizzes is more likely to get students to attend class and do their homework than is counting attendance and homework in the grading scheme. Early evaluation not only makes course goals and standards understandable to students but also enables them to determine whether their study activities are adequate before it is too late. We recommend giving shorter tests or written assignments and scheduling some form of evaluation every two or three weeks at least during the first few months of the first semester. Once students have negotiated the transition from high school to college, there will be time enough to wean them from dependence on tests.

Should I Grade on a Curve or Set Standards at the Outset?

Before addressing this issue, let us agree on the procedures being considered and debated. Grading on a curve involves determining grades by comparing each student's performance to the performance of others in the class (norm-referenced grading). Although several variations on this approach exist, the most sensible one calculates the mean for a set of scores and uses the standard deviation to establish cutoff points for various grades. Scores at least two standard deviations above the mean might receive an A, scores one standard deviation above the mean might receive a B, scores within one standard deviation above and below the mean receive a C, and so on. When we determine grades this way, an A means a student performed better than most students; an F means its recipient scored worse than most students. Grades based on a curve do not indicate how much or how little a student learned, however.

When we set standards at the outset, we determine grades by comparing each student's performance to the predetermined set of standards. Variation exists here too, but a widely used approach expresses the standard in terms of points. For example, if 100 points are possible, students who accumulate 90 to 100 points might receive an A, those who earn 80 to 89 points receive a B, and so on. An A means the student met the standard for outstanding work; an F means the student did not meet a minimum standard for passing. Grades determined in this way say nothing about whether the student did better or worse than other students in class.

Which grading approach should be used? We favor grading according to predetermined standards and making those standards explicit at the outset. Appropriate standards may be difficult to determine, and care should be taken to make sure they are reasonable, but grading according to standards holds more potential for communicating the extent to which students have achieved the course objectives. This seems especially likely in an introductory course, where curve grading often leads faculty to give satisfactory grades to students who have at best a precarious grasp of the material and too often not a clue about what is going on. Students are often all too willing to settle for this, but in the long run it does no one any favors.

Furthermore, students are more likely to achieve high standards if they know what those standards are, if their attention is focused on meeting the standards rather than on competing with one another, if they participate fully in class activities, and if they are willing to help one another learn. Grading according to standards tends to promote these conditions for learning; grading on a curve tends to undermine them.

Finally, grading according to standards is more likely to point up problems and lead to improvement in teaching and testing practice. If several students do poorly on an exam, the low grades usually prompt some serious soul searching. Was instruction inadequate? Was the exam poorly constructed? Or did students simply not study enough? We can correct such problems, but only if we detect them. Grading on a curve too often hides ineffective teaching, poor testing, and inadequate learning. So long as we give a reasonable number of A's and B's and not too many D's or F's, no one makes a fuss.

Grading Problems

As faculty plan their courses, their questions tend to focus on determining grades. Once classes begin, however, faculty attention tends to shift to solving problems that grading seems inevitably to produce.

Half My Students Are Failing—What Should I Do?

Even without experiencing it, we all know we do not want to be in this situation. The desire to avoid it probably accounts for why so many faculty continue to grade on a curve. When grades are assigned according to predetermined standards and the first one or two tests produce many low scores, both students and faculty see the writing on the wall. Unless something changes dramatically, a large number of students will receive a D or F in the course. We do not view this as a mark of merit or evidence that the course is rigorous; the situation indicates something has gone terribly wrong.

Students often pressure us to "scale the grades," by which they mean convert the predetermined grading scale into one with lower cutoff points for each grade. A typical scaling practice takes the highest score earned and regards it as the total number of points possible in a course. The instructor then determines new cutoff points by calculating percentages of the highest score earned or by looking for gaps in the distribution. Measurement texts do not discuss such procedures, and for good reason. Anchoring a grading scheme around one student's score—highest, lowest, or otherwise—is a questionable practice, and gaps in a distribution of scores are as likely to be produced by measurement error as by anything else. If original grading scales must be modified, we advise consulting someone with expertise in measurement for proper procedures for converting scores from one scale to another.

Even with this precaution, we are not in favor of scaling grades. Although the practice may placate students and spare faculty the angry complaints, it neglects the important issues. Why are so many students doing poorly? What can be done to increase their learning? Are our expectations reasonable and our tests fair? We cannot afford to skirt these issues in an introductory course, where the knowledge and skills taught are often essential for further study or important components of general education. Moreover, giving passing grades or higher marks to students who miss a third or half of the questions on an exam undermines claims that we are teaching and testing essential or important learning outcomes.

One way to avoid this predicament is to be more careful in setting standards and constructing tests. We can save ourselves a peck of trouble by consulting colleagues about what we can reasonably expect first-year students to accomplish in one term and by asking others to review tests before administering them. This is especially good advice for new faculty and for faculty who have been away from first-year students for a while.

Assuming we have reasonable standards and well-designed tests, a high failure rate points to problems in instruction. Both we and our students tend to underestimate the amount of practice deep learning requires. We include too few in-class exercises and homework assignments; students do not do the ones we assign. Such problems call for immediate attention and drastic action, and that is what we propose.

If many students do poorly on the first (or second or nth) exam, immediately scheduling another exam on the same material a week or so later sends a message to students that the material is important. To help them prepare for the retest, we might devote the intervening days to intensive review and practice: exercises in class, homework problems or questions to be answered in writing, practice quizzes, consultation with small groups during office hours, extra help sessions, and scheduled times when students may meet and study together. These activities require time, and we may have to revise the syllabus, but the alternatives—compromising reasonable standards or facing a potentially volatile political situation—are not pleasant to contemplate either. Reteaching and retesting hold promise that students will learn what they need to learn. Scaling grades only passes the problem on.

What Should I Do About Cheating?

When conversation turns to cheating, we hear faculty views along a continuum. There are some who would avoid the topic altogether, claiming they do not have problems with cheating and intimating something is wrong with those who do. At the opposite extreme are faculty who believe cheating is rampant and devote almost as much energy to catching cheaters as they do to teaching their classes. In between are faculty who suspect or recognize that cheating goes on in their courses but are unsure how to prevent it and less sure what to do about it should they discover it.

We think it fair to say that most students would prefer not to cheat. We would have to bury our heads in the sand, however, to say that most students do not cheat. Most research studies report half to three-fourths of college students admit to cheating (Center for Academic Integrity, 2004; Diekhoff and others, 1996; Genereux and McLeod, 1995; Pulvers and Diekhoff, 1999; Whitley, 1998). What, then, should we to do about academic dishonesty? In offering suggestions, we try to strike a balance between expecting and assuming the best from students while recognizing the pervasiveness of cheating.

Talk about academic integrity and why we value it. Given the importance of the issue, it is surprising how little many of us say about academic integrity. We do not define it except by negative example, we rarely articulate a case for it, and we are not willing to do much to protect it. We tell students that if they cheat they will only be cheating themselves, but we are hard-pressed to specify what exactly they are cheating themselves *of*. To define and discuss academic integrity in more positive terms, the Center for Academic Integrity suggests faculty talk with students about the values on which research and education depend: *honesty* in one's work and dealings with others, *trust* that others will behave honestly and fairly, *fairness* in assessing faculty and student work, *respect* for diverse opinions and ideas, *responsibility* to uphold the integrity of scholarship and research. (For a fuller discussion of these values and suggestions on how to discuss them with students, see *The Fundamental Values of Academic Integrity*, published in 1999 by the Center for Academic Integrity and available as a portable document at http://www.academicintegrity.org/fundamental.asp.)

Identify and discuss forms of academic dishonesty. Most students know that sneaking a peek at someone else's exam (or instant-messaging answers among friends), copying an assignment, or submitting a purchased term paper are forms of cheating. They are not so clear about what constitutes plagiarism, however—especially in the copy-and-paste environment of Web-based research. Students' ambiguity about plagiarism has prompted several institutions to hold workshops, seminars, and tutorials on the issues. Especially helpful, we think, are materials and tutorials that include excerpts from original sources followed by two or three summarized versions, with commentary about why each would or would not be regarded as plagiarism (see, for example, B. G. Davis, 1993; Princeton University, 2000).

Nor are students always clear about the line that faculty draw between collaborative study and individual assessment. A common practice tells students, "Study together; write the essay on your own." When students submit essays or problem solutions that contain the same arguments or reflect the same processes, we rightly wonder if someone has copied. Perhaps, but it is also possible that students listened closely in study groups, took careful notes, and were attentive to the decision their group reached. Rather than accusing them of cheating, it may be more appropriate to instruct them about properly citing their study group's contributions to their work.

Create new tests and essay assignments each term. We have yet to devise a foolproof system for keeping past exams and papers out of the hands of students. Efforts to develop ever more elaborate security measures would be better spent writing new tests and assignments. Doing so allows us to return papers to students and make previous exams available to all students for review and practice. Creating new tests need not be an overwhelming task if we write questions on a week-by-week schedule rather than the night before the exam.

Use alternatives to the essay. Make paper and project assignments less prone to plagiarism or the paper mill by asking for something other than an academic essay. The suggestions in Chapter Eleven—specifying particular genres, audiences, and purposes—not only create more authentic assessment practices but also make it more difficult for students to purchase a paper or copy and paste from the Internet.

Reduce pressure on students. When students knowingly cheat, they usually have "reasons"—and pressure to get good grades heads the list. There are several ways we could reduce the pressure and still maintain high standards. We offer four suggestions especially suited to introductory courses.

First, *schedule more opportunities for students to demonstrate their learning.* When we base a grade on only two or three exams or papers, stakes are high, failure is costly, and the pressure can be overwhelming to students. Using more assessment opportunities has the added benefit of increasing reliability (see Chapter Eleven).

Second, *consider distributing test questions beforehand.* Many faculty who use essay exams distribute the essay questions beforehand or give several questions from which a smaller number will be included on the exam. This strategy can also work for multiple choice exams by distributing the stems of the multiple choice questions before the exam. Although students eventually must select the answers from choices given, distributing the question stems encourages students to prepare for the exam in the same way they might prepare for an essay exam (by constructing answers) and gives them some time to do so.

Third, *think about offering opportunities for some collaboration on exams.* Convinced that tests are the only time students write essays without first bouncing ideas off someone else, a colleague in art history allows ten minutes at the beginning of an exam period for students to discuss the exam's interpretive essay question (Holmes, 1988). Ten minutes is enough time for students to identify key ideas for the essay, but not so much time that they could write a complete interpretation in a group. In addition to helping some students get past a moment of panic if they draw a blank on a question, this practice is especially useful for those whose learning style favors talking things through before writing.

Finally, *build in opportunities for students to rewrite papers or to retake comparable forms of exams.* Most faculty are aware that rewrite and retake opportunities both reduce pressure and increase learning, often dramatically. The rub comes if students catch on that they need not try their hardest the first time and decide to slapdash something together, wait for the feedback about what is on the first exam or comments on their essay or lab report, and then commence serious work. Fearing that less-than-ready exams and papers might quickly overwhelm them, some faculty strike a compromise by telling students they will average their grades on first and subsequent rewrites or retakes.

Testing more frequently, distributing questions beforehand, allowing discussion before writing an essay, and permitting students to rewrite papers or retake exams are practices that make sense because they reduce the pressures students feel in testing situations. They also convey the message that the instructor cares about student learning and is not out to get them. Most fundamentally, these strategies promote learning.

Take preventive measures in a testing situation. Some faculty and graduate teaching assistants balk at preventive measures because they think they communicate lack of trust. Apparently, inattention to preventive measures communicates the opposite. Many students who admit to cheating say they do so because "everyone cheats" and because they can "get away with it" (Genereux and McLeod, 1995; Whitley, 1998). We do not advocate making the classroom feel more like a maximum-security prison than a hall of learning, but we do recommend taking ordinary precautions.

Ask students to sit in alternate seats during tests. When students sit elbow to elbow, it takes some concentration to avoid the inadvertent glance at someone else's work and a substantial commitment to academic integrity to avoid the deliberate one.

Create different forms of multiple choice tests. Scramble the order of the questions and the order of the choices. Computers make it easy to create and to score multiple forms of one exam.

Proctor examinations. Although proctors rarely detect cheating, failure to proctor exams probably invites it. When we leave the room or refuse to line the walls with proctors, we assume that we communicate our trust in students. Apparently, students take such behavior to mean we do not care about either them or the test; they believe that most other students are cheating, and they feel disadvantaged or foolish or both if they themselves do not cheat (Diekhoff and others, 1996; Genereux and McLeod, 1995).

Supplement assessments completed outside class with in-class tests or essays. Take-home exams, papers, lab reports, and other projects completed outside class enable us to see what students can do when they have time to think and work. Unfortunately, they have one major drawback: we can never quite be sure students are submitting their own work. Periodic in-class assessment can help us lay such doubts to rest.

Take formal action on discovering violations of academic integrity. Suppose we discover that cheating has occurred despite our best efforts to discourage it. What then? Most institutions have a policy governing what faculty may do. Typically, the options range from failing the student on a particular assignment to failing for the course, to dismissal from the institution. By and large, faculty have been reluctant to exercise any of these options. Some sympathize with the plight of students and are satisfied if students promise never to do it again; others prefer to avoid the legalistic procedures and confrontation often involved in taking formal action (Diekhoff and others, 1996). Research documenting the prevalence of cheating and suggesting that today's students do not regard some forms of academic dishonesty to be serious offenses is prompting many of us to rethink our response.

Incidents of academic dishonesty are never pleasant, but we think everyone needs to step up to the plate on this issue. Some faculty show more sympathy for students who cheat than they do for students who do not understand. Truth be told, we suspect students are more likely to be dismissed from a postsecondary institution for ignorance than for dishonesty. Surely dishonesty is the more serious offense. In conversation, all of us agree that we want our students to value honesty and eschew corruption. If, however, we are unwilling to put forward a case of academic dishonesty and invoke sanctions, students get the message that academic integrity is not so important after all. We need to hold our sympathy in check and initiate formal action when we discover violation of academic integrity.

Do I Need to Worry About Grade Inflation?

We confess that grade inflation is not an issue that keeps us awake at night. However, it seems that every few years someone sounds an alarm about grade inflation and panic sets in. News that many students at Harvard receive A's and graduate with honors appears to have initiated one such panic ("Harvard Releases Report . . .," 2001). We do not intend to dwell on the history of this wave of concern, but two contemporary stories illustrate the depth of emotion around the issues and the length to which some will go.

On April 26, 2004, the Princeton University faculty voted (156 to 84!) to limit the number of A's faculty may award in undergraduate courses to 35 percent and cap the percentage of A's at 55 percent in junior and senior independent work. The report on this vote is especially surprising, given how protective faculties are of academic freedom in their work. Equally astonishing was a *Chronicle of Higher Education* report (Smallwood, 2004) that six professors at Point Park University in Pittsburgh had their merit awards cut by half because they had given too many A's in the previous semester. We do not think these are representative actions in higher education, but they document the fact that concern about grade inflation *does* keep some people awake at night.

Such actions also prompt us to advise faculty (especially part-time and untenured faculty who often teach first-year courses) to think through the issues involved in conversation about grade inflation. Underlying many of the arguments are beliefs about the purpose grades serve. Harvard's dean of undergraduate education explained, "We rely on grades not only to distinguish among our students but also to motivate them, and . . . by narrowing the grade differential between superior and routine work, grade inflation works against the pedagogical mission of the faculty" (S. G. Pederson, quoted in "Harvard Releases Report . . .," 2001). As we said at the beginning of this chapter, we do not view motivating students and ranking their achievement as primary functions for grading; nor do we believe they should cloud the main purpose: communicating the extent to which students have achieved objectives. It is entirely conceivable to us that half or three-quarters or even 90 percent of Harvard students, or Princeton's, or any other college's students, might demonstrate outstanding achievement of objectives. As we also said at the outset, people disagree about the primary purposes of grading.

Faculty who are unsure about grade inflation or who teach on a campus concerned about it may want to delve deeper into discussion of the issues. Catherine Shoichet (2002), relying on a 1999–2000 Department of Education report, says that reports of grade inflation are "inflated," at least nationally; her methodology for consulting government records offers an approach for getting accurate national data that are beyond Harvard, Princeton, and other headline institutions. In the most comprehensive discussion of grade inflation we have read, Alfie Kohn (2002) addresses questions about whether or not grades have actually changed over the years. Kohn also discusses what comparing grades to SAT scores might or might not tell us, epistemological issues (for example, if we discover that students today receive higher grades than earlier, does that mean lower standards today or more valid and reliable assessment practices?), and the relationship between grades and the various purposes they might serve.

Conclusion

Assessing student performance and assigning grades are complicated tasks. Not only does grading require time and expertise in constructing and evaluating assessment measures but it also brings us into contact with our students in a way that may go beyond how they did on the midterm or the last essay. Grades often strike at the heart of the first-year student's sense of self. They have been successful students in high school, and as we have seen, they come to college confident of their academic ability. Good grades confirm both their past accomplishment and their sense of efficacy. Poor grades can, and often do, have an impact well beyond the assignment that we think is just a small portion of our course.

We are not suggesting that faculty view grading as a form of therapy designed to build or sustain student self-confidence. We should be aware, however, that assessment and grading are critically important aspects of students' first-year experience, and the effect of grades is not simply academic but personal as well. We owe it to our students to develop assessment practices and construct grading systems that are thoughtful in design, careful in conduct, fair in application, and appropriate to the learning outcomes of our course. If we can accomplish those things, then both faculty and students will be better able to put the outcomes, good or bad, in proper perspective.

For Further Exploration

- Bean, J. C., and Peterson, D. "Grading Classroom Participation." In R. S. Anderson and B. W. Speck (eds.), *Changing the Way We Grade Student Performance: Classroom Assessment and the New Learning Paradigm.* New Directions for Teaching and Learning, no. 74. San Francisco: Jossey-Bass, 1998.

  Bean and Peterson pack a number of creative suggestions for grading participation into a small space. Although we remain of mixed minds about counting participation in course grades, the suggestions here offer a variety of ways to bring some reliability to the practice.

- Center for Academic Integrity (http://www.academicintegrity .org; retrieved Nov. 2004).

  Cheating and plagiarism can undermine the best grading practices. The Center for Academic Integrity researches the problem and offers a number of practical suggestions for reducing the incidence of academic dishonesty.

- McKeachie, W. J. *Teaching Tips* (11th ed.). Boston: Houghton Mifflin, 2002.

  McKeachie's treatment of grading is useful and to the point. He includes many of the topics we have discussed, among them grading on the curve and what to do about cheating.

PART THREE

Opportunities and Challenges in First-Year Instruction

Part Three calls out three aspects of higher education that deserve focused attention because of the special opportunities and challenges they present to those who teach first-year students. Chapter Thirteen explores how the issues of difference and diversity play themselves out in the first-year classroom. We have emphasized the importance of diversity in materials and approaches throughout the previous sections, but given the importance of race, gender, religion, and sexual orientation in our society, some attention to how the dynamics of difference affect first-year instruction is warranted. Chapter Fourteen takes on large-class instruction, something first-year students experience much more frequently than do their more advanced counterparts. We make several suggestions to help faculty move beyond the usual "all lecture, all the time, what else can I do" approach to large-enrollment courses. Chapter Fifteen discusses the important contribution faculty can make to first-year students in the role of advisor or instructor of a first-year seminar course. Meaningful contact with faculty outside the classroom can significantly enrich first-year students' experiences and increase the likelihood they will persist in their studies. Finally, Chapter Sixteen offers our reflections on how institutions can build and sustain faculty communities to own the responsibility for creating first-year instruction that is challenging, supportive, and engaging.

CHAPTER 13

Creating Inclusion in First-Year Classrooms and Curricula

Perhaps the most visible transformation of college curricula in the last thirty years has been the infusion of courses, programs, majors, and full-fledged departments devoted to what is known as multicultural education. Beginning in the 1960s with African American studies, college and university faculty have produced a tapestry of programs to engage issues of diversity and difference as objects of analysis and arenas for action: women's studies, Latino studies, Asian studies, queer studies, hunger studies, white studies, and more. Although some programs have fared better than others, the multicultural movement has substantially altered the character of American higher education.

Three aspects of this transformation are especially relevant to the experiences of first-year students. First, of course, the study of difference attracts interest and is a viable option when the time comes to choose a major or minor. Along the way, such programs create variety in general education curricula and elective credits. Second, and perhaps more important, the presence of academic programs devoted to the study of difference serves as a reminder to faculty across the campus that difference—racial, ethnic, gender, sexual orientation—was not a sixties or seventies phenomenon but a permanent part of the academic community. The durable nature of this reminder is at least in part responsible for campuswide efforts to infuse courses across the curriculum with discipline-based considerations of diversity. Finally, programs of racial, ethnic, and gender study have performed an important advocacy function, insisting (if only by their presence) that new cohorts of incoming students be representative of the nation's population and that once admitted, all students be supported intellectually, socially, and emotionally.

In some respect, then, the increasing diversity of first-year college students is the product of the politics of the academy itself. The same, of course, is true of the transformation in curricula. Nevertheless, we believe it is a mistake to think about issues of multiculturalism and difference on college campus as a product peculiar to them. Rather, our discussion of difference, our effort to transform classrooms and courses of study, and our desire to include students' diverse life experiences in our frame of attention emerge from larger social processes that we often do not notice, but that have a significant effect on what happens on campus in general and on our encounters with students in particular.

A Background of Difference

This is not the place for an extended survey, but there are several facets of the national conversation about and confrontation with difference that may be particularly illuminating for those of us who confront first-year college students in classrooms and other campus settings. For example, in the last decade and a half the steady progress in desegregating American public schools has come to a halt and actually reversed, leaving the nation with its schools more segregated than at any time since the late 1960s. As a consequence, the average white student attends a school that is 80 percent white, while the average black student or Latino student attends a school that is 70 percent nonwhite. Moreover, nearly 40 percent of Latino and black students are enrolled in schools that are more than 90 percent nonwhite. These developments have occurred in spite of the fact that the proportion of minority students in public schools continues to grow, recently surpassing the 40 percent mark (Frankenberg, Lee, and Orfield, 2003).

Against this backdrop, the racial diversity of recent cohorts of first-year college students looks a bit different in comparison to the composition of the entering class of a generation ago. Higher education finds itself in the odd position of, on average, providing a more "integrated" experience for incoming white students, although (again, on average) for black, Latino, Asian, and Native American students the college campus environment is more white than their previous public school experiences. This differential reality was captured poignantly in the documentary "Skin Deep," as two University of Massachusetts students reflected on their experiences on the Amherst campus. Marc Mazzone, a white student, finds there are "a lot more minority students" than there ever were at his high school, while his African American classmate, Brian Allen, was "shocked" to find so few minorities on campus or in his classes ("Skin Deep," 1995). Given the forces at work in public education, such disparate impressions are probably more common than we would like to imagine.

Another broad trend worth noting is the change in the experiences, expectations, and views students report having and holding regarding race, gender, and other aspects of difference. In the last thirty years, there has been a significant drop in the proportion of first-year students who think "homosexuality should be illegal" and in the number who believe "married women's activities are best confined to the home." Yet, in both cases a significant minority of students, about 30 percent, continues to hold those views. On race matters, the picture is similarly mixed. About two-thirds of incoming students report "frequently socializing" with a person of another race or ethnic group, and 63 percent report they expect to do so while in college. The encouraging signs we might see in those numbers, however, are mitigated by the fact that both have declined over the last four years. A more substantial change has occurred in the number of students rating "promoting racial understanding" as an "essential or very important" goal. From a peak of more than 42 percent in 1992, the 2002 proportion dropped to just under 30 percent, the lowest point since data collection began in 1977. There are significant racial differences here as well: more than a third of Native Americans, more than 40 percent of Latinos, and more than half of African American students viewed promoting racial understanding as important, while fewer than a quarter of their white classmates did (Astin, Oseguera, Sax, and Korn, 2002).

In addition to these changes in attitude and experience, there is a growing sense among many observers that the nation in general and students in particular are suffering from what might be called "diversity fatigue." Although this phrase may be a bit glib, it does capture a sense—especially among many white students—that they have dealt with issues of diversity enough. Although nearly all acknowledge that racial and gender discrimination are wrong, many feel much less need to continue to examine difference and its effects. Diversity fatigue is the foundation of the plaintive comment of an anonymous college administrator who, after extended discussions about racial, gender, and cultural difference, remarked "When are we going to get back to normal?" (Jones, 2005, p. 142).

Administrators are not alone in the desire to "get back," if not to "normal" then at least to something more familiar and more comfortable. One can certainly sense in trying to engage students in conversation about race, gender, or sexual orientation that the most common position is "been there, done that." Arthur Levine and Jeanette Cureton (1998), for example, point out that their effort to engage students about issues of race and race relations on campuses was most often met by silence. In our own experience, even when the silence about race—

or gender, or religion, or sexual orientation—is broken, students offer little more than platitudes. "Deep down, we're all the same," they say; if pressed, they add, "Everybody should accept everyone for who they are"; and when the stock of phrases is exhausted they pleadingly quote Rodney King, "Can't we all get along?"

Sometimes, however, the silence is shattered by student expressions that are more aggrieved than weary. For example, at the conclusion of a developmental psychology course in which students were asked to read Henry Louis Gates's memoir *Colored People* and Jonathan Kozol's *Savage Inequalities*, the instructor, Jack Meacham, received an e-mail from a student. It began, "You wouldn't believe how relieved I am that this class is over. For the past month I've been totally offended and disgusted at what we as a class have been asked to read and learn." The student's message continued, angrily indicting both Gates and Kozol, and blaming Meacham for transforming a perfectly good developmental psychology course into "Racism 101" (Meacham, 1998).

All of this makes dealing with issues of difference a high-stakes game for faculty. The needs of the nation and the world demand that college graduates be able to function effectively and humanely in an increasingly diverse world. As a consequence, faculty must be intentional in efforts to develop student capacity to cross the lines of race, gender, religion, and sexual orientation. Yet our attempts to engage students in discussion, revamp courses, and alter curricular tracks often put us in a position that is unfamiliar, uncomfortable, even unnerving. Encountering difference is an essential aspect of students' first-year experiences, and no matter how disconcerting it may sometimes be, our job as faculty members is to make those encounters not only civil but intellectually productive as well.

A Three-Part Plan

Dealing with difference in an academic setting is, as we have seen, a complex task. There is no magic formula, and although good intentions and good faith are essential parts of the process they are not enough. Nevertheless, we think it is productive for faculty and first-year students to think about the academic experience of difference along three dimensions.

First, difference is experienced in the warp and woof of course design. The strategic choices of instructors—every text, topic, approach, analysis, assignment, and more—send a powerful message about the centrality of difference in a given course, perhaps in a given major, and possibly on the campus as a whole.

Second, difference is experienced in the day-to-day conduct of class, inside and outside the classroom. Here, the tactics we employ as faculty embody in a concrete way the practice of our discipline. Again, the examples we use, the exam questions we pose, the authorities we cite, the questions we ask students to discuss, the art we exhibit, and the comments we make send a clear signal about the role of difference as it actually affects our disciplinary inquiry.

Third, difference is experienced on a more intimate level as students and faculty interact in discussion, office visits, written materials and appended comments, and the chit-chat that fills the spare moments as classes begin and end. In these exchanges, difference is more than a topic of inquiry or the substance of an investigation. It is also a characteristic of persons, defining in part who they are, how they see the world, and where they stand in relation to others.

Thinking about difference along these three axes is a way for us as faculty to reflect systematically on how we might approach the diversity of race, gender, religion, sexual orientation, and more that we see in first-year students. Difference does not change the fundamental challenge that confronts us in teaching first-year students: meeting students where they are with reasonable rigor and appropriate support. Awareness of difference lends a richness to those encounters that demands both care and creative attention. More than that, however, it also reminds us that the sometimes expressed desire to get back to normal is nostalgia for an academy that should have been gone long before it was.

Course Design

First-year students initially confront difference (at least in a classroom setting) when they receive the syllabus for their first college course. Indeed, throughout the first few days of class students are introduced to the framework of study that will structure a substantial portion of their time and command a considerable amount of their attention. As we mentioned in Chapter Five, the syllabus and manner in which the first class session is conducted send explicit and tacit messages about what is important and what is not, what is valued and what is not, what is acceptable and what is not. This is especially true when the syllabus, the embodied expression of an instructor's sense of the course, deals with issues of difference. When difference is set at the center of a course (recall the excerpt from the course Families in Society in Chapter Five), students get one sense of who is important in the inquiry to come. They get quite another if the consideration of difference is confined to a particular unit, say two or three weeks devoted to "alternative families" or several class sessions given over to the "debate about same-sex marriage." Still another sense of who is important (and who is not) would be imparted to students through a course titled The Family, in which diverse family forms were treated as deviations from normal (there's that word again).

Margie Kitano (1997) has usefully crystallized these various ways of locating difference in our curricula. She identifies three broad categories of course design that reflect the movement of issues of difference from the margins of our curricular concerns to the very heart of our courses. Her scheme is implicitly critical of what she terms "exclusive courses," those designs that have "traditional, mainstream experience and perspectives" as the focal point of a semester's work; it not so subtly urges a movement to more "inclusive" designs, with a "transformed" course where difference lays the foundation for inquiry as the final destination.

Although Kitano's characterization of the exclusive course is a bit overdrawn (in its typical form it includes only content and avoids discussion of social issues), it does serve as a useful reminder to those of us who teach first-year students. Our course titles often include qualifiers such as "introductory" or "basic" or "general," and we (and our departments and programs as well) often approach them as a prelude to the more serious inquiry in the upper-division courses to follow. Once students get some foundational ideas, theories, or readings under their belt, our reasoning goes, they will be much better equipped to engage issues of difference as an economist or philosopher or sociologist or historian or chemist would. Although the approach may be understandable—there are some ideas that are basic to any discipline—it does send the message that difference is not a central concern for its practitioners.

Reworking the content of a course to make consideration of difference a central aspect of the semester's work is not easy, and some features of first-year courses make the process a bit more difficult. Many courses that enroll first-year students serve a dual purpose. On the one hand, they produce general education or distribution credit, satisfying curricular requirements for so many credits in social science, natural science, humanities, mathematics, and so on. On the other hand, they serve as the first course for those students who intend to major in a particular field, and as such programs expect them to impart the knowledge and skills necessary for further study. As a result, the goals embedded in course design often run at cross purposes. For general education, we might be willing, perhaps even eager, to center a psychology course around issues of gender, or a physical anthropology course around the nature and evolution of race, or a chemistry course on the structure and effects of environmental pollutants in low-income urban neighborhoods. But when the course must also prepare students for upper-division courses in developmental psychology, the human fossil record, and organic chemistry, we frequently lose both our will and our way.

Of course, some of the difficulties we confront stem from the fact that the courses we design and teach do not exist in isolation from the curriculum and the discipline in which they are embedded. Transforming the content of an introductory course in sociology, history, or literature is easier for us to imagine because at least to some extent the idea of difference has been embraced as central to the practice of the discipline. A transformed life science course is harder for us to envision, and a transformed physics or mathematics syllabus seems to elude our imaginative capacity.

In our current circumstances, it is probably too much to ask that every first-year course completely transform its content to place difference at the center. Nevertheless, there are some things we all can and ought to do to ensure that students confront difference in the content of first-year courses. Many of the suggestions that follow employ instructional practices we have discussed earlier. That is as it should be. The consideration of difference is not separate from the substance of our disciplines. The good practices that make the content of psychology or physics, engineering or economics, history or human development accessible to our students can also be used to ensure that they encounter difference at the same time.

Difference as invitation. Perhaps one of the most manageable ways to begin to transform the content of a course with the consideration of difference is to use discussion of difference as an invitation for students to engage the substance of the discipline. This approach is particularly useful in courses where the content seems least amenable to transformation. For example, Judith Rosenthal (1997) suggests using difference to introduce topics for consideration in a variety of natural science courses: using ethnic music and musical instruments to open a unit on sound and sound waves; demonstrating the international variety in electrical plugs on appliances to introduce a section on electricity; asking a question about the frequent exclusion of women from major medical studies to kick off an inquiry in microbiology; using an account of deforestation in Brazil to jump-start a discussion of global warming in an environmental science course. By themselves, of course, these invitations to students will not do much more than remind them that they live in a world where difference matters. Nevertheless, the reminder is important, especially in courses where they expect to encounter objective truth about the way things are.

Difference as context. Another related way to infuse consideration of difference into course content is to use the dimensions of, say, race, gender, or religion in a problem that forms the basis for the inquiry in a particular segment of the course. In the problem-based learning example discussed in Chapter Ten, students in a composition course are asked to develop an account of a congressional representative's position on stem cell research. The focus of the course is expository writing, but the problem that sets the context for instruction compels students to confront issues of difference: disabilities and their potential cure through medical research, differences in religious commitment, and deep cultural differences in the understanding of life itself. Issues of difference do not overshadow the substance. Rather, they are a backdrop against which clear expression of ideas, the logic of argumentation, and clarity and use of evidence take on new and heightened meaning.

Examples such as this one are easily multiplied: DNA evidence, sickle-cell anemia, AIDS, women's roles in traditional societies, and more (see Rosenthal, 1997, for further examples). The point here is to use difference to create the substance for disciplinary inquiry, not to resolve the debate swirling about any of these issues. If we can use difference to shape the context of our courses, we teach students the principles of this or the basics of that, and we also encourage them to see that our disciplines offer useful tools for looking into and thinking about those differences that are so much a part of our lives.

Difference as prism. Finally, we can use difference to refract the substance of a course so that the effects of difference on development and practice of a discipline are revealed. In an example discussed by Kitano (1997), the life and career of Barbara McClintock, the Nobel prize winning geneticist, presented a way for students in a life science course to think about the effects of gender on how the problems of science are actually engaged. In addition, through their discussion of McClintock students also had the opportunity to see that scientists and science itself do not exist unaffected by difference but, like everyone and everything else, are very much part of a world where difference matters.

Bannister (2000) reports a similar tactic used in a criminal justice course. As part of their work, students read *Eight Bullets: One Woman's Story of Surviving Anti-Gay Violence.* Following completion of the assignment, the instructor asked students to respond to the deceptively simple prompt, "Why do you think I assigned this book?" The ensuing discussion put the experience of crime victims, police investigations, and impartial pursuit of justice in a new light.

All of these uses of difference do run the risk of making consideration of race, gender, religion, or sexual orientation seem tangential to the "real" substance of the course. Even so, the risk is worth taking. Considering difference if only for a bit sends a much better message to first-year students than postponing it until later in their academic career.

Conducting an Inclusive Course

Reworking the content of our courses to be more inclusive is perhaps the best way to deal with difference in the long run. That, however, is the rub. Reorienting the substance of a curriculum is a complex process and, as we have noted, not something that a single course or a single faculty member can accomplish alone. Nevertheless, there are other, more immediate ways to transform the nature of students' encounters with difference in our classrooms. As Kitano (1997) points out, we can make a course more inclusive not only through the transformation of the content but also through changes in what she terms "instructional strategies and activities and assessment practices." In some ways, transformation of assignments, exam questions, and classroom activities can be even more powerful than the deeper changes in disciplinary content. Students' primary interactions with a discipline and an instructor come through the day-to-day practices that constitute the actual conduct of a course. If we can infuse difference into those things we routinely ask students to do, it stands to reason they will confront difference regularly as a normal part of their academic lives.

There has been a good deal of work invested in developing classroom activities and other assignments that are "difference-enriched." The American Association of Colleges and Universities (http://diversityweb.org) has compiled an extensive inventory of classroom practices, faculty development activities, examples of curricular transformation, and other reflective pieces. These resources offer easily accessible suggestions about conducting courses in ways that are inclusive of a broad spectrum of students and that encourage durable consideration of difference. This literature is rich and varied, yet we think it might be useful to distill from it some general observations that can help guide design and implementation of inclusive instructional practices.

Making discussion inclusive. The advice most often repeated about creating an inclusive classroom is to employ multiple instructional methods to engage the various learning strengths and styles present in a diverse classroom. The underlying logic of instructional variety as a means of including difference is relatively transparent: the communities that emerge in classrooms between instructors and students reflect those characteristics that distinguish one individual's style from another and also embody the broader cultural differences that characterize larger society. In light of the cultural and individual complexity of the classroom, any one instructional strategy is unlikely to attract the attention and sustain the engagement of all students. Lee Knefelkamp (1997) puts the matter this way: "To teach students to participate effectively in a democratic and pluralistic society, one needs to respond to the needs of various groups within our classes as well as to the individual students." This emphasis on participation puts a premium on those instructional strategies that rely on collaborative effort. Small-group work, for instance, is a good place to begin, but we need to do more than merely ask students to form groups, to work on an assignment, and then report back. We need also to attend to how groups are formed, who speaks (and who listens) as they collaborate, which groups report substantively and which merely respond "we had what they had." Although we discussed some of these issues in earlier chapters, we return to them here to highlight the effects of difference on class participation.

Raymond Wlodkowski and Margery Ginsberg (1995) argue that many college classrooms are structured such that they deprive students of color and women of the opportunity to be "heard in their own way and on their own terms, reflecting their own interests" (p. 111). Although collaborative learning strategies may help break down these structural impediments, without careful attention on our part they may also reproduce the patterns of interaction that have historically marginalized certain groups. For example, research suggests that white men are more likely than women or minority men to dominate classroom discussion, and other work also indicates that faculty members tend to favor men through such nonverbal means as eye contact and patience while waiting for a response (Wlodkowski and Ginsberg, 1995).

The danger of "silencing" is probably most acute in whole-class discussion, but it lurks in every classroom when students are asked to work collaboratively. Moving from group to group, pausing to assess the interactions, and intervening to make space for those who seem to be marginalized is a simple but informal technique to encourage and support participation. Likewise, creating a "space-making" selection pattern (for example, asking for one part of an answer from one group, another from the next, and so on) can ensure substantive contribution from all groups during the process of reporting back.

Myra Sadker and David Sadker (1992) outline a more structured technique to avoid unequal participation. Each student receives a number of chips that serve as an entrée to and a brake on discussion. To participate, a student must contribute a chip; by the time the task is completed, each student's chips must be spent. However, once his or her chips are gone, a student must wait for the next task before participating again. The chips serve to regulate the more talkative students by tacitly asking they choose only their most significant responses, while at the same time affording an opening (and a gentle demand) for the more reticent to contribute. Distributing chips may seem a little stilted, but the technique does shift the burden of making space from an intervening instructor to the students themselves.

Another fairly common way to ask students to monitor their own participation is through publication of a set of rules or guidelines for classroom collaboration. Such guidelines may contain generic expectations ("Please come to class prepared") as well as those that have an impact on the discussion of difference ("no racial or ethic slurs, even as means of illustration"). Other principles appear frequently: no blaming, speak from a personal rather than universal perspective ("I think that . . ." rather than "Most people think . . ."), and various cautions about the use of humor (Wlodkowski and Ginsberg, 1995). In Chapter Nine, we suggest techniques for engaging students in establishing their own guidelines for participation. However the guidelines are established, the purpose is the same: creation of a space where all students are encouraged to participate.

Two questions about group formation frequently surface when instructors become intentional in the use of collaborative techniques to enhance participation of all students. "Should I let students self-select which group they join?" "Should I purposely balance groups along race and gender lines?" Although there is some variability, the general consensus is that we ought to ensure that each student working group embodies the dimensions of difference present in the classroom without unintentionally isolating students underrepresented in the class (Cuseo, 1998; Rosser, 1998; Sadker and Sadker, 1992). Although the reasoning here is clear—students will more fully encounter difference if they work in groups that are diverse—creating and sustaining diverse student groups is often easier said than done.

Left to their own preferences, students often sit in clusters that reflect the gender and race lines in larger society. If self-selected groups are formed on the basis of such seating arrangements, they are likely to include very little diversity. The use of a seating chart can, of course, overcome these patterns, but the effort to ensure varied groups can lead to the day-to-day isolation of some students, especially in a classroom where numbers are imbalanced along race or gender lines. Shari Saunders and Diana Kardia (n.d.) suggest a variety of tactics to produce diverse groups that work even in a classroom with a clustered seating pattern, such as randomly assigning students to groups by drawing group numbers from a container or by simply counting off. Of course, instructors themselves can intentionally assign students to groups so that each group reflects the diversity of the classroom.

Our own sense here is somewhat mixed. We agree that diverse groups are beneficial to all students and should be encouraged. At the same time, we recognize that students sometimes need the comfort and assurance of a self-selected group, even if the group lacks some of the dimensions of difference. Our best advice is to use a combination of tactics throughout the semester. Perhaps begin by random assignment, then move to an activity in which groups are self-selected, then develop a Jigsaw-like activity (see Chapter Nine) where self-selected groups work on a portion of a problem, then split to reform new groups where all portions of the problem are represented. Whatever techniques we use to form collaborative groups, we need to be vigilant and prepared to intervene to be sure that all group members participate as thoughtful speakers and respectful listeners.

Making materials inclusive. Encouraging and supporting the participation of all students involves more than designing collaborative learning practices. Ultimately, students participate in a course if the materials they work with—discussion activities, cases, examination questions—are relevant to their lives and experiences. This is seldom a problem for majority students; examples and other instructional materials are usually derived from the experiences and circumstances of people very much like them. For students who historically have been underrepresented on our college campuses, the situation is very different. Our examples often overlook their presence, and our materials often assume that all students approach the problems they pose from a similar vantage and with comparable points of view. For students whose first weeks on campus are already a period of significant adjustment, the effect of course materials that marginalize or exclude their experiences and perspectives can be particularly estranging.

As we noted, transforming the content of a course may work best to address this issue, but there are ways short of that to make the day-to-day materials of our course more inclusive of the diversity in our classrooms. Phillipa Kafka suggests that the questions we ask about the materials we assign are one means of introducing a wider range of experiences and perspectives. Using *Othello* as the content vehicle, she suggests that a series of questions revolving around issues of race, class, and stereotypes can elicit broader student participation than more traditional lines of inquiry (reported in Kitano, 1997). In a similar vein, Joseph Cuseo (1998) suggests that our questions to students ask them to personalize course concepts by situating them in some circumstance of their own lives: "How would you apply these stress management strategies to a stressful situation you are currently experiencing?"

In addition to asking questions that allow students to bring their own experiences to our course work, we might invite them to collaborate with us in constructing assignments or selecting problems. Asking them to select a topic of particular interest to them for an assignment or two is one way to do this. To give a bit more guidance, we might offer them a list of topics from which they can choose. Likewise, we might offer a series of readings for a particular unit and invite students to select those they wish to complete according to their judgment of which texts seem most relevant to their interests. The lists we compile, of course, should incorporate a variety of voices and approaches so that students will see their choosing as an honest invitation to link their own interests to the course content (Cuseo, 1998).

Having students simultaneously read different texts presents a challenge to maintaining a cohesive sense of community in the classroom. Our colleague in sociology Helen Mederer, who employs this strategy, uses a Jigsaw (see Chapter Nine) to take advantage of the diversity of student choices to enrich discussion. She begins by asking students who chose the same texts to form groups with one another. Following the work of those same-text groups, she asks students to regroup, this time in clusters where each text is represented by a student who chose it. In this way, students get a double benefit. They have their own choice validated as they become the expert on a particular reading, and they have the opportunity to hear from other expert voices about choices that were different from their own.

We should also be attentive to difference when we use examples, draw inferences from course materials, or make an effort to attune our content to contemporary concerns. Saunders and Kardia (n.d.) suggest, for example, that we construct illustrations that permit students to see content from multiple perspectives. A discussion of medical practices in an introductory sociology or nursing course could, for instance, be shown from a variety of perspectives: those of the physician, a patient who has only limited or no health insurance, or a recent immigrant family whose culture sees health care very differently from how it is in the West. For an interesting example, see Anne Fadiman's *The Spirit Catches You and You Fall Down* (1998). In creating these examples, we need to exercise care that groups and individuals be portrayed in as rich a context as possible. If our illustrations employ difference unreflectively, glossing over the complexities of life (efficient Japanese businesses, HIV-positive gay men, unemployed African American teenagers), we run the risk of undermining the very inclusion we seek to foster.

Constructing inclusive exam questions. Creating full-faceted and inclusive examples is especially important as we begin to draft problems, scenarios, and vignettes for an examination. Not surprisingly, students are more attentive to the material that appears on an exam than they are to other materials in a lower-stakes setting. Moreover, they probably engage exam problems more seriously than they do those cases and scenarios that shape "ordinary" class activities. If our class sessions are inclusive of diverse viewpoints and voices but our exams consist of problems in which actors appear only in generic guise, stripped of those human factors that in part make us who we are—race, gender, sexual orientation—students receive a clear indication about how much the consideration of difference matters when things count.

Patricia Williams (1991, p. 88) adds that such generic descriptions often send a tacit message: "I am struck, for example, by the general absence of white people in exams written by people who do specify race when they are referring to nonwhites. . . . 'White' is used only to distinguish from blacks and other nonwhites. The absence of 'white' thus signals that 'everyone' is white." The point Williams makes here about race can also be extended to gender, sexual orientation, class, and other axes of difference.

One relatively easy way to ensure that examinations represent the same commitment to diversity as other class activities is to invest time in searching for texts that lie outside our disciplinary boundaries for material that can be fashioned into questions. Memoirs, biographies, op-ed pieces, popular films, and other not-for-classroom-use genres often contain voices and perspectives that with a little massaging can be fashioned into exam items in which difference plays an integral part. For example, consider this item, written in the style so familiar to us:

> Describe the concepts we would use to explain a person's sense of identity. Be sure to include some discussion of how we "create a self" both through the choices we make and how we respond to the views others have of us.

The "person" in question is generic (and if Williams is right, we envision *him* as *white* and *straight*). Even though we can easily imagine that the class sessions from which this task is drawn focused on gender and race and more, those important dimensions that affect creation of self have been pushed to the margins now that the exam has arrived.

In trying to get students to think about what it means to create a self, instructors might spend some time scanning current memoirs, reading periodicals, searching the Web for interview transcripts, and looking in on various public affairs television programs. Just such a process led us to essayist and PBS commentator Richard Rodriguez's recent memoir, *Brown* (2002), and a piece in the *Chronicle of Higher Education* (Rodriguez, 2003), along with several online interviews with the author. Using those bits and pieces as raw material, we refashioned the question into one in which difference plays a central role:

> Richard Rodriguez, whose parents immigrated from Mexico to the United States and who has often been introduced as "a Chicano intellectual," tells the following story: "On his interview show, Bill Moyers [who is white] once asked me how I thought of myself. As an American? Or Hispanic? I answered that I am Chinese, and that is because I live in a Chinese city [San Francisco] and because I want to be Chinese. Well, why not? Some

> Chinese-American people . . . paint their houses in colors I once would have described as garish. . . . But I have lived in a Chinese city for so long that my eye has taken on that palette. . . . I see photographs in magazines or documentary footage of China, especially rural China, and I see what I recognize as home. Isn't that odd?"

> Describe the concepts we would use to explain Rodriguez's sense of his identity. Be sure to include some discussion of how we "create a self" both through the choices we make and how we respond to the views others have of us.

The task here is the same: we ask students to think about the process of self-creation. Unlike the earlier version, however, the reformulated question establishes a context that compels students to engage difference as central to the task of analyzing of just how we create a self.

Whether we create examination items from scratch using materials we assign or those we find outside the bounds of the classroom, or whether we select them from a commercial or departmental test bank, it is important to be attuned to the profound impact examinations can have on students' sense of inclusion. Wlodkowski and Ginsberg (1995, pp. 258–259) present a useful checklist for preparing exams that can help us avoid some of the more painful pitfalls. They suggest we monitor construction of our test items along these lines:

- *Invisibility*: Are only certain groups referred to in testing materials?
- *Stereotyping*: Does the depiction of groups cast them in rigid roles that deny the richness of their lives?
- *Selectivity*: Is the item structured so that it allows only one interpretation of an issue or situation?
- *Unreality*: Do items lack a context such that they are divorced from the complexities of historical development and contemporary life?
- *Fragmentation*: Are questions that ask about the dimensions of difference separate from other items on the exam?
- *Linguistic bias*: Does the phrasing on the exam reflect dominant cultural views about the occupants of particular roles or positions?

The list of questions is also useful when we select text or other readings for our courses.

Examinations are only one avenue along which students in our courses encounter difference, but the encounter is likely to be especially salient, particularly for first-year students. Although she writes from the halls of a law school, Patricia Williams (1991) has, we think, made this point as eloquently as anyone. As teachers, she says, we:

> create miniworlds of reality. . . . We define the boundaries of the legitimate and the illegitimate, in a more ultimately powerful way than almost anyone else in the world. It is enormously important therefore to consider the process by which we include, as well as the process by which we exclude. It is thus that an exam, which includes only three problems, two of which feature black criminality and the third of which deals with gay criminality, constructs a miniworld that reinforces the widely held misperception that blacks commit most of the crimes, that only gays carry AIDS, or that all gays are promiscuous [p. 88].

Difficult Dialogues

Sooner or later, in spite of our best efforts (or perhaps because of them) to make our classrooms and courses inclusive, nearly all of us will find ourselves engaged with students in circumstances where difference is not merely present but a point of contention. A discussion on DNA testing may turn toward racial profiling, with students arguing heatedly along racial lines about the legitimacy of such practice. The report of a small group may include reference to "true families" set in opposition to the "artificial families" of gay households, bringing angry responses that question just who gets to decide what a true family is. A question that interrupts a lecture may begin with a reference to "welfare queens," eliciting exasperated sighs from several parts of the room.

Moments such as these often catch us off-guard. We were thinking about how to move the discussion forward, about how to respond to a group's report, about an example that would illustrate the point we have just made. Instead we are listening to an angry exchange and raised voices, or confronting a chilly silence where a phrase just hangs, waiting for us to say or do something.

What ought we say, what ought we do when the dialogue we have encouraged turns difficult? There are no simple three- or eight-step answers to these questions, a fact that often discourages us from seeking to engage students in this sort of conversation in the first place. If dealing with difference is going to produce difficult dialogue that leaves us groping for a solution (and we are pretty sure it will), would we not be better off to avoid this sort of dialogue in the first place?

That may seem a safe approach, but it is not. Classroom interactions, no matter how routine we may think they are, can turn difficult in the twinkling of an eye. A random comment, an ill-chosen word, a humorous remark that goes awry can infuse even the blandest discussion with the potential to ruin a semester's work. Difference is present in our classrooms, in our students, between our students, in us, and between our students and us. If our courses are going to invite all students to participate, we need to develop some effective and inclusive ways to deal with those dialogues that turn difficult.

Lay a Constructive Foundation

We can often help ourselves and our students deal with difficult dialogue by spending some time at the beginning of a course talking about what sorts of issues are likely to come up during the semester and how we can constructively discuss them. As we noted earlier, one way to do this is to publish a set of guidelines in the syllabus that help students speak and act so as to produce respectful interaction. Less formally, we might orally remind students to avoid some of the things that often trigger difficult dialogue: blaming, stereotyping, certain slang phrases, and so on. Depending on the nature of our course, we might want to refocus on guidelines of this kind as we approach a particularly provocative topic or unit. We do need to be clear that the purpose of the guidelines is not to hamper debate or disagreement, but rather to foster a climate in which disagreement can be intellectually productive. Issues of difference produce a variety of views that are often passionately held. Rules to guide classroom work can help us and our students manage that variety and passion constructively (IRC, 2003a).

Play for Time

Even if we have established rules and even if students make their best efforts to follow them, debate can become argument and disagreement a shouting match. At this point, many recommend stopping the action in the hope that things might cool down. To do this, we might interject ourselves into a conversation ("Let's wait a minute. There's some interesting stuff going on here, but we need to relax a bit") or we might gesture like a referee and literally call "Time out!" (IRC, 2003b).

Once the exchange is interrupted, we have a number of options. We might rephrase what students have said less provocatively, correcting language that may be offensive. We might buy a bit more time by outlining the dimensions of the disagreement on the board or overhead. We might even gently suggest that discussion would go better if everyone were just a bit calmer. Lee Warren (2003) suggests that we ask students to reflect on just what they might learn from the interrupted exchange. Often, she says, this question helps students shift gear and begin to reflect on the difficulties that difference presents in everyday life.

Invite Broad Participation

As with other heated exchanges, interrupting a difficult dialogue often defuses the situation. A few remarks from us and the discussion can resume as a productive exchange. Sometimes, however, the dispute simply restarts, especially if the same students continue to hold the floor. Here we can use the nature of the dispute, rephrasing it to invite more students to participate. For example, if students were embroiled in an exchange over the propriety of same-sex marriage, we might halt the conversation and ask something like: "Many people in this society think that their own marriages will be damaged if we permit same-sex marriage. Let's see if we can sort out why they might think that, and then let's see what some more of us think about that" (IRC, 2003b).

Have Students Write

We might at this point need to be rather directive, either calling on students who have yet to participate or perhaps forming groups to have all students begin to work on the newly posed question. Another strategy is to have students do some quick writing on the problem posed (Warren, 2003; IRC, 2003b) or even on the nature of the dispute itself. The writing serves a dual function: it asks all students to engage the issue, and it allows them to do so in a more private and less threatening manner. Additionally, it takes some time, allowing things to cool down and giving us some time to think.

Keep the Dialogue Going

However we seek to manage the difficult moments in our classroom, it is important not to truncate them or conclude them prematurely. Once the waters have been oiled, we can often fashion the dispute into a genuine learning experience. If students have done some writing, we might collect it and bring excerpts to our next class session. Alternatively, we might ask them to do some additional investigation outside class and bring their results to class with them (IRC, 2003b). For our own part, we might rethink the next few class sessions and plan on devoting some attention to addressing the dimensions of the dispute, bringing in additional information or another perspective.

It is also important to keep the dialogue going with individual students. We might talk to the initial participants in the dispute informally after class or before the next session. These conversations can offer encouragement, guidance, and support that may be essential if students are to continue to engage with and learn from the views of others (Warren, 2003).

See Ourselves as Participants

It is tempting to think about difficult dialogues from the vantage of a referee: we watch for low blows, break the clinches, and give a standing eight count when the action gets too hot. There is some truth to metaphor, as the preceding suggestions indicate. Nevertheless, we are not merely bystanders in these dialogues, we are participants; we have our own strongly held views, and we, like our students, can be wounded or angered by the words and actions of others. To manage the difficult dialogues of the classroom effectively, we first need to manage ourselves.

Warren (2003) suggests four checkpoints in this regard. First, we need to be calm and steady amid the confusion a difficult dialogue creates. Our steadiness during an angry exchange makes it more likely that students will be able to control themselves and learn something from the experience. Second, we should take time to "breathe deeply." After interrupting a dispute among students, a few moments of silence may be just what they and we need. Third, we should keep our personal feelings under rein and resist the urge to take remarks personally. Again, we need to model for students the behavior we hope they will display. Finally, we need to be reflective about our own bias and vulnerability. Thinking in advance about what is likely to get under our skin reduces the likelihood that we will be caught off-guard should a difficult dialogue turn our way.

Conclusion

Creating and sustaining inclusive courses and inclusive classrooms are among our most important obligations. Our responsibilities in this regard do not stem from fashionable politics or the latest educational theory. Rather, they stem from those basic commitments we have made as faculty: to meet our students where they are, engage them with reasonable rigor, and support them in their efforts to succeed. We can no longer afford to include some students while others are marginalized. The task of higher education is not only to produce graduates; it is also to nurture citizens who can understand, respect, and deal equitably with those who differ from themselves. If our courses include different experiences, communities, and cultures as central to their inquiry, and if we invite expression and consideration of those differences, we and our students move closer to fulfilling that calling.

For Further Exploration

- American Association of Colleges and Universities Diversity Web, n.d. (http://diversityweb.org; retrieved Jan. 2006).

  This site, sponsored by AACU, has been a durable presence on the Web for many years. It is a treasure trove of ideas for incorporating diversity into classrooms and curricula. There are links to an extensive array of campus-hosted sites that offer additional resources, including sample syllabuses, classroom discussion guidelines, suggestions for dealing with classroom conflict, and much more.

CHAPTER 14

Teaching Large Classes

The lecture hall with its tiered seats, projection screens, and fixed lectern has become a cultural icon. In scene after scene in both film and television, the collegiate educational process is represented by brief glimpses of a lecturer set in front of dozens and dozens (if not hundreds and hundreds) of students. The scenes work because most of us have experienced at least some of our education in just this manner. Whether we remember those lecture hall experiences fondly or not, things are quite different if we move from the tiered seats to the lectern, from being one of several hundred students to being the instructor charged not only with teaching such a throng but controlling them as well.

It is probably safe to say that none of us relishes the prospect of having to teach a class of one hundred or two hundred or more first-year students. Our sense of education as a personal encounter between faculty member and student, where essays and conversation are at the heart of the process, quickly fades. Instead, we find ourselves thinking about the mundane but suddenly threatening issues of attendance, record keeping, microphones, unruly students, computer grading, and a host of other clerical issues. Students who find themselves trooping into a lecture hall with hundreds of their peers are probably no keener on the large class than their instructor is. For them too, large classes seem to push more meaningful issues to the margin of consciousness while a sense of all-lecture, all-memory, always a number, never a name comes to the fore.

The trepidation most faculty and students feel about the prospect of conducting a large class is not misplaced. Important instructional goals probably are more difficult to achieve as class size expands to auditorium proportions, and this is especially true when our goals involve more than retention of information. If we want to develop thinking skills or effect change in motivation or attitude, a large class simply is not as effective as a small one (McKeachie, 2002; Bligh, 2000). Why, then, are large classes so prevalent, particularly in universities? A simple trade-off supplies the answer. At many institutions moderately large (say, one hundred to two hundred students), or even very large (three hundred to five hundred or more students), courses permit an economy of scale that underwrites a number of small, more intimate classes in which professors and students get down to the supposed real stuff of education. Of course, first-year students and general education courses commonly bear the brunt of this exchange.

Although we might wish for an academic world without large first-year classes so that personal contact with faculty members would characterize a student's collegiate career from the initial semester until commencement, eliminating large-enrollment courses seems an unlikely prospect. Given that fact, we should spend our time trying to get the most out of the large-class environment rather than bemoaning its existence. We believe that large-class instruction can be more effective, more engaging, and more productive of student learning than is generally the case. Indeed, much of the research on how class size affects learning is difficult to interpret because large-class instruction tends to proceed through lectures ("What else can I do?" the first-time large-class instructor asks), while small classes rely somewhat more on discussion and other more interactive methods. Research tells us that lecturing is less effective in promoting understanding, thinking, or attitude change (Bligh, 2000). We could, perhaps, significantly reduce the difference in student learning between small and large classes if we incorporated similar activities to engage students in both settings.

This, of course, is the heart of the matter. Can faculty teaching large classes use instructional methods that promote understanding, thinking, and problem solving? We are convinced the answer is yes. Most of the practices and methods discussed in previous chapters are suited to large classes as well as small ones. Indeed, many of the specific ideas and examples presented earlier were contributed by colleagues who teach large classes.

Clearly, however, large classes are not merely small classes only larger. Class size does make some difference. For example, if 10 percent of the students in a small class miss a class or do poorly on an assignment or seek extra help, we can probably give them the individual attention they request. In a large class, the percentage of students seeking or needing attention may be the same, but the sheer number of students—now twenty or fifty—needing our time and attention quickly surpasses our ability to provide it. Even with the ease of electronic communication (and, oddly, perhaps because of its "24/7" capacity), it is draining to respond to that many individual students each week, every week. Those who teach large classes *do* face problems not confronted by their colleagues teaching small classes. Faculty who are faced with those challenges can nevertheless be successful, and the large class may have some characteristics of its own that they can put to sound educational use.

Anonymity

Anonymity, the sense students have that no one—especially not the instructor—will notice them, attend to their needs, or care about them, is probably the chief challenge in large-class instruction. The anonymity of the auditorium fosters a sense of disaffiliation, eroding the motivation, commitment, and personal responsibility essential to student learning. A large class often leaves students feeling disconnected from their classmates, the professor, and the classroom and course itself. They miss class for flimsy reasons, wander in and out during class sessions, neglect assignments, avoid seeking extra help, cheat on exams—with little sense that something is awry because, after all, this is what one does in the nameless and faceless world of the large class.

For our part as faculty, we find ourselves unable to combat effectively the restiveness and disconnection that we see (and that often disturbs our concentration and derails our train of thought). Most of our strategies for doing so have been developed in small classes where we can call students by name or appeal to personal relationships to sustain engagement and maintain or even restore the productive order of the classroom. But what works with a small community gathering in the seminar room will not work with the crowd that populates the auditorium.

The anonymity of the large class seems on the face of it to be inevitable. Yet some faculty manage to create a large-class environment that clearly conveys to students that they care about them, both collectively and as individuals, and that they are committed to student learning. Naturally, they do not learn the names of hundreds of students, or establish personal relationships with them, but their course evaluations are sustained testimony that students feel cared about as well as cared for. When we ask these large-class instructors how they account for such student comments as "The professor really cares about students," they are initially puzzled and often protest: "How can I care about them? I don't even know who they are." Upon reflection, many of them offer speculation frequently phrased as hypothesis: "Maybe they think I care because. . . ." Those faculty reflections tend to coalesce around two strategic principles. First, they suggest that large-class instructors actively seek to bridge the distance between the lectern and the seating of the lecture hall. Second, they point clearly to the importance of creating opportunities for students in large classes to make connections with each other. These principles lie behind our more specific recommendations.

Get out among students. The ten minutes or so between class periods can be used to break down the barrier that the fixed seating and fixed lectern structure of most auditoriums erects. Greeting students as they arrive for class with a simple "Hi, how are you doing?" can be a surprisingly effective way of demonstrating an interest in students. Additionally, circulating through the tiers of an auditorium, up one aisle, across the mezzanine, and down another aisle, stopping to chat with students, even if briefly, can create a personal touch in an otherwise impersonal setting.

A colleague at the University of Massachusetts told us he imagined his role during the short period between classes as a director on a cruise ship, seeking to ensure his passengers' journey was pleasant and that their needs were attended to. We are not certain of the metaphor, but the underlying advice is sound. Of course, talking informally with students before class means we need to come to the classroom a bit early and be ready to teach (rather than using the ten minutes to sort notes, start up presentation software, and so on). That little bit of extra organization will be well repaid.

Incorporate small-group discussion and activities. There is a strong tendency for instructors to view a large class as a setting in which only one instructional method—the lecture, aided by the various wonders of presentation software—can succeed. This is very much not the case. Although using small groups in a large-class setting requires some careful planning and attention to detail (something we address later in this chapter), such activities do give students a chance to talk to one another, exchange ideas, and even form relationships that may blossom into study groups as well as friendship.

In spite of the numbers, the process of small-group discussion proceeds in a large class as it does in a smaller one. We begin by posing a question, problem, or case, with a specific set of tasks articulated, and then ask students to form groups and get to work. In a small classroom, students move chairs or desks; in a lecture hall or auditorium, students swivel in their seats, lean down to a lower row or back to a higher one to accomplish the same effect. Sometimes they will even leave their seats to form a small circle on the floor nearby. We might think that fixed seating is an impossible barrier to small group work, but it is not. After all, students have no problem talking with their neighbors several seats away as they wait for class to begin.

As students begin to work on the discussion question, the instructor can move among the groups, pausing to talk with students a bit more personally about the substance of the course. In much the same manner as the simple greeting mentioned earlier, these interactions break down the barrier that the auditorium seems to impose. Although such conversation is usually brief, faculty say they learn at least something about the students and feel more connected with them. If faculty feel more connected, we suspect the students do as well.

Johnson and Johnson (1987) suggest creating "base groups" of four or five to reduce student anonymity and its erosive effects. The purpose of a base group, a small group in which membership is stable, is to provide support for its members. At the beginning of each class, students meet in their base groups, tell one another about pleasant or stressful experiences since last they met, and report how much of the homework they completed. Each student gives a brief summary of the reading and his or her thoughts about it. Together, they summarize the main points and identify things they do not yet understand.

Later, when the instructor pauses to give a discussion question or problem-solving exercise, base groups function like any other small group. During the last five minutes, students meet in their base groups once again to outline the major ideas of the lecture and make sure everyone understands the assignment. Incidentally, having base groups ensures productive use of time while papers are being returned or handouts distributed. The stable membership of base groups has the potential for reducing isolation, creating a sense of responsibility to and for other students, and making support readily available. When using this technique, it is probably a good idea to give students one week to decide where they will sit for the rest of the term, and then form the base groups.

Think about using audience response technology. Audience response technology, sometimes called "classroom communication systems" (Beatty, 2004), where students use wireless handheld devices to respond to questions and problems posed by an instructor, is another way to break up presentations and invite student participation. The electronics required for wireless audience response are quite simple and are available through commercial publishing houses (with some textbook adoptions) or through stand-alone providers. Each student is supplied with (usually through bookstore purchase) an inexpensive handheld device (a clicker) that communicates with a receiver linked to a notebook computer. Students use the device to respond to questions the instructor poses, and the receiver quickly tabulates results, often directly importing them into presentation software for immediate display to the class. Using this technology, an instructor could, for instance, collect a class's responses to a question derived from a short presentation, conduct a brief pre-presentation quiz to be followed by a post-presentation quiz to see how well students understood the material, or do some simple polling to see where students collectively stand on some issue related to the course.

The immediate availability of results is the great strength of an audience response system. Students no longer have to wait until we have had time to process the information we have collected before we provide them feedback. As a trade-off, the systems are not yet an efficient means for more discursive responses, and they do not involve the more personal, hands-on aspects of other techniques to engage students. Nevertheless, the immediacy such systems offer is something to look into.

The ability to get individual students to participate actively and publicly is another advantage of an audience response system, one that may be especially important for some learning styles. By combining audience response techniques with small-group work, other collaborative practices, and writing to learn, the instructor transforms a passive learning environment into an active one while at the same time bringing variety to instructional methods.

Assertively invite students to office hours. Faculty teaching large classes often report that office hours are a lonely time. In small classes the personal contact between instructor and student is usually sufficient to encourage students to use our office hours as we hope; when they need our attention, they seek it. In a large class, this is much less likely to be the case. The anonymity of the auditorium combined with the anxiety many first-year students have about interacting with college faculty members creates the paradox many large-class instructors confront: the more students they have, the less likely it is that any of them will visit. Office hours seem to be a largely untapped resource for reducing the distance between large-class instructors and their students.

Our colleagues have tried to address this issue in several ways. One requires each student to meet with him privately for at least fifteen minutes during the semester. Another tells students that she wants to see every student in her office at least once during the semester. They have the option of coming alone or with up to three classmates (the number of chairs in her office), but they should plan to spend at least thirty minutes there. Another brings an appointment sheet to class each week and encourages students who have not yet been to see her to sign up for an appointment.

Some of these strategies do seem limited to classes that are moderately large, but the idea that underlies them can be adapted to courses with larger enrollments. For example, McKeachie (1986) has tried announcing that he will meet over coffee or soft drinks with any students who are free, and periodically he hands out an invitation to students to join him for refreshments in order to get better acquainted. At other times, he distributes class observation forms to a small number of students at the beginning of class and asks them to discuss their observations with him afterward. None of these methods can ensure that every student in a large class will encounter the instructor personally. Nevertheless, they can and do give evidence to students that the course is not quite so anonymous and the instructor not quite so distant as might first appear.

Schedule extra sessions during the semester. We make this recommendation with some hesitation because we believe faculty who teach large classes are already harried and frequently overworked. In some respects, however, extra sessions scheduled in the evenings can become a viable alternative to office hours, especially for a very large class. One of us (C. B. Peters) regularly teaches a course with five hundred first-year students and has done the math: fifteen minutes spent with each student would be full-time work for nearly a month. Scheduling extra sessions with students may be more productive use of time. Peters, for example, offers a series of workshops during the first two weeks of the course on how to read the texts, how to learn from lectures, and how to prepare for exams. Additionally, he schedules extra help sessions before each exam, which adds five or six extra meetings during the semester. These are not intimate gatherings; attendance, which is voluntary, usually runs two hundred to three hundred students. He is not sure that students who attend improve their performance on exams, although students report the sessions are indeed helpful. Students do, however, seem to have a good time, often arriving together in ad hoc study groups, and it does seem likely that the extra time he is willing to spend demonstrates to students the fact that he cares about them and wants them to succeed.

Getting Students Involved

Anyone who has taught a large class knows that the tried-and-true method for getting students involved—a class discussion—does not work in the lecture hall. On a good day, 10 students might volunteer contributions, but the remaining 90 or 190 or 490 students quickly settle into a passive state and eventually tune out altogether. For large-class instructors, nothing can be worse than facing scores of vacant stares and bored expressions, so it is understandable that they return to the teaching method they know best: the lecture.

Twenty years ago, art historian Wendy Holmes (1985) wrote of her early attempts to teach a large class and in a recent conversation reconfirmed her experience: "After some desultory attempts at general discussions, question and answer sessions, and optional discussions for interested students, that [talking *at* students] is exactly what I settled into in Introduction to Art, a class in art appreciation which I teach to two hundred students every semester. I clarified and refined my lectures. I distributed mimeographed sheets bearing artists' names and dates and the main points of each lecture. I showed slides of paintings and talked about them." The lectures, though they were well organized and always accompanied by visual aids, did not yield the desired response from students. She continued: "What I disliked about the large classes was the passivity and literalness of the students, their desire for precise answers to questions for which there are no precise answers, their tendency to busy themselves recording every word I uttered rather than really looking at the paintings, the poor quality of their interpretive essays, and the resentment that was inspired by exams. I came to believe that the speaker/listener dispenser/receiver structure of the lecture format . . . bred fear and hostility toward doing anything" (pp. 159–160). In the end, she turned to two methods that we believe are indispensable tools for instructors of large classes: small-group discussion and writing-to-learn exercises (Holmes's essay includes examples of both).

John Stevenson, now the chair of the Department of Psychology at the University of Rhode Island, responded to our query about how he got students involved with an outline listing twenty-five of the small-group activities and the writing exercises he uses. Although we can include only a few of his examples, they are worthy of attention because they were designed for an introductory psychology course that regularly enrolls more than five hundred students.

- Small-group discussion following a vignette in which I act out how two very different people spent their time at the same party: "Develop two or three plausible explanations for what caused these differences." Follow-up discussion codifies the answers to develop theories about the causes of human behavior and illustrates that students already have complex theories about the causes of human behavior.

- Preliminary out-of-class assignment: "Read the case study and write a short answer (one to three sentences) to this question: 'What central aspects of Carol O'Brien's personality have remained constant over time?' Provide three supporting quotations from the case study."

- Small-group discussion: "How are current students the same as or different from the woman, Carol O'Brien, described in the case study?"

- Small-group discussion: "If you were trying to select the ideal roommate, what kinds of things would you look for and what would be the best way to find out about each?" Follow-up discussion leads to lecture on prediction and personality assessment.
- After identifying four major sources of information and illustrating each using examples from the "ideal roommate" task, a writing-to-learn exercise: "List one advantage and one disadvantage for each of these four sources of information about personality." Follow-up discussion produces a summary chart.

Not surprisingly, these examples look very much like discussion and writing activities used in small classes. Nearly all of the small-group discussion, case-study, role-playing, writing-to-learn, and structured homework assignments we discuss in Chapters Seven, Eight, and Nine are suitable in large classes. There are, however, some challenges in using such activities as enrollment grows larger. Our advice here is, in many respects, the same sort of guidance we would give to all instructors regardless of class size. Large-class instruction has a smaller margin for error, however, because our ability to clear up confusion, redirect attention, and refocus a discussion is affected by class size. Accordingly, attention to organizational detail is of paramount importance when planning active learning projects for a large-class setting.

Prepare explicit instructions for any activity. First-year students need structure and direction, and in a large class this is often especially the case. Articulating specific tasks to be accomplished ("List three things that . . ."), specific evidence to be cited ("Reference two particular passages in your text . . ."), and the particular product to be produced ("Submit one paragraph that . . .") can help ensure that discussion is focused on the content of the activity, rather than on just what it is that students are supposed to be doing or supposed to hand in. In a smaller class, faculty might clarify or elaborate as questions arise, but the number of questions that can come up in a large class will quickly undo even the most patient instructor.

Put instructions in writing. Complicated tasks may require handouts with complete instructions. Alternatively, if the activity and accompanying instructions are concise enough, the information can be projected using presentation software. The point here is that if instructions are only presented orally, many students will miss some or all of them. Having to stop a discussion to repeat the question or clarify what the task requires is both distracting to students and frustrating to the instructor.

Look at samples of student work. Do not try to visit every small group or read every student's response to a writing-to-learn exercise. Instead, develop a procedure for sampling. These activities offer an excellent opportunity for instructor–student interaction, but that can become overwhelming if we try to be in too many places at one time or read too many pages of first-year student prose. One handy way to collect these exercises is on 4x6 note cards. They are inexpensive and easy to distribute (students can pick them up on the way to their seats), but the real advantage is that they permit easy review. An instructor can quickly scan a stack of cards, even a large one, to reveal the general tenor of student responses, select a sample of good answers to read in class, and identify those that seem confused or misinformed.

Once a few answers have been identified as especially good, an instructor can use them for feedback in the next class session. Excerpted responses can be projected or even distributed as a handout. "Here's what some of you said last time . . ." is a simple way to connect one class to the next, as well as give students a sense of what they and their classmates have said and offer instructor feedback. We can also use student responses to correct widespread misimpressions ("Many of you said things like this . . . but if we think a little bit, we can see that this approach sidesteps an important issue . . .").

In using this feedback strategy with a class of five hundred first-year students, we have discovered that attaching students' names to the good responses has a powerful effect. "Suzanne and Matt had this to say . . ." adds a personal touch without identifying students in a way that might prove embarrassing (a benefit of a large-enrollment course). In our experience, students come to regard this first-name identification to be a reward worth seeking. They often cheer when what they have said appears on the projection screen, and many of them speak for their group in saying things like, "This is really good; we're sure you'll want to put it up" as they pass in their responses.

Encourage participation. Experiment with strategies for encouraging students to participate in these activities. Even though there are several strategies designed to reduce the sense of disconnection inherent in the lecture hall, many first-year students are not all that eager to become actively involved in learning, and their anonymity in a large class makes it easier to sit back and wait. Start with gentle encouragement: "You should try this because it will help you know how prepared you are." If this does not work, introduce subtle persuasion: visit with students or groups who appear idle and ask if they need some help. Using the feedback method just discussed may also lend some encouragement along these lines.

Of course, even when such activities constitute a small portion of the points available, grading remains a reliable motivator. Holmes

(1985) recounts her decision to begin grading her in-class activities: "I collected all class exercises and used them to spot-check attendance. I instituted a new grading policy, awarding 'extra-credit' points for some group and individual exercises. All students or groups handing in an assignment received an attendance check, but one or two points were awarded only for adequate or superior answers to questions. Attendance was excellent, class morale high, and the interpretive essays on exams were much better. I believe that the single most important factor in the students' improvements from first to second semester was my decision to collect and grade in-class assignments" (p. 162).

Grading several hundred activities in any reliable way may seem a daunting task, and in some ways it is. However, if the task is sufficiently focused so that requirements can be met in a paragraph or less (or perhaps two), if the grading system does not ask for more distinction than pass or fail (*acceptable* or *unacceptable* may be better language), and if the portion of the course grade devoted to in-class activity is an appropriate reflection of course objectives, then grading class activities regularly throughout the semester is a manageable task. For example, when C. B. Peters teaches a course that enrolls five hundred students, he devotes a modest portion of his course grade to points that can be accumulated throughout the semester by thoughtful participation in classroom activity. Students submit a response to each one. Using the notecard technique described earlier, he can sort a day's worth of submissions into those that are acceptable and those that are not, in a relatively short time (an hour or so for five hundred students). Each submission is worth 1 point (the semester total is 100), and he allows students to earn up to 15 points in this manner. In addition to gleaning information about what students are thinking, this system sends the message that class activity and discussion are worthwhile and encourages students to participate meaningfully.

Do not despair if you notice some students do not participate or else drift in and out of a small-group discussion. Even in small classes, some students engage actively while others withdraw or make only a sporadic effort to contribute. For the most part, we are used to that. We can encourage participation in a variety of ways and, if we must, even call directly on those who appear to be drifting. Things are different in a large class, but not so different as we might first think. If fifteen students in a class of twenty were active participants in a discussion or small-group activity, most of us would be pleased that the class had gone so well. Seeing 50 quiet while 150 carry the burden of the task, would trouble many of us. Yet the ratio of active to withdrawn students is the same in both cases.

Again, we have more options to encourage and perhaps require student participation in a small course than we do in a large one. Still, a well-structured activity, collected and perhaps graded, followed by feedback from an instructor who has moved from group to group assisting students, asking them to focus, and responding to questions can go a long way toward allaying the feeling that too many students have taken the easy way out.

Riskier Strategies to Engage Students

We think that most, if not all, instructors in large classes can incorporate small-group activities and other nonlecture classroom practices with little risk of failure. Of course, there will be times of uncertainty, and times when things do not go exactly as planned, but for the most part those ragged edges can be dealt with successfully even in a very large course. The benefit—a more engaging, less anonymous classroom alive with active learning—certainly justifies the risk of an occasional snag. There are some other approaches to enhancing large-class instruction that do come with higher risk. For an instructor with substantial successful experience in large-class instruction, these risks may be worth taking because when these approaches work, the benefits can be substantial.

Large-Class Problem-Based Learning

The large class might not seem to be a likely setting for an instructional technique as free-flowing as PBL, but with a few adjustments and some focused effort it can be an effective addition to instruction. As with nearly everything associated with large-class instruction, planning is essential. The problem employed must be more structured than might be the case in a small course, and the stages through which students move toward its solution require more guidance as well. In some respects, a PBL unit in a large course resembles a series of small-group activities that are linked together, with completion of one leading to the next, so that once the sequence is completed students have arrived at a solution to the problem that began the unit.

We have employed PBL in a very large introductory sociology course. Students self-select into groups of three to six that work together throughout the problem-based unit. A brief introduction of the problem (formulating policy responses to demands for reparations for slavery, for instance) opens the unit, and from that point on class time is devoted entirely to group work. Each day students receive instructions specifying the task. They work together to complete the task and submit their group's work at the end of the hour. Students then receive another stage of the problem, again with specific tasks, to be completed outside class. The solution to that stage of the problem must be typed and submitted at the beginning of the next class session.

The groups of students work outside class, either in face-to-face meetings or through e-mail interaction to complete the stage of the problem distributed for homework. The rhythm of in-class work followed by out-of-class work is punctuated by feedback at the beginning of each class session ("Here's what some of you said . . ." "Here's where we are in this process . . ." "Here's where we're headed next . . ."). Students are motivated to participate because each activity contributes to the course grade. The in-class portion is part of an ongoing tally of in-class points (as discussed earlier) and the out-of-class portion is credited toward a student's score on the examination that concludes the problem-based unit. The examination, like the rest of the work in the unit, is a group project. The working groups of students take it together, with each student submitting his or her own answer sheet.

Student responses on a survey designed to assess the PBL unit are generally positive. They like the change of pace in the all-discussion format, and they especially enjoy the group work that results in a collaborative examination. They also report investing more time outside class than is usually the case. Perhaps most important, the majority of students report learning "a lot" during the PBL portion of the course. These are encouraging results, but PBL in a large class is not easy to pull off. The course we have described already had a substantial array of student activities that required talking and writing together beginning with the first session. In addition, the instructor had a long history of large-class instruction, so the mechanics of distributing, collecting, and evaluating materials (no simple task) were well rehearsed, as were any number of other techniques and tactics essential to dealing with a large number of small groups working at the same time. (For more discussion of PBL in large classes, see Rangachari, 1996; Woods, 1996; Shipman and Duch, 2001.)

e-Learning

Another strategy we recommend with some caution is use of Web-based, e-learning courseware as a means of fostering student discussion and exchange and student-instructor contact. The advantages of e-learning are obvious. With little technical expertise, an instructor can establish a chat room, hold online discussion, distribute materials and course information, post grades, and more. Students can take quizzes, get practice, and see their progress at anytime, from anywhere. The instructor can monitor visits to the course site and evaluate student work without the clutter of paper or stacks of note cards.

The immediacy of access to course information and materials is a good thing, and probably more of us than do should take advantage of these aspects of e-learning. So why the caution? Large-class instruction founders when the anonymity of individual students and the distance of the instructor make learning a private act rather than part of a process in which a community of learners is engaged. When e-learning is used to engage students with one another and with the instructor (for example, continuing a class discussion in a chat room format later in the day or initiating a discussion that extends beyond the classroom), it can be a powerful enhancement to large-class instruction. If, however, students begin to see that they can complete the course from a remote site (e-mailing assignments, downloading classroom presentations, taking quizzes in their dorm room or apartment), the power of the technology begins to undermine the process of learning we had hoped to nurture.

In some respects, our advice about these risky strategies is the same. Before employing them, the instructor should work to make the large class an active and engaging environment, becoming comfortable with the steady attention that needs to be paid to the threats to learning inherent in the auditorium (anonymity, disaffiliation, distance). If those issues seem under control, faculty should be willing to take a few risks. The rewards are likely to be worth it.

Testing and Grading

Assessing student learning is one of the most challenging, and frustrating, tasks in large-class instruction. It seems beyond the ability of even the most dedicated instructor to manage essay exams and papers, even short ones. Accordingly, faculty who teach large classes come to rely more heavily on multiple-choice tests than their colleagues who teach small classes. This is as it should be. If the questions test understanding and thinking, not merely memorization, multiple-choice exams need no apology.

The more difficult matter is persuading students that the tests demand understanding and thinking. As we noted in Chapter Eleven, this is always the case, but especially in a large class first-year students expect to memorize and little else. One way to combat this sort of complacency is to include sample test questions on the syllabus and augment this information by distributing additional samples as the first test approaches. In this way, the instructor can alert students not only to the form the exam will take but also to the sort of learning required.

Unfortunately, for many first-year students the distinction between items that test for memory and those that require a higher order of learning is not an easy one to make, even with examples given. To address this issue, some faculty teach the difference more actively. They describe the types of questions, offer examples, and give students practice in classifying sample questions according to the type of thinking required.

In one particularly useful workshop we conduct, we ask students to study a few paragraphs of a required text. After several minutes, we ask three questions that merely require students to recall the factual information they have just studied. Most students recognize that what they have done is memorize. After a brief discussion, we ask students to resume studying, and this time they know another short exam is forthcoming. Although the next three questions are a bit more difficult, they too can be answered through memorization. After some discussion, students come to see that the two sets of questions they have confronted require only that they memorize. We then pose three more questions, based on the same few paragraphs the students have worked with. These questions ask students to apply ideas, recognize examples, and extend the material to a new context. Coming as they do in the wake of memory items, the difference in question style and in the sort of learning required is much clearer to students (for a more complete discussion, see Peters, 1990).

Other forms of evaluation are difficult in a large class, and as enrollment climbs they may become impossible. Assigning essays or papers in a large class quite obviously creates a heavy burden, but some instructors do it and still lead a relatively normal life, most often with the help of graduate or advanced undergraduate assistants who do at least some of the grading. Of course, this necessitates carefully training them, preferably in the use of a scoring guide (see Chapter Eleven). Faculty who do not have grading help, as is often the case in a class of one hundred or more, might want to proceed cautiously in thinking about essay exams, but there are ways of dealing with short student papers that may be worth trying.

We have, for example, used a course design that requires two hundred students to write one essay during the semester, though not all on the same topic at the same time. At the beginning of the term, we assigned students to eight essay groups and announced the date on which each group would be asked to submit their papers. We assigned the first group its topic two weeks before the papers were due, and a week later we informed the second group of its topic with their due date two weeks out. We repeated the staggered process through the next weeks until each group was assigned a topic. Eventually, of course we read and responded to two hundred essays, but the task was manageable because the staggered assignments produce only twenty-five essays in a given week. Even so, the process was relentless. It began in the fourth week of the semester as the first group submitted their essays and did not conclude until the twelfth week, when the last of the essays were returned to the students (for a brief—and youthfully enthusiastic—description, see Peters, 1985).

Albert McLeod of California State University at Fresno developed another strategy that might be manageable in large classes. At the beginning of the term, he divides his class into "home groups." Once a week the members of each group put their written work (summaries of readings and lectures) into a large envelope. The instructor collects the envelopes and redistributes them, making sure no group gets its own work back. One student in each group does the grading, and every student gets to grade at least once. At the end of the course, students submit a file of all their summaries, and the instructor awards the final grade (Watkins, 1990).

The benefit of the peer grading is obvious: regular feedback can be given to each student without overwhelming the instructor. McLeod noted a close correspondence between his own grades and those of the students. His impression is supported by research. A major review of peer assessment practices in postsecondary education found high reliability and concluded that peer-assessment of writing is "at least as good as teacher assessment, and sometimes better" on measures of achievement and attitudes toward learning (Topping, 1998, p. 268).

Although McLeod uses these written assignments in lieu of examinations, the technique can easily be adopted as a companion for exams or other forms of graded work. In the end, of course, the instructor must deal with a substantial quantity of student writing, but the feedback and guidance provided by peer assessment may lighten the load just enough to make the task doable.

As with so many things involved with large-class instruction, the investment of time in responding to student writing and its benefits to students must be weighed against other uses of that time (developing and evaluating in-class activities that are engaging, writing multiple choice exam items that test higher-order learning, meeting regularly with small groups of students) and their possible benefits to students. Although we would never advise against requiring students to write in a moderately large class (where the instructor is without assistants), careful consideration of costs and benefits is necessary. It is also useful to remember that no course, regardless of size, can incorporate practice in *all* those skills we expect students to develop during their college years. Developing assessment strategies in large classes requires considerable discernment in this regard.

Working with Teaching Assistants

In many colleges and most universities, advanced undergraduates and graduate teaching assistants (TAs) have taken on major responsibility in first-year instruction. They assist faculty in grading, tutor individual students, lead the recitation or discussion section of a large course, supervise laboratories, and perhaps conduct extra help and study skills sessions. Some graduate TAs have full responsibility for teaching courses, particularly general education staples such as first-year composition or college algebra. At some universities, it is possible for a first-year student to complete the two initial semesters without ever encountering a full-time regular member of the teaching faculty; at others, first-year students may be graded only by teaching assistants. Our principal concern here is not so much that TAs, temporary faculty, and per-course instructors have assumed a major portion of the responsibility for teaching first-year students (though that does concern us) but rather with offering suggestions to those faculty who suddenly find that the assignment to teach a large class comes bundled with an inexperienced TA or two.

Training and supervising would-be college teachers is not a role to which most of us are accustomed, and it is a formidable task. Few graduate students have had any prior preparation for college teaching. They know little about the factors that affect learning and less about the skills required for effective teaching. Many will make their first attempt to present a lecture or lead a class discussion on the first day of class, and in the absence of any alternatives they approach the task by trying to imitate professors they liked. They forget, naturally enough, that they themselves are not very much like the vast majority of incoming college students. As Donald Ross reminds us, graduate students "are unusual in their achievements as undergraduates: they did well in most of their courses; they had well-defined and academic career goals; they wished to be like their professors in many ways. To a significant degree they need to be reminded of the students who sat next to them in introductory courses, those who went on to major in something else, those who got C's, and those who dropped out of college" (1986, p. 47).

Working with international TAs poses an even more complex challenge. Unfamiliar with the philosophy and teaching practices of American higher education, they may be surprised—and even insulted—when students interrupt a lecture to ask questions, offer opinions, or challenge them. Most international TAs passed a test of their ability to read and write in English and many passed tests in spoken English. Nevertheless, it is rare to find a new international student who understands American slang or is practiced in the quick interchanges, casual conversation, and small talk that American students expect from their instructors.

Although we depend on teaching assistants to help us solve the problems that come with large-course enrollment, inexperienced graduate students cannot be expected to assume major instructional responsibilities without training, guidance, and support. Providing training and supervision for TAs may not have been part of the bargain when we agreed to teach a large class; however, it may be necessary. Our first suggestion is to follow the general maxim, "When faced with a difficult task, share it."

Working with colleagues rather than in isolation reduces duplication of effort and often makes the time spent more fruitful. On our campus, for example, faculty from the sciences, mathematics, engineering, and computer science work with the Instructional Development Program to sponsor a program for their TAs that includes an introductory workshop series and department-based follow-up programs.

During the week before classes begin, new and returning TAs meet with faculty in their department during the morning and attend five workshops on college teaching in the afternoon. In the department, assistants meet faculty and other students, find out about their teaching responsibilities, review departmental policies and procedures, and begin to discuss the specific content they will be teaching. The afternoon workshops focus on aspects of teaching and learning that cut across departments: the characteristics of first-year students, meeting the first class, clarifying goals, presenting and explaining, and getting students involved. Faculty and experienced teaching assistants from each department attend all workshops and share responsibility for conducting the sessions. Workshop activities include a variety of demonstrations, simulations, role-playing exercises, and discussions, but half of each session is devoted to microteaching. By the end of the week, every teaching assistant has practiced teaching at least five short lessons, seen himself or herself on videotape, and received feedback from peers and faculty.

Once the semester begins, each department offers a follow-up program that continues throughout the year. Although department activities vary considerably, most departments (1) videotape their TAs and review the tapes with them, (2) collect student evaluations and discuss the results in individual consultation, and (3) hold regular meetings to discuss course content, teaching strategies, and the problems students are likely to have in understanding the material. The department-based program is the heart of our effort. Orientations and workshops, no matter how good they are, quickly fade to a faint memory if that is all there is.

On many campuses, the center or program supporting instructional development offers training programs for graduate student instructors. Most programs include an initial one-or-two-day orientation meeting. Many also offer seminars on a variety of instructional topics during the semester, individual consultation with TAs, and services to obtain student feedback. Center personnel are often available and eager to work with the department or individual faculty to develop a TA training and supervision program tailor-made to specific circumstances. Faculty assigned responsibilities for a large course and for teaching assistants should take full advantage of these opportunities where they exist.

Conclusion

None of the challenges in teaching a large class are new, but the convergence of two national trends has, perhaps, created a new environment in which those challenges can be addressed. Concern about the costs of higher education has driven more and more institutions to seek the efficiency of large-class instruction, while concern about the quality of undergraduate education has pushed institutions to ensure that student experiences inside and outside the classroom are intellectually challenging and educationally sound. If the joining of our concern for efficiency with our desire for quality causes us to address creatively the design and conduct of large classes, first-year students are sure to be among the beneficiaries.

For Further Exploration

- Stanley, C. A., and Porter, M. E. (eds.). *Engaging Large Classes.* Bolton, Mass.: Anker, 2002.

  The challenges of large classes are varied, and there are many ways in which they can be addressed. Stanley and Porter have compiled essays that discuss the unique characteristics of large-class instruction and lay out an array of practical techniques for addressing them.

- MacGregor, J., Cooper, J. L., Smith, K. A., and Robinson, P. (eds.). *Strategies for Energizing Large Classes: From Small Groups to Learning Communities.* New Directions in Teaching and Learning, no. 81. San Francisco: Jossey-Bass, 2000.

  This short collection addresses the most important aspect of large-class instruction: transforming the inherent passivity of the lecture hall into an active learning environment. The suggestions here are both wise and creative.

CHAPTER 15

Sustaining Engagement Outside Class

Office Hours, Advising, and First-Year Seminars

> I expect that college will be similar to high school in that one has the ability to have a close rapport with one's faculty; I expect it to be different in every other way. (first-year student)

Having a "close rapport with one's faculty" unfortunately may be a major loss that students experience when they enter college. Reports from the National Survey of Student Engagement (NSSE), administered to students at the end of their first year, indicate that a significant number of first-year students have little or no contact with faculty outside class. According to the NSSE 2004 Annual Report:

- Forty-four percent of first-year students indicated they *never* "discussed ideas from your readings or classes with faculty members outside of class."

- Twenty-six percent of first-year students said they *never* "talked about career plans with a faculty member or advisor."

- Sixty-five percent of first-year students said they *never* "worked with faculty members on activities other than coursework (committees, orientation, student life activities, etc.)."

These are disturbing data because we know that student-faculty contact outside class makes an enormous difference. Drawing upon interviews with students about their college experiences, Light (2001) lets us hear how students talk about these out-of-class conversations, and their stories are powerful testimony to the importance of student-faculty interaction. To be sure, such evidence is anecdotal and possibly not representative. Yet most faculty can recall occasions when out-of-class conversation with their own professor had a similar impact. Then too, there is the now ample research indicating that *personal contact with instructors outside class* correlates strongly with student satisfaction with college experiences, higher educational aspirations, higher academic achievement, and persistence in college (Astin, 1993; Pascarella and Terenzini, 2005; Tinto, 1997).

This chapter explores how faculty might use the contexts in which they already meet with students outside class—office hours, advising session, first-year seminar—to create the sense of personal contact so important to students. Light's research (2001) is particularly helpful in imagining how to make the most of such occasions by identifying a key theme: conversation that mattered to students was often initiated when a faculty member asked a question or posed a challenge that forced students to think about the "relationship of their academic work to their personal lives" (p. 88). These "bigger questions," as Light refers to them, ask in one form or another, "How does what you are studying fit into the bigger picture of your life?" No one expects faculty to become every first-year student's best friend, mentor, or substitute parent. Faculty may, however, make a big difference in the first-year student's academic life by initiating and making time for conversation about these bigger questions.

Office Hours

Most faculty schedule weekly office hours when students in their courses may drop by to ask questions or discuss course content. Many go to considerable lengths to be available at times convenient to students whose schedules differ from one another and from the professor's normal working hours. That so few students take advantage of the opportunity is a source of bewilderment, frustration, and sometimes annoyance to faculty.

If we look at office hours from the student's viewpoint, however, perhaps we can empathize. Few things are more frightening to a student—especially to a first-year student—than a one-on-one meeting with a professor. Successful and struggling students alike recognize that the professor is far more knowledgeable than they are. Reason may tell students that this is as it should be, but fear of appearing foolish is a powerful emotion and deters many from seeking help. Then too, there is a question of trust. Most faculty are sensitive, caring, and eager to help students succeed, but a few are not (those, for example, who see their mission as "weeding students out"), and their comments in one-on-one interaction can be quite devastating. Truth be told, when we think about the courage students have to muster to take advantage of office-hour opportunities, it is a bit surprising that so many do.

Nonetheless, office hours are a chance for the type of personal interaction with students outside class that research has shown to be so important for learning. Here we take some time to talk about how to make office hours work, focusing first on how to get students to visit during office hours and second on how to make the time productive.

Getting Students to Come to Office Hours

Recognizing that many first-year students are fearful of meeting with a professor one-on-one, faculty may have to issue invitations more than once and take extra steps to reassure students. Our suggestions are based on strategies that colleagues say worked for them.

- *List office hours on the syllabus.* Write the most gracious invitation you can muster encouraging students to visit and indicate what kind things you are interested in discussing during office hours.

- *On the first day of class, orally reiterate the invitation to visit during office hours.* Repeat the invitation often throughout the term, highlighting topics and issues you are especially interested in discussing as the course progresses.

- *Talk with students informally before and after class.* Asking students what they think about the Red Sox (a favorite topic in New England) or about various campus events or music they listen to—the more varied the topics, the better—can be a good entrée for casual conversation and go a long way toward convincing students you are approachable.

- *Bring office hour sign-up sheets to class.* Ask students to sign up for an office visit individually, in pairs, or in small groups. Asking students to draft an agenda for this meeting not only puts control in their hands but also may encourage them to reflect on their studying activities and learning.

- *If the course uses cooperative learning activities, invite or require that those groups meet with you during office hours.* Again, asking groups to set the agenda for the meeting encourages reflection on their learning and group work.

- *Survey students about their interest in topics or issues related to course material.* Designate some office hours for discussing those topics in more depth than you plan to give in class. Some colleagues recommend moving these meetings out of the office and calling them a "coffee hour" to create a more informal ambiance.

- *Require students to meet with you during office hours at least once during the course.* Make it preferably during the first few weeks of the semester. Scheduling at least one meeting (individual or in a small group) early in a term can be especially helpful in making sure first-year students are on track.

- *Write "please see me during office hours" on returned exams or papers.* Apparently, such notes produce a 75 percent response rate (Unruh, 1990, as reported in B. G. Davis, 1993). "Please see me" messages need not be limited to students having difficulty. The invitation might also go to students who raised an issue in their paper or journal that you would like to explore further or to students who performed especially well on an examination and might be able to help identify useful study strategies.

- *Incorporate an electronic version of office hours.* Many of our colleagues report that students seem much more likely to ask for help via e-mail than they do in face-to-face conversation. This may be due to the odd sense of anonymity e-mail permits; it often disassociates names and faces. It is also possible that e-mail interaction fits student schedules better. They can fire off questions when (often in the wee hours) and where they actually do their studying rather than having to wait for scheduled office hours. Not all questions or issues are easily addressed via e-mail, but faculty can always invite students to meet with them to discuss the more complicated issues.

Conducting Office Hour Meetings

Some colleagues, annoyed by students' vague entreaties for help or by suspicion that students are using office hours as a substitute for attending class, ask students to come with written questions or other evidence—a problem partially worked, text marked up, a draft of an assignment—that they have put in a fair share of effort to understand (B. G. Davis, 1993; McKeachie, 2002; Nilson, 2003). Such a requirement may be useful if one discovers students are not putting in much effort, but it serves as an additional deterrent for students who already feel hesitant about meeting the professor privately. Admittedly, the suggestions given here are geared more toward welcoming a hesitant student than they are toward deterring a slack-off.

- *Welcome students and try to put them at ease.* Welcoming students includes letting them know that whatever else one is working on when they arrive is less important and easily put aside. It is not, "Give me five minutes to finish up this paragraph or e-mail message." It is more like, "Good to see you! Come in and let me just save this." Putting students at ease is more of a challenge. If the meeting is planned, taking time to review whatever information you have about the student's interests or out-of-class activities can help identify possible small-talk topics. Otherwise, go with the weather, parking problems, or the Red Sox.

- *Invite the student to identify the focus for the meeting* ("What can I do for you today?"), but expect that his or her answer may be vague: "I don't get any of this," or "I was hoping you could explain this chapter." Rather than sending students away to develop more specific questions, try helping them pinpoint the trouble spots ("Let's look at the reading. Show me which parts you understand and where you begin to feel puzzled" or "Let's look at the homework problems. Show me which you're having trouble with. What have you tried?").

- *Be prepared to offer study strategies.* Depending on students' issues, it may make sense to recommend that they visit the writing center, learning skills center, tutoring center, or other campus services. Remember, however, if students are to transfer skills learned in these settings, they need instruction and practice in how to use those skills in the context of specific disciplines (see Chapter Eight for a more thorough discussion).

- *If there is time, try to raise some of the bigger questions.* "Now that we've talked about some things you might try, do you have time to talk with me about some more general questions? Have any of the topics we've discussed so far in the course resonated with things in which you're personally interested?"

Advising

Although individuals other than faculty provide advising services in many institutions, faculty remain the primary source of academic advising on most campuses. According to recent surveys of advising practices conducted by the American College Testing program, faculty are *solely* responsible for academic advising at nearly half the institutions surveyed; if one factors in shared advising arrangements, faculty are responsible for somewhere between 75 percent and 90 percent of all advising (Habley, 2003; King and Kerr, 2005).

The continuing reliance on faculty for academic advising is good news; advising sessions create additional opportunities for the types of meaningful faculty-student interactions that correlate with student success. To capitalize on these opportunities, however, advising sessions must involve something more than students coming to an advising meeting with a list of courses they might like to take and faculty advisors signing off on them. Effective advising recognizes the overlap between advising and teaching and involves a broader array of advising tasks. Helping students make course selections remains an important task, but it should occur *after* more fundamental conversation focused on such tasks as determining and clarifying their educational goals; identifying the knowledge and skills they will need to accomplish their goals; assessing their strengths, weaknesses, and readiness for courses; and exploring curricular and cocurricular activities that might enable them to move toward achieving their goals.

The next paragraphs discuss each of these tasks in a bit more detail, including strategies for initiating and facilitating discussion about them. Our discussion focuses on advising first-year students, but we want to stress that these advising tasks are iterative. Faculty and their advisees cycle through conversation about them in ever more sophisticated versions several times during a student's stay. We also emphasize that first-year advising takes place in a variety of contexts: during a summer orientation session, in group and individual meetings, in first-year seminars, in a learning community, occasionally in the context of a service learning project, and increasingly via electronic communications. Strategies for facilitating conversation in these contexts vary, and faculty may have to adapt strategies discussed if they wish to use them in another context.

Helping Students Identify and Clarify Their Educational Goals

Establishing educational goals is among the most difficult tasks when working with first-year students. Some students come with no idea about what they want to gain from college or what they want to do afterward. At the opposite extreme are students who have a definite idea that they want to be a teacher or engineer or owner of a business, often with only the vaguest notion about what those professionals actually do. To complicate advising matters further, faculty increasingly see students whose parents also have definite ideas about what their son's or daughter's educational goals should be. Speaking to a meeting of academic advisors, the president of one university sympathized with the challenges these "helicopter parents" (parents who hover a lot) create when they pressure students to major in an area they think appropriate, when they second-guess advisors on what courses students should take, and when they urge their son or daughter not to take courses that meet on Fridays so that they can come home on weekends (Spanier, 2004).

For a variety of reasons, then, helping students identify and clarify *their* educational goals is likely to be an ongoing process in which students change their minds (and their majors) as they learn more about tentatively chosen (and not chosen) fields and reflect on their experiences and interests. Given that, how might we initiate conversation about educational goals?

Take a direct approach. Some faculty ask, "What majors are you considering? What interests you about those majors?" Discussion of course selection and sequences proceeds from the answers students supply.

Talk about interests first and majors afterward. Other faculty ask, "What experiences in the past year or two have you found especially interesting and perhaps have you thinking about possible majors?" Incidentally, students fresh out of high school often talk about courses they found interesting or did well in, but asking about recent experiences rather than high school courses allows room for students to talk about other experiences—at work, in the family, in the community—and to have those experiences recognized as legitimate reasons for pursuing a college degree.

Ask who they want to be. Ask students to think beyond what they might major in and envision the person they want to be when they graduate. Drew Appleby (2001), for example, describes an assignment that asks students in his first-year seminar to write a major paper addressing four questions: (1) Who am I now? (2) Who do I want to become? (3) How must I change to become the person I want to be? (4) How can I use my college education to become the person I want to be?

As we noted earlier, most first-year students are just beginning to think about educational goals, and many will change their mind about a major at least once before they graduate. Advisors can be most helpful by initiating conversation about goals early in their meetings with advisees, by working with what students say at the time and by revisiting the questions often—at least before each registration period.

Discussing Knowledge and Skills Needed to Achieve Goals

Faculty know, of course, a good deal about the knowledge and skills needed to work in their areas, to be responsible citizens, and to live fulfilling lives. We spend considerable time discussing such matters, debating what is essential and important, and translating those decisions into curricula of required and elective courses. Having given it so much thought, we often find it tempting simply to tell students what they need to know and be able to do, lay out the curricular requirements, and get on with the business of mapping out a schedule of courses. Students, especially those in the early developmental positions described in Chapter Two, will quite likely welcome such direction and structure (unless, of course, it conflicts with what their parents advise).

We should try to resist the temptation to lay everything out for students, however. If they participate in envisioning the knowledge and skills they need and in identifying courses in which they might acquire those abilities, they are more likely to see the value of those experiences and less likely to view them as hurdles to jump or requirements to get out of the way. How, then, might we engage students in thinking about the knowledge and skills they might need?

Encourage thinking about needed knowledge and skills. Build on earlier conversation about goals by asking students to begin identifying the knowledge and skills they need in order to achieve their goals. A follow-up activity then asks them to compare their list with the college's and program's statements of student outcomes. Where is the overlap? What are the discrepancies between the two lists? Identification of discrepancies can be especially important for further exploration, so it is wise not to truncate the conversation by jumping in too soon to explain the institution's expectations, or by allowing students to accept institutional requirements without really understanding or endorsing them. Instead, encourage students to consult others: upper-division students in their intended major, potential employers in the fields they are interested in pursuing, and people they admire (including parents). Asking students who they talked to and what they found out is a good opening for subsequent advising sessions.

Begin thinking about jobs. We might ask groups of advisees during orientation meetings to think about jobs they want. Appleby (2001) helps students clarify goals by distributing recent newspaper advertisements for job openings suitable for college graduates, invites students to select those that appeal to them, and then asks them to list on the board the knowledge, skills, and characteristics these preferred ads seek in applicants. In the second phase of the activity, students review the department's and college's lists of learning outcomes (including those for general education), compare them to the knowledge skills and characteristics gleaned from job advertisements, and circle those that overlap. Finally, students identify specific course requirements that will help them develop the circled items.

Once students identify, albeit tentatively, the knowledge and skills they need in order to accomplish their goals, good advising encourages another round of self-reflection to assess students' readiness for particular courses before they actually develop a course schedule.

Helping Students Assess Readiness

Are students ready to begin the calculus sequence they will need, or should they start with a precalculus course? Did their achievement in a high school advanced placement course really prepare them to jump into one beyond the introductory level? Helping students assess their readiness for a particular course can spare them the disappointment or boredom that often result from selecting one with too much or too little challenge. Good advice can also save them time and money.

Advisors of first-year students usually receive or have access to some information about students from the admission office: high school courses students have taken and their grades, high school class rank, ACT or SAT scores, academic honors, and so on. At best, such data offer only a *starting* point for considering students' talents and potential success at the postsecondary level. High school curricula, standards, and grading practices vary widely. Standardized tests continue to be challenged on the grounds of validity and equity. We do not advocate ignoring these data altogether, but we caution against making too much of them.

Assessing a student's readiness for a particular college course is further complicated because many first-year students place a lot of faith in what high school grades and standardized tests have told them. Students who earned A's in high school language or math courses, for example, may not believe they should enroll in a beginning language or math course in college, despite what their performance on a placement test might suggest. It can also work the other way; those who score high on a college placement exam but received lower grades in high school or on standardized tests may be reluctant to register for a more advanced course.

Helping students determine their best entry point in college curricula is often difficult, and conversation about options can quickly turn sensitive with first-year students because many are quick to conclude they will not be able to do the work and do not belong in college. Still, we think faculty are best prepared to help students consider the options; we offer these suggestions for how to go about it.

Self-assessment of readiness. Asking students to assess their own readiness for particular courses is one starting point: "You will need the calculus sequence for both the majors you are considering. You have a choice between a two-semester sequence and a three-semester sequence. Which do you think is the better fit for you?"

List courses for discussion. Alternatively, ask students to identify a tentative list of courses that can serve as a starting point for discussion.

Advisors can then use the data they have to affirm or raise questions about students' tentative choices: "You completed two years of French in high school with a B average. Why are you thinking about an introductory-level rather than an intermediate French course?"

Encourage investigation. When in doubt, ask students to investigate further the courses they are considering: "Let's be sure we're constructing a schedule that will work for you. Look at syllabi [often online] and readings [in the bookstore] for courses you're considering. How comfortable are you with the readings? Does the pace seem manageable? Talk to other students about the work. Several of the orientation advisors have taken these courses; what did they find challenging?"

Helping Students Develop Academic Plans

In the past, providing accurate information about curricular options and requirements was an academic advisor's major concern, one that left many feeling overwhelmed by what they needed to know and daunted by the possibility that they might miss something. It is still true that failing to inform students about key requirements, neglecting to alert them to alternate semester scheduling patterns for some prerequisites, or giving them misinformation can be costly to students, both in time-to-graduation and in tuition dollars. Fortunately, technology has reduced the amount of information faculty advisors must keep in mind as they help students develop a curricular plan. On most campuses, program requirements and course offerings are available online, and up-to-date information is usually only a keystroke or two away. What many faculty advisors once found to be the most time-consuming and off-putting aspects of advising—learning and remembering details about various curricular programs and requirements—are no longer necessary. Freed from, or at least substantially supported for, these course-selection aspects of advising, many faculty have time to talk with students about their hopes and plans without getting bogged down in which chemistry course is which.

We all know that advising takes time, and we suspect that we all also know that good advising takes even more time. Scratching out a course schedule is one thing; building an advising relationship with a student is another. We can't achieve all that good advising offers in a meeting or two. We are probably better off trying to create enduring contact with students. One way to do this might be to schedule some group sessions interspersed with individual meetings. The groups can address issues common to students' experience, while our attention can be devoted to individual interests in our one-on-one encounters. However we do it, it is worthwhile to make time to talk with students about things that matter.

First-Year Seminars

Results from the Second National Survey of First-Year Academic Practices (Barefoot, 2002) indicate that 94 percent of postsecondary institutions in the United States offer some form of first-year seminar in which the primary goals include helping students negotiate the transition to college and fostering development of their academic skills. Characteristics of these seminars vary considerably. Some are basically an extended orientation seminar focused on topics such as time management, study skills, campus resources, diversity, and health and wellness issues. Others are more like a traditional academic seminar, organized around an academic theme or issue but also addressing critical academic skills and transitional issues. Mary Stuart Hunter and Carrie Linder (2005) give a comprehensive overview of first-year seminar types. Here, we want to focus more on how first-year seminars, regardless of type, offer a context and opportunity for those faculty-student interactions that are so important for student success. On the basis of conversations with colleagues at our own campus and elsewhere, we share four activities that seem especially effective in initiating meaningful dialogue with students.

Inventory of Expectations and Practice

As we have seen, first-year students enter college with vague expectations that things will be different and that they will have to do more studying than they did in high school. This expectation, of course, is not wrong, but it affords no real guidance about how different things will be, how much more work is required, and how well a student's habits, practices, and skills equip them to deal with the alien landscape they now inhabit. One way to sharpen students' awareness of what they need to do to succeed (and what might stand in their way) is to engage them in a systematic assessment of their expectations for college and their array of academic skills.

Although there are any number of home-grown ways to encourage this sort of reflection, two sophisticated instruments, the Perceptions, Expectations, Emotions, and Knowledge About College Inventory (referred to as PEEK; Weinstein, Palmer, and Hanson, 1995) and the Learning and Study Skills Inventory (referred to as LASSI; Weinstein, Schulte, and Palmer, 1987) collect and report meaningful information about study expectations and skills. Although both inventories must be purchased (print and Web-based versions are available), the cost is relatively low given the depth and breadth of assessment.

PEEK surveys student expectations in three broad categories: academic, personal, and social. The instrument asks students to respond to various prompts according to their expectations for their emerging college experiences (for example, "The material presented by my instructors will simply repeat what is in my textbooks"; "Most of my classmates will have values similar to mine"). The feedback from the inventory allows students and faculty to see how likely it is that student expectations will be matched by the realities of campus life. The areas of mismatch that are identified generate a list of topics likely to lead to fruitful discussion and reflection. PEEK can be previewed at www.hhpublishing.com/_assessments/PEEK/index.html.

LASSI is a comprehensive assessment of students' study skills, habits, and practices that yields information along ten dimensions ranging from attitude and motivation to concentration and the ability to identify main ideas. Much like PEEK, students respond to a series of prompts (for example, "When I am studying a topic, I try to make everything fit together logically"; "I find it hard to stick to a study schedule") by rating the statements as more or less descriptive of their experience with academic work. The feedback indicates to students which activities they seem to have well in hand and those that merit close attention. The instructor can use the data from LASSI about study habits and skills to develop discussion, workshops, or other activities that address potential trouble spots.

Time Logs

How first-year students spend their time, competing demands on their time, and their feeling of being overwhelmed are recurrent themes in previous chapters and in other discussion of first-year students. Time management is a challenge for many of them. Several faculty on our campus and elsewhere (Angelo and Cross, 1993; Light, 2001) have found time log assignments useful in helping students take control of how they spend time. In brief, the assignment asks students to record in half-hour intervals how they spend their time over a week or two and then debrief the logs with the instructor. Instructions for keeping a time log usually encourage students to be specific; rather than entering "Studied for class," they should say "Studied for economics," or better still, "Studied for economics—read the chapter for 15 minutes and worked problems for 15 minutes."

As is the case with many such exercises, debriefing questions are the key. In preparation for discussing a time log with an instructor an assignment might ask students:

- How much time did you spend in each of these activities: attending classes; doing homework; socializing; exercising; meeting with faculty outside class; working; recreational activities (e.g., watching TV, listening to music, playing video games)?
- How much time did you spend per week preparing for each of your courses?

- Where do you think you need to spend more time? Where can you spend less time? Where can you find time?
- What changes would you like to make?

Campus Activity Sampler

As we noted in the opening chapter, first-year students are often concerned about fitting into their new environment. One way to help them address that worry is to develop a list of campus activities and then ask them to attend at least one event in each of several categories. For example, we might create a menu of events—an athletic event, an artistic exhibition, an academic colloquium, a social gathering—and then establish a two-or-three-week period for students to attend and write brief reviews. Asking that students go in pairs or small groups is an option to consider. This way, not only do they get out and about on the campus, but they can also make more lasting connections with their peers.

The benefits of the campus activity sampler are readily apparent. First-year students often have difficulty finding the rich resources of campus life and too often conclude that "nothing really happens here." This simple exercise dispels the myth. Further, once they have attended some of the same events as their classmates, they discover they have more in common than they first thought. Finally, students' accounts of their experience at various campus venues have the potential for creating links with us. We may have attended the theater production or the field hockey game or the gallery exhibition (and it probably is a good idea for us to attend at least some of the events on the list). If we share our response and compare our reaction to theirs, we can enhance early on those faculty-student connections so essential to student success.

Write a Letter to Next Year's First-Year Students

Our introduction to this activity was through our university's first-year seminar, URI 101. Our colleague, W. Lynn McKinney, now dean of the College of Human Science and Services, shared some very informative student comments with us. When we asked about the assignment that produced them, he said, "Simple, I just asked them to write a letter to next year's incoming class telling them all the things they wish they'd known when they arrived." What a good idea.

Deceptively simple, these letters tap a rich lode of student experiences, academic and social. The letter format allows students to write in an authentic voice, and the audience—fellow students, not parents or instructors—creates a level of informality that is revealing. The letters paint a vivid picture of students' lives, their thoughts, their worries, and of course their successes. The assignment is easy to make, and although it was originally designed to be a final assignment it could be used at the midpoint of the semester as well.

In borrowing this activity, we phrased the assignment this way:

> You are now a seasoned veteran of nearly one semester of university life with all its ups and downs, successes and failures, joys and sorrows (and we hope the ups, successes, and joys far outnumber the downs, failures, and sorrows). This assignment asks you to draft a letter to an imaginary first-year student at the university focusing on what you now know that you wish you'd known back in September. You can focus on those things you think are most important for first-year students, but it would be good if some of your advice was academically oriented and some focused on the more personal issues of life on a university campus.

A brief catalogue of some responses reveals the rich possibilities for conversation and points of faculty-student connection inherent in the letter-writing assignment.

> Most college work is your own responsibility to do on your own free time. It's easy to put things aside, because you have no parents to scold you and tell you what to do and when to do it. It's important to have self-discipline, so you know when it's time to go out and have fun and when it's time to stay in and study. (Maggie)

> Another thing I learned is not to expect to be able to study in your room. I set up a desk with my computer, a lamp, and every school supply known to man, determined to sit down and hit the books. This never works, especially during the first few weeks of school At least in my dorm, it is never quiet, friends are always around, and it is so easy to become distracted by the TV or radio. (Marissa)

> For academic advice, I would suggest going to all of your classes. Once you miss one you are going to be off track for a while, one step behind trying to catch up. I learned this the hard way. I missed a mathematics class and couldn't catch up and ended up dropping the course. (Mark)

> My last piece of advice is to get involved on campus. There are so many groups on campus; everyone can find at least one that they love. I am involved in Habitat for Humanity and the Student Entertainment Committee, and I love them both. It is just a great way to meet more people. (Bijitha)

Conclusion

These comments bring us back to where we began: the voices of students. These voices, like those we heard at the outset, embody the rich complexity of the first-year college experience. But now, near the end of their semester, the students sound a bit different: more confident, more seasoned, a bit wiser, more capable of navigating college life in and out of the classroom. They seem well on their way to becoming the sort of students we hope for.

It has been quite a journey for them. Their initial encounters with classes and professors are probably forgotten in the blur of assignments completed, exams taken, parties attended, papers written, friends made, courses dropped, and much more. But those encounters and the sustained attention faculty members paid to their learning and their lives has been the foundation for their success. The attention comes at a price; the time invested in creative instruction and caring interaction with first-year students is time taken from those other faculty activities often more valued by both colleagues and institutions.

Yet we know we must invest in our first-year students if we are to begin shaping the academic skill essential for success in college and the habits of mind necessary for productive and engaged citizenship. We also know that the investment of faculty time and energy in first-year students demands strong institutional support. We offer some reflections on this issue in our final chapter.

For Further Exploration

- Kramer, G. L. (ed.). *Faculty Advising Examined.* Bolton, Mass.: Anker, 2003.

  This collection is a range of reflection on effective advising practices. The contributed chapters include practical advice for faculty advisors as well as suggestions and strategies for improving institutional support for advising.

CHAPTER 16

Strengthening Commitment to First-Year Instruction

As we look back over the preceding chapters and our recommendations for engaging first-year students with reasonable rigor and appropriate support, we are reminded of the considerable challenge faced by faculty who teach first-year courses. None of what we have recommended can be achieved without a good deal of effort. The time necessary for reworking courses, for meeting and talking with students, and for providing useful and frequent feedback on assignments has to be carved out of faculty schedules that are already filled with the various demands of an academic career.

Most faculty we know work very hard, and national data confirm our observation. A total work week of fifty hours or more is typical of faculty regardless of rank or institutional type, and on average more than thirty hours per week are already invested in teaching (NCES, 2001). Although some of the time faculty already commit to teaching could be redirected to activities more likely to engage first-year students, we are well aware that implementing many of our recommendations requires faculty to invest more time in instructional activities.

Even the most devoted faculty have limits beyond which (sensibly) they are unwilling to go. Improvement of first-year instruction cannot depend on the willingness of faculty to devote more of their nights and weekends to teaching. Nor can it depend on persuading them to shift time and effort away from those research and creative activities valued by the institution only to invest it in first-year classrooms, unless teaching first-year students becomes central to the institution's culture and faculty reward structure.

Hopeful Signs

In the first edition of this book, we lamented the paucity of institutional support for first-year instruction and agreed with William Arrowsmith's assessment (quoted in Smith, 1990, p. 219) that faculty devoted to first-year students would find the college and university campus as congenial to them as the "Mojave Desert would be to a clutch of Druid priests." Fortunately, the last two decades have seen many colleges and universities make a concerted effort to put first-year students and first-year instruction in a new and much more prominent light. Although there remains much to be done, especially at large, research-oriented institutions, the emerging focus on the needs and support of first-year students in a variety of institutional settings is a hopeful sign.

In an ambitious study, Betsy Barefoot, John Gardner, and their associates have identified thirteen colleges and universities that attained "institutional excellence" in programs for first-year students (Barefoot and others, 2005). The criteria Barefoot, Gardner, and colleagues employed in their determination are useful reminders of the sort of institutional commitment needed for faculty to engage first-year instruction with the time and energy it deserves. As they point out, colleges and universities with excellent first-year programs have "strong administrative support for first-year initiatives" that results in an "equitable share of fiscal and personnel resources" for those projects. In addition, such institutions have made students' first-year experiences a "centerpiece of campus marketing" (Barefoot and others, 2005, p. 8).

Institutions committed to excellent first-year programs also share a variety of programmatic initiatives (Barefoot and others, 2005). Many of those initiatives, from advising to experiential learning, from supplemental instruction to learning communities, from mentoring to faculty development, touch in one way or another on the challenge, support, variety, and engagement of first-year students that we have advocated. Of course, by themselves efforts to improve the quality of first-year students' experiences do not translate into better-conceived, better-delivered instruction. They do, however, foster a climate (or, to return to Arrowsmith's metaphor, they plant a few trees) in which faculty may be more willing to make efforts to enhance the quality of what goes on in and outside of first-year classrooms.

Campuswide commitment to first-year students is an important first step, but because the academic lives of faculty are often lived in a scholarly community defined by departments, disciplines, or even the readership of particular journals, they may effect less change in how courses are conducted in the classroom than they do in graduation requirements, cocurricular activities, and living arrangements. The disciplinary heritage of academic departments militates against significant investment in first-year courses. Faculty are experts in their fields, trained and rewarded (through publication and promotion) to work at the edge of a discipline rather than the foundation. As a result, first-year courses are usually seen as less desirable assignments than courses for majors or graduate students.

It is, of course, too much to ask faculty to give up their attachment to majors and graduate students. It is not, however, inappropriate to ask them to reflect on the consequences of departmental practices that assign responsibility for introductory chemistry or general psychology or communication fundamentals only to those who can find no way to avoid it. When first-year instruction—and very likely a substantial component of any general education program—is seen as something to be endured only if it cannot be evaded, students are introduced to college work by the newest and least experienced instructors, or by those who see their current duties as at best serving their time.

This view of first-year instruction can be challenged in two different but related ways. First, as we have noted before, students' academic careers are deeply affected by their experiences during their first semesters on campus. The significant institutional resources used to identify and recruit an incoming class can be easily squandered by indifferent or even hostile instruction, persuading far too many first-year students that college is not the place for them. More engaged and engaging first-year instruction would allow the time and effort currently invested in replacing students who have left to be expended instead in enriching the experiences of those who remain.

But there is more to taking first-year instruction seriously than the benefits of an improved retention rate for an institution's bottom line. The demands of an information economy and an increasingly complicated global society make college education integral to life as a productive and engaged citizen. As George Kuh and his associates (2005) point out, in response to the global market and international political realities our nation is engaged in an unprecedented effort to extend "high quality post-secondary education to more than three-quarters of the adult population" (p. xiii). First-year instruction that is engaging, challenging, and supportive cannot ensure the success of this undertaking, but without it we in higher education cannot expect to produce a sufficient number of graduates who possess the skills and commitments necessary for leading fulfilling lives or meeting their obligations as citizens.

Second, first-year instruction need not be the drudgery that it is frequently imagined to be. The same lectures, the same facts, the same plug-and-chug problems year after year are not the obligatory substance of first-year curricula, nor the required practice in first-year classrooms. As we have tried to make clear throughout our discussion, we believe that varied instructional activities that engage first-year students actively and challenge them appropriately are much more suited to introductory courses than the common "forty lectures and a couple of exams" vision allows.

We have offered dozens of ideas and practices that improve first-year instruction. There are many more. The journal *College Teaching* and the newsletter *The Teaching Professor* are both good sources of practical ideas and advice. More sophisticated but still accessible is the Jossey-Bass series *New Directions for Teaching and Learning*. The volumes are topical, focusing on such issues as problem-based learning, using small groups, teaching large classes, and so on. The chapters are written from a variety of perspectives and permit some triangulation on the effectiveness and appropriateness of particular instructional practices. In addition to these cross-disciplinary sources, many professional associations also publish journals devoted to teaching in their disciplines.

Whatever the source of good teaching practice, we believe that engaged and engaging first-year instruction is truly a win-win situation. Clearly first-year students win: they learn more, they enjoy learning more, and they are better prepared to continue to learn, as students and as citizens. But faculty win too: classes are more interesting, student work is more thoughtful, and students are more likely to become the majors and graduate students who attract so much of our attention.

Building Supportive Faculty Communities

Effective first-year instruction can then be seen as an academic and citizenly obligation, as well as an opportunity for faculty to make their teaching lives more enjoyable and rewarding. Nevertheless, it remains hard and time-consuming work that is likely to be abandoned without the support of a face-to-face community of like-minded faculty. Some institutions (our own included) have addressed this issue through the work of a center for teaching and learning, or instructional or faculty development. Indeed, many of the institutions whose programs for first-year students were identified as excellent were colleges and universities that had emphasized faculty development programs (Barefoot and others, 2005).

The workshops, seminars, and consultation services run by instructional development professionals or the experienced faculty who staff such centers are occasions when the community of faculty committed to effective first-year instruction can gather for insight, support, and revitalization. In addition, of course, faculty development centers are a visible symbol of an institution's commitment to effective teaching and student learning. As such, they clearly indicate to faculty that should they choose to invest their time in revamping first-year courses to make them more challenging, more supportive, more engaging, they will have at least some institutionalized approval and support.

Formal faculty development centers are not the only way to sustain the work of faculty in first-year courses and with first-year students. If attention to first-year instruction is to become part of the culture of an institution, conversation about teaching and learning must be diffused throughout a campus community. Some of this can and does occur informally, over lunch or drinks, or around the coffee pot. Other aspects of the conversation are more formal, often beginning as a spin-off from some structured faculty development activity: a faculty book discussion (using, say, *Student Success in College* by Kuh and colleagues, or *Teaching Tips* by McKeachie, or, we hope, this book) organized by a vice provost for undergraduate education; a luncheon series where large-class instructors gather to share their experiences and ideas (and lick their wounds!) hosted by a dean of arts and sciences; a regular brown bag gathering convened by science department chairs where faculty who teach first-year courses can demonstrate especially effective and engaging classroom activities.

Another way to sustain the faculty community essential for improvement of first year instruction is to encourage and support a systematic program of classroom research. K. Patricia Cross, who pioneered the idea, and Mimi Harris Steadman see classroom research as "ongoing and cumulative intellectual inquiry by classroom teachers into the nature of teaching and learning in their classrooms" (Cross and Steadman, 1996, p. 2). Three aspects of classroom research are especially suited to nurturing improvement in first-year instruction. First, of course, is the attention it focuses on assessing the effectiveness of particular instructional practices using one's students as the research population. As we have noted, first-year students differ from more advanced students. They have unique needs and respond in their own way to classroom activities. A concerted effort to assess which assignments, which illustrations, what sort of feedback work best with the students in our introductory classrooms (and why) is a useful way to tailor general teaching strategies to the particular needs of first-year students.

Using classroom research for this purpose may seem a bit daunting. After all, it is difficult enough to develop a new, actively engaging classroom exercise without having to design a research project to judge the reasons for its effectiveness. Yet classroom research need not be an overly elaborate process. Cross and Steadman (1996) present some sophisticated examples of the use of classroom research to diagnose problems and evaluate curricular design, but embedded in the discussion are some compact "classroom assessment techniques" (Angelo and Cross, 1993) that can be used without much scaffolding.

For example, "punctuated lecture" (Angelo and Cross, 1993, pp. 303–306) is "designed to provide immediate, on-the-spot feedback on how students are learning from a lecture or demonstration," by "punctuating" a presentation with a pause where students are asked reflect on their learning behavior and offer anonymous written feedback to the instructor. The descriptions of students' listening processes collected through this simple technique can be a useful "window on how students learn." The feedback from this and other classroom research efforts not only yields valuable information but also encourages development of "all those little connections that move teaching and learning closer together" (Cross, 1988, p. 4).

Second, a program of classroom research can also create a forum for exchange of ideas and good practice among faculty who teach first-year students. The products of even modest classroom research are suitable for presentation in colloquia and seminars and can also form the basis for an ongoing community of faculty who agree to employ and evaluate new approaches and new strategies systematically. We have for the last decade conducted a three-hour-long, pre-semester workshop in which faculty who have developed and evaluated creative assignments and practices that "get students involved" are asked to host concurrent roundtable discussions. The sessions have been extremely well attended and well liked. In addition, they have often planted the seeds for new assignments and new classroom research undertakings. Perhaps most important, however, is the visibility the workshop gives to those faculty who take teaching seriously and who see it as an object worthy of scholarly inquiry.

The clear connection that classroom research draws between teaching and inquiry is the third way it can encourage and support improvement in first-year instruction. Since its introduction by Ernest Boyer (1990), the "scholarship of teaching" has attracted attention on campuses across the country. Cross and Steadman (1996) argue persuasively that classroom research is multifaceted, weaving together the scholarships of discovery, integration, application, and teaching itself (see Boyer, 1990). As we've seen, classroom research can advance the cause of good teaching through findings that show us what works and why. Equally important, however, is its identification of classroom practice as an object worthy of study not just by educational researchers but by disciplinary practitioners. Lee Shulman (2004, p. 141) observes that teaching is often seen as something that is laid "on top of what you *really* do as a scholar in a discipline." Classroom research belies that illusion.

Of course, raising the status of instructional activity in disciplinary settings is advantageous for all undergraduate instruction, especially at research-intensive institutions. It is, however, especially important for first-year instruction. As we noted earlier, an introductory course is not often seen as a plum assignment, in part because it seems removed from the current research that draws faculty attention. Classroom research holds out the promise that teaching first-year students (disciplinary apprentices?) can be seen as a valued scholarly endeavor in its own right.

Sustaining high-quality first-year instruction requires that first-year teaching, to use Shulman's phrase, become "community property" (2004). The communities that matter most here are those faculty directly involved in delivering the first-year curricula. It is one thing (and a good one) to have broad institutional commitment to first-year students. It is quite another to have those disciplinary and departmental communities that lie close to the heart of faculty life begin to own their obligation to provide instruction to first-year students that is challenging, engaging, and supportive.

Departmental or programmatic ownership of high-quality first year instruction can be encouraged from outside by a dean or provost, but unless senior, respected faculty sign on to the process it is unlikely to take root. Peer reviews by senior scholars that ask for evidence of teaching excellence—student evaluations, to be sure, but also syllabi, assignments, exams, reflective essays on teaching philosophy—can send a broad message that the departmental community takes teaching seriously. More powerful than that, however, are staffing assignments that have energized senior faculty willingly taking on the responsibility for first-year courses. The presence of respected faculty engaged in creative, challenging, and supportive instruction in introductory courses can probably do more to enhance the status of first-year instruction than initiatives emanating from a central administrative office.

The good news is that we know it can be done. The accounts of those institutions with excellent first-year programs (Barefoot and others, 2005) are replete with evidence that departments and programs have acknowledged their responsibility for high-quality first-year instruction and responded to the challenge with creative and engaging courses and curricula. At small and large institutions alike, excellent first-year programs were characterized by deep involvement of departmental faculty with other campus professionals to create a comprehensive program of instruction linking, in various ways, substantive departmental instruction with integrative first-year seminars. There are, of course, many other departments on campuses across the country that have responded to the challenge of first-year instruction with equal creativity and engagement, but without the same national recognition (at least yet).

A Troubling Trend

There is some worrisome news in this, though. Over the past thirty years, full-time faculty, those who create and sustain a departmental community, have begun to disappear from college and university campuses. In 1970, more than three-quarters of the nation's college and university faculty were full-time; by 2000, the figure had dropped to 57 percent (Allen, 2004). The increasing number of part-time and often "per-course" faculty that has resulted from this shift in faculty employment status presents some significant challenges for higher education in general, but many of those issues have special relevance for first-year courses and first-year students. Part-time and per-course faculty are primarily hired to teach entry-level, general education courses whose rosters are heavily populated by first-year students. As a consequence, the effects of part-time and per-course faculty work are felt in the main by first-year and other relatively inexperienced students.

We are not indicting part-time and per-course faculty. They are our colleagues, well-trained and often talented and committed teachers. The conditions of their work, however, make it difficult for them to invest the time needed to engage first-year students, challenge them reasonably, and support them appropriately. For instance, many part-time faculty teach courses on multiple campuses, a fact that compels them to use time that could be spent meeting with students or providing feedback on assignments for travel instead. Moreover, because of the transient nature of their employment, part-time and per-course faculty are much more loosely connected to the departmental community than their full-time colleagues. The challenge is to integrate even those who teach a single section into the culture of a department that is committed to high-quality first-year instruction.

Our own campus is a case in point. Part-time and per-course faculty contribute significantly to first-year instruction at the University of Rhode Island, and over the years we have developed several programs to enrich and support their instructional activities. One of our more effective efforts has been the development of a provost-sponsored set of workshops conducted by full-time faculty focusing on how to involve students actively in general education courses. Part-time and per-course faculty receive a small stipend (and a free lunch!) to attend. The results have been encouraging. The exchange of ideas and practices is, of course, a good thing, but the camaraderie that develops between the part-time and full-time faculty and among the part-time faculty themselves around entry-level instruction also sends a message that good teaching is community property, and that all who teach are part of that community.

Coda

First-year students present an array of challenges to those who teach them. Throughout our discussion we have tried to spell out what we as faculty members must do if we are to meet those challenges and set students on the road to academic success and enlightened, reflective, and engaged citizenship. College attendance is on the rise, but unless we do a better job of engaging, supporting, and educating first-year students the increase will come to naught. We can no longer afford to admit students only to have them lose their way.

Our world is an increasingly complex and dangerous place. A highly educated population is indispensable if we are to sustain prosperity, establish peace, and lay the groundwork for worldwide human flourishing. College education has never been more important. Because a student's initial encounters with faculty in the classroom, laboratory, and recital hall lay the foundation for ultimate success or failure, rigorous and supportive first-year instruction must be a priority in every higher education setting. Our first-year students, our nation, and our world deserve no less.

REFERENCES

Allen, H. L. "Employment at the Margins: Nonstandard Work in Higher Education." *NEA 2004 Almanac of Higher Education.* Washington, D.C.: NEA, 2004.

Allen, H. P. "The Mainstreaming College Mathematics Project." *National Teaching and Learning Forum,* 1999, *9*(1), 1–4.

American Association of Colleges and Universities Diversity Web, n.d. (http://diversityweb.org; retrieved Jan. 2006).

American Diploma Project. *Ready or Not: Creating a High School Diploma That Counts* (executive summary). Washington, D.C.: Achieve, 2004.

Anderson, L. W., and Krathwohl, D. R. (eds.). *A Taxonomy for Learning, Teaching, and Assessing: A Revision of Bloom's Taxonomy of Educational Objectives* (abridged ed.). White Plains, N.Y.: Addison-Wesley Longman, 2001.

Angelo, T. A., and Cross, K. P. *Classroom Assessment Techniques: A Handbook for College Teachers* (2nd ed.). San Francisco: Jossey-Bass, 1993.

Appleby, D. "The Teaching-Advising Connection." *Mentor: An Academic Advising Journal,* 2001, *3*(1-2). Pennsylvania State University Center for Excellence in Academic Advising (http://www.psu.edu/dus/mentor, Feb.–Apr. 2001; retrieved Mar. 2005).

Astin, A. W. *What Matters in College: Four Critical Years Revisited.* San Francisco: Jossey-Bass, 1993.

Astin, A. W., Oseguera, L., Sax, L., and Korn, W. S. *The American Freshman: Thirty Five Year Trends.* Los Angeles: Higher Education Research Institute, University of California, Los Angeles, 2002.

Astin, A. W., Vogelgesang, L. J., Ikeda, E. K., and Yee, J. A. *How Service-Learning Affects Students.* Los Angeles: Higher Education Research Institute, University of California, Los Angeles, 2000.

Bannister, S. "Teaching Challenges: Sexual Orientation in the College Classroom." Fall 2000 (http://diversityweb.org/Digest/F00/orientation.html; retrieved Mar. 2005).

Banta, T. W., Black, K. E., and Kline, K. A. "PBL 2000 Plenary Address Offers Evidence for and Against Problem-Based Learning." *PBL Insight,* 2000, 3(3) (http://www.samford.edu/pbl).

Barefoot, B. "Second National Survey of First-Year Academic Practices." Policy Center on the First Year of College. 2002 (http://www.brevard.edu/fyc/survey2002/findings.htm; retrieved Mar. 2005).

Barefoot, B., and others. *Achieving and Sustaining Institutional Excellence for the First Year of College.* San Francisco: Jossey-Bass, 2005.

Barkley, E. F., Cross, K. P., and Major, C. H. *Collaborative Learning Techniques: A Handbook for College Faculty.* San Francisco: Jossey-Bass, 2005.

Baxter Magolda, M. B. *Knowing and Reasoning in College: Gender-Related Patterns in Students' Intellectual Development.* San Francisco: Jossey-Bass, 1992.

Baxter Magolda, M. B. "Epistemological Reflection: The Evolution of Epistemological Assumptions from Age 18 to 30." In B. K. Hofer and P. R. Pintrich (eds.), *Personal Epistemology: The Psychology of Beliefs About Knowledge and Knowing.* Hillsdale, N.J.: Erlbaum, 2002.

Bean, J. C. *Engaging Ideas: The Professor's Guide to Integrating Writing, Critical Thinking, and Active Learning in the Classroom.* San Francisco: Jossey-Bass, 1996.

Bean, J. C., Drenk, D., and Lee, F. D. "Microtheme Strategies for Developing Cognitive Skills." In C. W. Griffin (ed.), *Teaching Writing in All Disciplines.* New Directions for Teaching and Learning, no. 12. San Francisco: Jossey-Bass, 1982.

Bean, J. C., and Peterson, D. "Grading Classroom Participation." In R. S. Anderson and B. W. Speck (eds.), *Changing the Way We Grade Student Performance: Classroom Assessment and the New Learning Paradigm.* New Directions for Teaching and Learning, no. 74. San Francisco: Jossey-Bass, 1998.

Beatty, I. "Transforming Student Learning with Classroom Communications Systems." *Educause Research Bulletin*, 2004, 3.

Belenky, M. F., Clinchy, B. M., Goldberger, N. R., and Tarule, J. M. *Women's Ways of Knowing: The Development of Self, Voice, and Mind.* New York: Basic Books, 1986.

Bligh, D. A. *What's the Use of Lectures?* San Francisco: Jossey-Bass, 2000.

Boyer, E. L. *Scholarship Reconsidered: Priorities of the Professoriate.* San Francisco: Jossey-Bass, 1990.

Bransford, J. D., Brown, A. L., and Cocking, R. R. *How People Learn: Mind, Brain, Experience, and School.* Washington, D.C.: National Academy Press, 2000.

Bredehoft, D. J. "Cooperative Controversies in the Classroom." *College Teaching*, 1991, *39*(3), 122–125.

Brookfield, S. D. *The Skillful Teacher: On Technique, Trust, and Responsiveness in the Classroom.* San Francisco: Jossey-Bass, 1990.

Brookfield, S. D., and Preskill, S. *Discussion as a Way of Teaching: Tools and Techniques for Democratic Classrooms.* San Francisco: Jossey-Bass, 1999.

Carskadon, T. G. "Student Personality Factors: Psychological Type and the Myers-Briggs Type Indicator." In K. W. Prichard and R. McLaren Sawyer, *Handbook of College Teaching: Theory and Applications.* Westport, Conn.: Greenwood Press, 1994.

Center for Academic Integrity. 2004 (http://www.academicintegrity.org/cai_research.asp; retrieved Nov. 2004).

Chickering, A. W. "Commentary: The Double Bind of Field Dependence/Independence in Program Alternatives for Educational Development." In S. Missick and Associates (eds.), *Individuality in Learning.* San Francisco: Jossey-Bass, 1976.

Choy, S. *Nontraditional Undergraduates.* No. 2002-012. Washington, D.C.: National Center for Education Statistics, 2002.

Claxton, C. S., and Murrell, P. H. "Learning Styles: Implications for Improving Educational Practices." *ASHE-ERIC Higher Education Report, 4.* Washington, D.C.: Association for the Study of Higher Education, 1987.

Clinchy, B. M. "Revisiting Women's Ways of Knowing." In B. K. Hofer and P. R. Pintrich (eds.), *Personal Epistemology: The Psychology of Beliefs About Knowledge and Knowing.* Hillsdale, N.J.: Erlbaum, 2002.

Connolly, P., and Vilardi, T. (eds.). *Writing to Learn Mathematics and Science.* New York: Teachers College Press, 1989.

Consulting Psychologists Press. *Myers-Briggs Type Indicator: Report Form* (6th printing). Palo Alto, Calif.: Consulting Psychologists Press, 1990.

Cottell, P. G., Jr., and Millis, B. J. "Complex Cooperative Learning Structures for College and University Courses." In R. Wadsworth (ed.), *To Improve the Academy: Resources for Faculty, Instructional, and Organizational Development,* Vol. 13. Stillwater, Okla.: New Forums Press, 1994.

Cross, K. P. "In Search of Zippers." *American Association for Higher Education Bulletin,* 1988, *40*(10), 3–7.

Cross, K. P., and Steadman, M. H. *Classroom Research: Implementing the Scholarship of Teaching.* San Francisco: Jossey-Bass, 1996.

Cuddy, L. "One Sentence Is Worth a Thousand: A Strategy for Improving Reading, Writing, and Thinking Skills." In J. R. Jeffrey and G. R. Erickson (eds.), *To Improve the Academy: Resources for Student, Faculty, and Institutional Development.* Professional and Organizational Development Network. Stillwater, Okla.: New Forums Press, 1985.

Cuseo, J. B. "Capitalizing on Student Diversity." 1998 (http://amath.colorado.edu/carnegie/pubs/diversity.pdf; retrieved Jan. 2006).

Davis, B. G. *Tools for Teaching.* San Francisco: Jossey-Bass, 1993.

Davis, J. R. *Better Teaching, More Learning: Strategies for Success in Postsecondary Settings.* American Council on Education Series on Higher Education. Phoenix, Ariz.: Oryx Press, 1993.

deWinstanley, P. A., and Bjork, R. A. "Successful Lecturing: Presenting Information in Ways That Engage Effective Processing." In D. Halpern and M. D. Hakel (eds.), *Applying the Science of Learning to University Teaching and Beyond.* New Directions for Teaching and Learning, no. 89. San Francisco: Jossey-Bass, 2002.

DeZure, D., Kaplan, M., and Deerman, M. A. "Research on Student Notetaking: Implications for Faculty and Graduate Student Instructors." Center for Research on Learning and Teaching, Ann Arbor: University of Michigan, 2001 (http://www.math.lsa.umich.edu/~krasny/math156_crlt.pdf; retrieved Jan. 2006).

Diekhoff, G. M., and others. "College Cheating: Ten Years Later." *Research in Higher Education* 1996, *37,* 487–502.

Duch, B. J., Groh, S. E., and Allen, D. E. (eds.). *The Power of Problem-Based Learning: A Practical "How to" for Teaching Undergraduate Courses in Any Discipline.* Sterling, Va.: Stylus, 2001.

Edens, K. M. "Preparing Problem Solvers for the 21st Century Through Problem-Based Learning." *College Teaching,* 2000, *48*(2), 55–60.

Evans, N. J., Forney, D. S., and Guido-DiBrito, F. *Student Development in College: Theory, Research, and Practice.* San Francisco: Jossey-Bass, 1998.

Eyler, J., and Giles, D. E., Jr., *Where's the Learning in Service Learning?* San Francisco: Jossey-Bass, 1999.

Fadiman, A. *The Spirit Catches You and You Fall Down.* New York: Farrar, Straus, and Giroux, 1998.

"Faculty Approves Proposals to Establish Grading Standard." *News@Princeton,* Apr. 26, 2004. (http://www.princeton.edu/main/news/archive/S07/51/49G20/index.xml; retrieved Jan. 2006).

Farber, E. I. "Alternatives to the Term Paper." In T. G. Kirk (ed.), *Increasing the Teaching Role of Academic Libraries.* New Directions for Teaching and Learning, no. 18. San Francisco: Jossey-Bass, 1984.

Felder, R. M. "Reaching the Second Tier: Learning and Teaching Styles in College Science Education." *Journal of College Science Teaching,* 1993, *23*(5), 286–290 (http://www.ncsu.edu/felder-public).

Felder, R. M. "Matters of Style." *ASEE Prism,* 1996, *6*(4), 18–23 (http://www.ncsu.edu/felder-public).

Felder, R. M. and Soloman, B. A. "Learning Styles and Strategies." n.d. (http://www.ncsu.edu/felder-public; retrieved Feb. 2005).

Fincher, C. "Learning Theory and Research." In J. C. Smart (ed.), *Higher Education: Handbook of Theory and Research*. New York: Agathon Press, 1985.

Fink, L. D. *Creating Significant Learning Experiences: An Integrated Approach to Designing College Courses*. San Francisco: Jossey-Bass, 2003.

Frank, O. M. "Effect of Field Independence-Dependence and Study Technique on Learning from a Lecture." *American Educational Research Journal*, 1984, *21*(3), 669–678.

Frankenberg, E., Lee, C., and Orfield, G. *A Multiracial Society with Segregated Schools: Are We Losing the Dream?* Cambridge: Civil Rights Project, Harvard University, 2003.

Frederiksen, N. "Implications of Cognitive Theory for Instruction in Problem Solving." *Review of Educational Research*, 1984, *54*(3), 363–407.

Friedman, L. "Introduction to Ethics." 2003 (http://www.apa.udel.edu/apa/governance/committees/teaching/viewpost.asp?submitid=59 retrieved Mar. 2005).

Gagne, R. M., Briggs, L. J., and Wager, W. W. *Principles of Instructional Design* (3rd ed.). Austin, Tex.: Holt, Rinehart, and Winston, 1988.

Genereux, R. L., and McLeod, B. A. "Circumstances Surrounding Cheating: A Questionnaire Study of College Students." *Research in Higher Education*, 1995, *36*(6), 687–704.

Graesser, A. C., Person, N. K., and Hu, X. "Improving Comprehension Through Discourse Processing." In D. Halpern and M. D. Hakel (eds.), *Applying the Science of Learning to University Teaching and Beyond*. New Directions for Teaching and Learning, no. 89. San Francisco: Jossey-Bass, 2002.

Habley, W. R. "Faculty Advising: Practice and Promise." In G. L. Kramer (ed.), *Faculty Advising Examined: Enhancing the Potential of College Faculty as Advisors*, Bolton, Mass.: Anchor, 2003.

Halpern, D. F., and Hakel, M. D. "Applying the Science of Learning to the University and Beyond: Teaching for Long-Term Retention and Transfer." *Change*, 2003, *35*(4), 36–41.

"Harvard Releases Report on Grade Inflation, Promises to Take Action." *Chronicle of Higher Education, Today's News*. Nov. 21, 2001 (http://chronicle.com/daily/2001/11/20001112103n.htm).

Herreid, C. F. "What Makes a Good Case?" *Journal of College Science Teaching*, Dec. 1997/Jan. 1998, 163–165 (http://ublib.buffalo.edu/libraries/projects/cases/teaching/good-case.html; retrieved Mar. 2005).

Hofer, B. K., and Pintrich, P. R. "The Development of Epistemological Theories: Beliefs About Knowledge and Knowing and Their Relation to Learning." *Review of Educational Research*, 1997, *67*(1), 88–140.

Hofer, B. K., and Pintrich, P. R. (eds.). *Personal Epistemology: The Psychology of Beliefs About Knowledge and Knowing*. Hillsdale, N.J.: Erlbaum, 2002.

Holmes, W. "Small Groups in Large Classes." In J. R. Jeffrey and G. R. Erickson (eds.), *To Improve the Academy: Resources for Student, Faculty, and Institutional Development*. Professional and Organizational Development Network. Stillwater, Okla.: New Forums Press, 1985.

Holmes, W. "Art Essays and Computer Letters." In J. Kurfiss and others (eds.), *To Improve the Academy: Resources for Student, Faculty, and Institutional Development*. Professional and Organizational Development Network. Stillwater, Okla.: New Forums Press, 1988.

Hung, W., Bailey, J. H., and Jonassen, D. H. "Exploring the Tensions of Problem-Based Learning: Insights from Research." In D. S. Knowlton and D. C. Sharp (eds.), *Problem-Based Learning in the Information Age*. New Directions in Teaching and Learning, no. 95. San Francisco: Jossey-Bass, 2003.

Hunter, M. S., and Linder, C. W. "First-Year Seminars." In M. L. Upcraft, J. N. Gardner, and B. O. Barefoot (eds.), *Challenging and Supporting the First-Year Student: A Handbook for Improving the First Year of College.* San Francisco: Jossey-Bass, 2005.

Intergroup Relations Center, Arizona State University [IRC]. "Conflict De-Escalation." 2003a (http://www.asu.edu/provost/intergroup/resources/classconflict.html; retrieved Mar. 2005).

Intergroup Relations Center, Arizona State University [IRC]. "Discussion Ground-rules." 2003b (http://www.asu.edu/provost/intergroup/resources/class-groundrules.html; retrieved Mar. 2005).

Ishler, J.L.C. "Today's First Year Students." In M. Upcraft, J. Gardner, and B. Barefoot (eds.), *Challenging and Supporting First Year Students.* San Francisco: Jossey-Bass, 2005.

Jensen, G. H. "Learning Systems." In J. A. Provost and S. Anchors, *Applications of the Myers-Briggs Type Indicator in Higher Education.* Palo Alto, Calif.: Consulting Psychologists Press, 1987.

Johnson, D. W., and Johnson, F. P. *Joining Together: Group Theory and Group Skills.* Upper Saddle River, N.J.: Prentice Hall, 1975.

Johnson, D. W., and Johnson, F. P. *Learning Together and Alone: Cooperative, Competitive, and Individualistic Learning.* Upper Saddle River, N.J.: Prentice Hall, 1987.

Johnson, D. W., Johnson, R. T., and Smith, K. A. *Active Learning: Cooperation in the College Classroom.* Edina, Minn.: Interaction Book, 1991a.

Johnson, D. W., Johnson, R. T., and Smith, K. A. "Cooperative Learning: Increasing College Faculty Instructional Productivity." *ASHE-ERIC Higher Education Report, 4.* Washington, D.C.: Graduate School of Education and Human Development, George Washington University, 1991b.

Johnson, D. W., Johnson, R. T., and Smith, K. A. *Academic Controversy: Enriching College Instruction Through Intellectual Conflict.* ERIC Digest (ED409828). Washington, D. C.: Graduate School of Education and Human Development, George Washington University, 1997.

Johnson, D. W., Johnson, R. T., and Smith, K. A. "Cooperative Learning Returns to College: What Evidence Is There That It Works?" *Change Magazine,* July–Aug. 1998, 27–35.

Jones, W. T. "The Realities of Diversity and the Campus Climate." In M. Upcraft, J. Gardner, and B. Barefoot (eds.), *Challenging and Supporting First Year Students.* San Francisco: Jossey-Bass, 2005.

Kesner, L., and Eyring, E. "Service-Learning General Chemistry: Lead-Paint Analyses." *Journal of Chemical Education,* 1999 76(7), 920–923.

King, A. "From Sage on the Stage to Guide on the Side." *College Teaching,* 1993, 41(1), 30–35.

King, M. C., and Kerr, T. J. "Academic Advising." In M. Upcraft, J. Gardner, and B. Barefoot (eds.), *Challenging and Supporting First Year Students.* San Francisco: Jossey-Bass, 2005.

King, P. M., and Kitchener, K. S. *Developing Reflective Judgment: Understanding and Promoting Intellectual Growth and Critical Thinking in Adolescents and Adults.* San Francisco: Jossey-Bass, 1994.

King, P. M., and Kitchener, K. S. "The Reflective Judgment Model: Twenty Years of Research on Epistemic Cognition." In B. K. Hofer and P. R. Pintrich (eds.), *Personal Epistemology: The Psychology of Beliefs About Knowledge and Knowing.* Hillsdale, N.J.: Erlbaum, 2002.

Kitano, M. K. "What a Course Will Look Like After Multicultural Change." In A. I. Morey and M. K. Kitano (eds.), *Multicultural Course Transformation in Higher Education.* Boston: Allyn and Bacon, 1997.

Knefelkamp, L. "Effective Teaching for the Multicultural Classroom." Fall 1997 (http://www.diversityweb.org/Digest/F97/curriculum.html; retrieved Jan. 2006).

Kohn, A. "The Dangerous Myth of Grade Inflation." *Chronicle of Higher Education,* Nov. 8, 2002, B7 (http://www.alfiekohn.org/teaching/gi.htm; retrieved Jan. 2005).

Kolb, D. A. "Learning Styles and Disciplinary Differences." In A. W. Chickering and Associates (eds.), *The Modern American College: Responding to the New Realities of Diverse Students and a Changing Society.* San Francisco: Jossey-Bass, 1981.

Kolb, D. A. *Experiential Learning: Experience as the Source of Learning and Development.* Upper Saddle River, N.J.: Prentice Hall, 1984.

Kolb, D. A. *Learning Style Inventory.* Boston: McBer, 1985.

Kuh, G. "Student Engagement in the First Year of College." In M. Upcraft, J. Gardner, and B. Barefoot (eds.), *Challenging and Supporting First Year Students.* San Francisco: Jossey-Bass, 2005.

Kuh, G., Kinzie, J., Schuh, J. H., Whitt, J., and Associates. *Student Success in College: Creating Conditions That Matter.* San Francisco: Jossey-Bass, 2005.

Kurfiss, J. G. "Critical Thinking: Theory, Research, Practice, and Possibilities." *ASHE-ERIC Higher Education Report, 2.* Washington, D.C.: Association for the Study of Higher Education, 1988.

Laufgraben, J. L., Shapiro, N. S., and Associates. *Sustaining and Improving Learning Communities.* San Francisco: Jossey-Bass, 2004.

Leamnson, R. *Thinking About Teaching and Learning: Developing Habits of Learning with First Year College and University Students.* Sterling, Va.: Stylus, 1999.

Levine, A., and Cureton, J. S. *When Hope and Fear Collide.* San Francisco: Jossey-Bass, 1998.

Lewis, R. B. "Assessment of Student Learning." In A. I. Morey and M. K. Kitano (eds.), *Multicultural Course Transformation in Higher Education.* Boston: Allyn and Bacon, 1997.

Lieux, E. M. "A Skeptic's Look at PBL." In B. J. Duch, S. E. Groh, and D. E. Allen (eds.), *The Power of Problem-Based Learning: A Practical "How to" for Teaching Undergraduate Courses in Any Discipline.* Sterling, Va.: Stylus, 2001.

Light, R. J. *The Harvard Assessment Seminars: Explorations with Students and Faculty About Teaching, Learning, and Student Life.* (2nd report). Cambridge, Mass.: Harvard Graduate School of Education, 1992.

Light, R. J. *Making the Most of College: Students Speak Their Minds.* Cambridge, Mass.: Harvard University Press, 2001.

MacGregor, J. (ed.). *Student Self-Evaluation: Fostering Reflective Learning.* New Directions for Teaching and Learning, no. 56. San Francisco: Jossey-Bass, 1993.

MacGregor, J., Cooper, J. L., Smith, K. A., and Robinson, P. (eds.). *Strategies for Energizing Large Classes: From Small Groups to Learning Communities.* New Directions in Teaching and Learning, no. 81. San Francisco: Jossey-Bass, 2000.

Maki, P. L. *Assessing for Learning: Building a Sustainable Commitment Across the Institution.* Published in association with American Association of Higher Education. Sterling, Va.: Stylus, 2004.

Martin, K. H. "Writing `Microthemes' to Learn Human Biology." In P. Connolly and T. Vilardi (eds.), *Writing to Learn Mathematics and Science.* New York: Teachers College Press, 1989.

Marton, F., and Säljö, R. "Approaches to Learning." In F. Marton, D. Hounsell, and N. Entwistle (eds.), *The Experience of Learning.* Edinburgh: Scottish Academic Press, 1984.

Masterton, W. L., Slowinski, E. J., and Stanitski, C. L. *Chemical Principles* (alternate ed.). Philadelphia: Saunders, 1983.

McKeachie, W. J. *Teaching Tips: A Guidebook for the Beginning College Teacher.* (8th ed.). Lexington, Mass.: D. C. Heath, 1986.

McKeachie, W. J. *Teaching Tips: Strategies, Research, and Theory for College and University Teachers.* (11th ed.). Boston: Houghton Mifflin, 2002.

McKeachie, W. J., Pintrich, P. R., Lin, Y., and Smith, D.A.F. *Teaching and Learning in the College Classroom: A Review of the Research Literature.* Ann Arbor, Mich.: National Center for Research to Improve Postsecondary Teaching and Learning, 1986.

Meacham, J. "Introduction to Racism: My Introduction to Student Resistance." Summer 1998 (http://diversityweb.org/Digest/Sm98/racism.html; retrieved Jan. 2006).

Messick, S., and Associates. *Individuality in Learning: Implications of Cognitive Styles and Creativity for Human Development.* San Francisco: Jossey-Bass, 1986.

Meyers, C. *Teaching Students to Think Critically: A Guide for Faculty in All Disciplines.* San Francisco: Jossey-Bass, 1986.

Michaelson, L. K. "Myths and Methods in Successful Small Group Work." *National Teaching and Learning Forum,* 1999, *8*(6), 1–5.

Miller, H. G., Williams, R. G., and Haladyna, T. M. *Beyond Facts: Objective Ways to Measure Thinking.* Englewood Cliffs, N.J.: Educational Technology Publications, 1978.

Milton, O. *Will That Be on the Final?* Springfield, Ill.: Thomas, 1982.

Milton, O., Pollio, H. R., and Eison, J. A. *Making Sense of College Grades: Why the Grading System Does Not Work and What Can Be Done About It.* San Francisco: Jossey-Bass, 1986.

Myers, I. B. *Introduction to Type: A Description of the Theory and Applications of the Myers-Briggs Type Indicator* (10th printing). Original type descriptions by I. B. Myers, revised by M. H. McCaulley; further revisions and additional material by A. L. Hammer. Palo Alto: Consulting Psychologists Press, 1987.

National Center for Education Statistics (NCES). *The Condition of Education 2001.* Washington, D.C.: U.S. Department of Education, 2001.

National Center for Education Statistics (NCES). *Statistical Digest of Education 2003.* Washington, D.C.: U.S. Department of Education, 2003.

National Survey of Student Engagement (NSSE). *Annual Report 2004.* Bloomington: Center for Postsecondary Research, Indiana University, 2004.

Nilson, L. B. *Teaching at Its Best: A Research-Based Resource for College Instructors* (2nd ed.). Bolton, Mass.: Anker, 2003.

Nist, S. L., and Simpson, M. "College Studying." *Reading Online.* 2000 (http://www.readingonline.org/articles/handbook/nist/; drawn from work in Kamil, M. L., Mosenthal, P. B., Pearson, P. D., and Bar, R. [eds.], *Handbook of Reading Research: Vol. 3.* Hillsdale, N.J.: Erlbaum, 2000.

Norman, D. A. *Learning and Memory.* New York: W. H. Freeman, 1982.

Park, O. "Example Comparison Strategy Versus Attribute Identification Strategy in Concept Learning." *American Educational Research Journal,* 1984, *21*(1), 145–162.

Parkyn, D. L. "Learning in the Company of Others: Fostering a Discourse Community with a Collaborative Electronic Journal." *College Teaching,* 1999, *47*(3), 88–90.

Pascarella, E. T., and Terenzini, P. T. *How College Affects Students: A Third Decade of Research.* San Francisco: Jossey-Bass, 2005.

Perry, W. G., Jr. "Notes on Scheme and Some Implications for Education." Unpublished note. Cambridge, Mass.: Bureau of Study Counsel, 1989.

Perry Jr., W. G. *Forms of Ethical and Intellectual Development in the College Years: A Scheme.* San Francisco: Jossey-Bass, 1999. (Originally published by Holt, Rinehart, and Winston, 1968, 1970.)

Peters, C. B. "Silk Purses." In J. Jeffrey and G. Erickson (eds.), *To Improve the Academy: Resources for Student, Faculty, and Institutional Development.* Professional and Organizational Development Network. Stillwater, Okla.: New Forums Press, 1985.

Peters, C. B. "Rescue the Perishing: A New Approach to Supplemental Instruction." In M. D. Svinicki (ed.), *The Changing Face of College Teaching.* New Directions for Teaching and Learning, no. 42. San Francisco: Jossey-Bass, 1990.

Pittenger, D. J. "The Utility of the Myers-Briggs Type Indicator." *Review of Educational Research,* 1993, *63*(4), 467–488.

Princeton University. "Academic Integrity at Princeton University." 2000 (http://www.princeton.edu/pr/pub/integrity/index.html; retrieved Feb. 2005).

Problem-Based Learning Clearinghouse, n.d. (https://chico.nss.udel.edu/Pbl).

Pulvers, K., and Diekhoff, G. M. "The Relationship Between Academic Dishonesty and College Classroom Environment." *Research in Higher Education,* 1999, *40*(4), 487–498.

Rangachari, P. K. "Twenty-up: Problem-Based Learning with a Large Group." In L. Wilkerson and W. H. Gijselaers (eds.), *Bringing Problem-Based Learning to Higher Education: Theory and Practice.* New Directions for Teaching and Learning, no. 68. San Francisco: Jossey-Bass, 1996.

Ratcliff, J. L. "Assessment's Role in Strengthening the Core Curriculum." In D. F. Halpern and Associates, *Changing College Classrooms: New Teaching and Learning Strategies for an Increasingly Complex World.* San Francisco: Jossey-Bass, 1994.

Reich, R. *Transforming American High Schools: Early Lessons and Challenges.* Palo Alto, Calif.: Aspen Institute, Stanford University, 2003.

Reynolds, N. "Using Post-Writing Effectively." Unpublished workshop document. University of Rhode Island Instructional Development Program Course Planning Workshops, 1999.

Reynolds, N. *Portfolio Teaching: A Guide for Instructors.* Boston: Bedford/St. Martin's, 2000.

Richmond, J. "The University of Rhode Island's New Culture for Learning." In E. Zlotkowski, (ed.), *Service-Learning and the First-Year Experience: Preparing Students for Personal Success and Civic Responsibility* (Monograph no. 34. Columbia: National Resource Center for the First-Year Experience and Students in Transition, University of South Carolina, 2002.

Rodriguez, R. *Brown: The Last Discovery of America.* New York: Viking, 2002.

Rodriguez, R. "'Blaxians' and Other Reinvented Americans." *Chronicle of Higher Education,* Sept. 12, 2003, B10.

Rosenthal, J. W. "Multicultural Science: Focus on the Biological and Environmental Sciences." In A. I. Morey and M. K. Kitano (eds.), *Multicultural Course Transformation in Higher Education.* Boston: Allyn and Bacon, 1997.

Ross, D. "Training Teaching Assistants to Use Active Learning Strategies." In S. F. Schomberg (ed.), *Strategies for Active Teaching and Learning in University Classrooms.* Minneapolis: Communication Services, Continuing Education and Extension, University of Minnesota, 1986.

Rosser, S. V. "Group Work in Science, Engineering, and Mathematics: Consequences of Ignoring Gender and Race." *College Teaching,* 1998, *46*(3), 82–88.

Sadker, M., and Sadker, D. "Ensuring Equitable Participation in College Classes." In L.L.B. Border and N. Van Note Chism (eds.), *Teaching for Diversity.* New Directions for Teaching and Learning, no. 49. San Francisco: Jossey-Bass, 1992.

Saunders, S., and Kardia, D. "Creating Inclusive College Classrooms." n.d. (http://www.crlt.umich.edu/gsis/P3_1.html; retrieved Mar. 2005).

Sax, L., and others. *The American Freshman: National Norms for Fall 2004.* Los Angeles: Higher Education Research Institute, UCLA, 2004.

Sedlacek, W. E. "Issues in Advancing Diversity Through Assessment" (Research report no. 5–93). Counseling Center, University of Maryland at College Park, 1993 (http://www.inform.umd.edu/EdRes/Topic/Diversity/General/Reading/Sedlacek/issues.html; retrieved Jan. 2006).

Seshachari, N. C. "Instructor Mediated Journals: Raising Critical Thinking and Discourse Levels." *College Teaching,* 1994, *42*(1), 7–11.

Shibli, A. "Increasing Learning with Writing in Quantitative and Computer Courses." *College Teaching,* 1992, *40*(4), 123–127.

Shilling, K. M., and Shilling, K. L. "Expectations and Performance." In M. Upcraft, J. Gardner, and B. Barefoot (eds.), *Challenging and Supporting First Year Students.* San Francisco: Jossey-Bass, 2005.

Shipman, H. L., and Duch, B. J. "Problem-Based Learning in Large and Very Large Classes. In B. J. Duch, S. E. Groh, and D. E. Allen (eds.), *The Power of Problem-Based Learning.* Sterling, Va.: Stylus, 2001.

Shoichet, C. "Reports of Grade Inflation May Be Inflated, Study Finds." *Chronicle of Higher Education,* July 12, 2002, A37.

Shulman, L. S. *Teaching as Community Property: Essays on Higher Education.* San Francisco: Jossey-Bass, 2004.

"Skin Deep." (Film). Berkeley, Calif.: Iris Films, 1995.

Smallwood, S. "Professors Lose Money for Awarding Too Many A's." *Chronicle of Higher Education,* Jan. 30, 2004 A9.

Smith, P. *Killing the Spirit: Higher Education in America.* New York: Viking Penguin, 1990.

Spanier, G. B. "Emerging and Persistent Issues for First-Year Students." *Mentor,* Oct. 22, 2004 (http://www.psu.edu/dus/mentor/041022gs.htm; retrieved Feb. 2005).

Springer, L., Stanne, M. E., Donovan, S. S. "Effects of Small-Group Learning on Undergraduates in Science, Mathematics, Engineering, and Technology: A Meta-Analysis." *Review of Educational Research,* 1999, *69*(1), 21–51.

Stanford, G., and Stanford, B. G. *Learning Discussion Skills Through Games.* New York: Citation Press, 1969.

Stanley, C. A., and Porter, M. E. (eds.). *Engaging Large Classes.* Bolton, Mass.: Anker, 2002.

Stevens, D. D., and Levi, A. J. *Introduction to Rubrics: An Assessment Tool to Save Grading Time, Convey Effective Feedback, and Promote Student Learning.* Sterling, Va.: Stylus, 2005.

Stice, J. E. "Using Kolb's Learning Cycle to Improve Student Learning." *Engineering Education,* 1987, *77,* 219–296.

Suskie, L. "Fair Assessment Practices: Giving Students Equitable Opportunities to Demonstrate Learning." *AAHE Bulletin,* 2000, *52*(9), 7–9.

Suskie, L. *Assessing Student Learning: A Common Sense Guide.* Bolton, Mass.: Anker, 2004.

Svinicki, M. D. *Learning and Motivation in the Postsecondary Classroom.* Bolton, Mass.: Anker, 2004.

Svinicki, M. D., and Dixon, N. M. "Kolb Model Modified for Classroom Activities." *College Teaching,* 1987, *35*(4) 141–146.

"Syllabus Tutorial," n.d. (http://www1.umn.edu/ohr/teachlearn/syllabus/index .html; retrieved Jan. 2006).

Taylor, K., Moore, W. S., MacGregor, J., and Lindblad, J. *Learning Community Research and Assessment: What We Know Now* (executive summary). National Learning Communities Project. 2003 (http://learningcommons.evergreen.edu/pdf/ pages_from_ImpactLC.pdf; retrieved Mar. 2005).

Terenzini, P. T., and others. "Making the Transition to College." In R. J. Menges and M. Weiner (eds.), *Teaching on Solid Ground.* San Francisco: Jossey-Bass, 1996.

Tinto, V. "Classrooms as Communities: Exploring the Educational Character of Student Persistence." *Journal of Higher Education,* 1997, *68*(6), 599–623.

Topping, K. "Peer Assessment Between Students in Colleges and Universities." *Review of Educational Research,* 1998, *68*(3), 249–276.

Vogelgesang, L. J., Ikeda, E. K., Gilmartin, S. K., and Keup, J. R. "Service-Learning and the First-Year Experience: Learning from the Research." In E. Zlotkowski (ed.), *Service-Learning and the First-Year Experience: Preparing Students for Personal Success and Civic Responsibility* (Monograph no. 34). Columbia: National Resource Center for the First-Year Experience and Students in Transition, University of South Carolina, 2002.

Wade, S. E., and Moje, E. B. "The Role of Text in Classroom Learning: Beginning an Online Dialogue." *Reading Online.* 2000 (http://www.readingonline.org/articles/handbook/wade/index.html; online version adapted from work in Kamil, M. L., Mosenthal, P. B., Pearson, P. D., and Bar, R. [eds.], *Handbook of Reading Research: Vol. 3.* Hillsdale, N.J.: Erlbaum, 2000.

Walvoord, B. E., and Anderson, V. J. *Effective Grading: A Tool for Learning and Assessment.* San Francisco: Jossey-Bass, 1998.

Warren, L. "Managing Hot Moments in the Classroom." 2003 (http://bokcenter.fas.harvard.edu/docs/hotmoments.html; retrieved Jan. 2006).

Watkins, B. "Ideas for the Classroom." *Chronicle of Higher Education,* Dec. 5, 1990, A18.

Weimer, M. *Learner-Centered Teaching.* San Francisco: Jossey-Bass, 2002.

Weinstein, C. E., Palmer, D. R., and Hanson, G. R. *Perceptions, Expectations, Emotions, and Knowledge About College.* Clearwater, Fla.: H and H, 1995.

Weinstein, C. E., Schulte, A. C., and Palmer, D. R. *Learning and Study Strategies Inventory.* Clearwater, Fla.: H and H, 1987.

Weinstein, C. E., and others. "Teaching Students How to Learn." In W. J. McKeachie, *Teaching Tips: Strategies, Research, and Theory for College and University Teachers* (11th ed.). Boston: Houghton Mifflin, 2002.

Whitley, B. E. "Factors Associated with Cheating Among College Students: A Review." *Research in Higher Education,* 1998, *39*(3), 235–274.

Williams, P. *The Alchemy of Race and Rights.* Cambridge, Mass.: Harvard University Press, 1991.

Witkin, H. A. "Cognitive Style in Academic Performance and in Teacher-Student Relations." In S. Messick and Associates, *Individuality in Learning.* San Francisco: Jossey-Bass, 1976.

Witkin, H. A., Oltman, P. K., Raskin, E., and Karp, S. A. *A Manual for the Embedded Figures Tests.* Palo Alto, Calif.: Consulting Psychologists Press, 1971.

Wlodkowski, R. J., and Ginsberg, M. B. *Diversity and Motivation: Culturally Responsive Teaching.* San Francisco: Jossey-Bass, 1995.

Woods, D. R. "Problem-Based Learning for Large Classes in Chemical Engineering." In L. Wilkerson and W. H. Gijselaers (eds.), *Bringing Problem-Based Learning to Higher Education: Theory and Practice.* New Directions for Teaching and Learning, no. 68. San Francisco: Jossey-Bass, 1996.

Zeakes, S. J. "Case Studies in Biology." *College Teaching,* 1989, *37*(1), 33–35.

Zlotkowski, E. (ed.). *Service-Learning and the First-Year Experience: Preparing Students for Personal Success and Civic Responsibility* (Monograph No. 34). Columbia, S.C.: University of South Carolina, National Resource Center for The First-Year Experience and Students in Transition, 2002.

Zubizarreta, J. *The Learning Portfolio: Reflective Practice for Improving Student Learning.* Bolton, Mass.: Anker, 2004.

Zull, J. E. *The Art of Changing the Brain: Enriching the Practice of Teaching by Exploring the Biology of Learning.* Sterling, Va.: Stylus, 2002.

INDEX